"*Edge of the World* brings readers to the cusp of longing. At the heart of this collection of travel essays is a queering of narrative, of point of view, of relationships between people as well as the relationship queer humans have to the nonhuman world around them. Underneath tourism an entire universe exists that teaches us how to see each other and the planet differently. This book will open eyes and hearts in the most astonishing, beautiful ways."
—LIDIA YUKNAVITCH, author of *Reading the Waves* and *The Chronology of Water*

"*Edge of the World* is one of those rare anthologies that will live alongside you for ages. What a joy to walk through so many worlds with our most gifted writers. Whether in Senegal or Cambodia or Holland or Key West, the insights and revelations in these essays offer endless food for thought. The travel is not just multigeographic dalliances, of course—instead *we* are the tourists exploring the psyches of these authors from all kinds of backgrounds. Alden Jones has brought together essential voices who span half a century in age and are rooted in all kinds of distinct cultures, concerns, inclinations, and styles. The result is a dazzling gift to our queer communities and a most loving invitation for all kinds of wandering souls to walk through the world on our too-often-overlooked magical margins."
—POROCHISTA KHAKPOUR, author of *Tehrangeles* and *Sick*

"In the pages of *Edge of the World* you'll find much more than travel advice. Each of these incredibly vulnerable and beautifully written essays reminds us that our identities can affect where we go, who we are expected to be in those spaces, and that beauty (and heartache) can be found almost everywhere. I'm grateful to each of this anthology's contributors for their stories, and I believe you will be, too—queer or not."
—DE'SHAWN CHARLES WINSLOW, author of *In West Mills* and *Decent People*

"If, like most queers I know, you're more yourself when you're *not* at home, and your sense of home itself is fraught, and most days find you simultaneously restless and dreamy and anxious about your thirst for adventure, these stories are your stories. Candid, wise, and filled with longing, *Edge of the World* is an essential compendium of the unique discoveries we've made on our most unforgettable journeys. I'm shocked this vital book hasn't existed until now."

—CHRISTOPHER CASTELLANI, author of *Leading Men*

"If I were curating a cohort to accompany me on my travels I could hardly do better than the writers assembled in this collection. Witty, intelligent, gossipy, and wise, these writers remind me of why I love to travel. Their essays beautifully trace the different ways queerness interacts with being a stranger in a strange land, alive to possibility and reinvention."

—ALYSIA ABBOTT, author of *Fairyland*

"*Edge of the World* is a mesmerizing feat. It honors the exquisite complexity of queer travel with immediacy, tenderness, and ferocious curiosity. I'm so grateful for these 16 authors who chart paths through cultures and languages, along the Baltic Sea, from Mérida to Amsterdam, across class strata, and even into the past, through family lineages and memory. This collection offers a new cartography of becoming, alert to the ways queerness shapes how we see, seek, and find. This collection is a vital contribution to the discourse, arriving at a crucial moment when the illusion of virtual 'connectivity' makes the nuance of travel more important than ever."

—MARGOT DOUAIHY, *USA Today* bestselling author of *Scorched Grace* and *Blessed Water*

# Edge of the World

# EDGE
## *of the*
# WORLD

---

## An Anthology of
## Queer Travel Writing

### EDITED BY ALDEN JONES

— BLAIR —

Blair is an imprint of Carolina Wren Press.

*The mission of Blair/Carolina Wren Press is to seek out, nurture, and promote literary work by new and underrepresented writers.*

We gratefully acknowledge the ongoing support of general operations by the Durham Arts Council's United Arts Fund and the North Carolina Arts Council.

Library of Congress Control Number: 2024950579
ISBN: 978-1-95-888851-3

# Contents

# Edge of the World

# We Find Each Other

## A Prelude

---

**ALDEN JONES**

**H**ow and why do queer people travel? We travel to find each other. To escape the places and people who reject us. Because somewhere, on a faraway beach, a party is being planned. Because we are displaced by violence or war. For the thrill of something new. To pursue an education. For love. To heal a broken heart. Because of some mysterious instinct to move and move and move. All the reasons human beings travel.

At a cocktail party in Los Angeles in 2016, I began a conversation with a fellow travel writer that became this book. We were at the party to toast Raphael Kadushin's retirement from the University of Wisconsin Press, where Raphy had built a unique list of gay and lesbian travel literature—the only such collection I was aware of. He had acquired my own travel memoir, *The Blind Masseuse*, a few months after a writers' conference at which I'd discovered a table stacked with gay and lesbian travelogues, anthologies, and place-based memoirs and boldly announced to him that my book belonged at his table. Raphy was a magazine travel writer in addition to being an editor. He'd acquired and in some cases edited books such as *Queer Frontiers: Millennial Geographies, Genders, and Generations*; *Something to Declare: Good Lesbian Travel*

*Writing; Wonderlands: Good Gay Travel Writing;* and *Big Trips: More Good Gay Travel Writing,* and he'd done this during a time when "queer travel writing" was so specialized a genre that few publishers believed a readership for it existed.

More room has been made for queer stories in publishing since the first gay and lesbian travel writing anthologies appeared. It was logical in the early 2000s to divide anthologies by "gay" and "lesbian," as these early collections were sorted. It made sense that purchasers of these anthologies might be looking for stories of same-sex romance set abroad: Before the internet, queer readers searched for stories of queer love and sex anywhere and everywhere, and if a story was billed as gay, there'd better be something *gay* about it. LGBTQ+ lit is no longer in the margins. Queer travel literature is in a position to forge new ground.

At the cocktail party, I posed a musing question: What if we didn't sort out these collections by gender and queer subidentity? What would we discover about travel writing if we considered it more expansively, through the lens of being *queer*? Why doesn't an inclusive anthology of queer-themed travel writing exist yet?

The conversation lasted the rest of the weekend, because I couldn't stop thinking about it, and everyone I ran the idea by also wanted answers. What themes could surprise us in a queer-forward travel collection? What *did* it mean to be queer and moving through the world? To get my answer, I'd have to pose the question to some queer thinkers and request their answers in the form of travel tales. I set out to create this book.

I became a travel writer because I was interested in what the genre could do that it wasn't already doing. (Also because in the '90s, when I was starting out as a writer, it was possible to make actual money writing for travel sections and magazines. Those were the days.) As a genre, travel writing has not always made room for all the ways human beings travel; it has tended to focus on pleasure and leisure, the lure of the exotic, and brief escapes. In *Edge of the World*, we offer some escape stories in that tradition. Travel writing *should* exist as entertainment, as microvacation. In *Edge of the World* it exists in the form of luminary Edmund White reminiscing about his years of visiting the gay mecca of Key West, and Texan KB Brookins inviting us along on a road trip to Mérida, Mexico, for a feel-good Pride. Of course, travel isn't always festive and fun, and danger presents itself to queer travelers in particular ways. As Sara Orozco discovers on a spontaneous trip to a gay bar in 1985, being gay and cavalier about the rules of an unfamiliar place might cause you to end up in handcuffs. Sara is not the only writer here who comes face-to-face with homophobia in the form of the law; in New Orleans, stopped for the alleged crime of kissing their girlfriend in public, Alex Marzano-Lesnevich must weigh how important it is to assert their legal rights to the officer shining his flashlight in their eyes. An emotional spectrum exists between those highs and lows.

Once I began to collect these essays, refrains arose—some expected, others more revelatory. There is dancing in *Edge of the World*. A recurring quest for a queer utopia. Returning to a foreign locale years after a first visit to confront how much both you and the place have changed. The push and pull of parental love. How many of us long for our original home, even when we've traveled far away from it for a specific reason. There are scenes in this book that seem almost to be doubles, repetitions, one writer's experience mirrored by another's. Travel has a tendency to conjure self-knowledge and bring it to the surface, and the best travel writing reflects this. I hope, in addition to exploring the expansive queer experience, that this collection asks not only what it means to be queer and moving through the world, but also what a queer perspective can do to expand or test the parameters of travel writing.

Queer communities do not generally form at home. More often, queerness sends us searching.

And we find each other. That is what we do.

―――――――――◆―――――――――

The year I spent in Costa Rica I lived in the highlands in an ad hoc community near the sugar refinery in Juan Viñas. I taught English to the children of families whose work fueled the sugar industry, mostly the cutting of cane. Trucks piled with caña groaned down the one street in town, and my students ran behind to collect the stalks that bounced off the truck. Some women earned money by hand-sewing baseballs for the nearby Rawlings factory. I loved my students and had many friends in town. The loneliness I felt, particularly those first few months, did not come from being alone. It was just that I didn't feel completely like *myself.*

On Thursday afternoons, after teaching my six classes, I walked to the highway to catch the bus to San José. From the stop in San José I walked to another bus stop and caught the local bus to Alajuela, where Lisa, another English teacher, lived in a modern apartment with a couple named Rainer and Ronald. Our employment arrangement required that we live with a family as part of integrating into our communities. After Lisa's original family assignment hadn't worked out, she moved in with a tico English teacher and his boyfriend, arguing that Rainer and Ronald were a family. "My two dads," she called them, winking when she said it, since Rainer and Ronald were in their twenties like us. I ached for such a situation. The family I lived with was lorded over by a distrustful, child-sized patriarch who counterbalanced his small-ness with constant aggression. He was periodically cruel to his daughters, whom I adored, and he was controlling with his wife, though she seemed warm towards him. The dynamic put me on edge. Lisa, Rainer, and Ronald made room for me in their apartment. By the year's end I was there nearly every Thursday night. I found myself revisiting this time after reading Genevieve Hudson's "Myth Maker," in which Genevieve discovers a weekly queer cooking collective in Amsterdam after a period of loneliness and isolation—the way we find each other and create these little pockets for ourselves in places all over the world.

We found each other at Rainer and Ronald's apartment: Lisa, Rainer, Ronald, me, Brent, and Shari, a posse of bilingual queers who didn't notice when we slipped from one language to the other. We found each other in what Tripadvisor now calls the "gay district of San José," at the gay club Déjà Vu, or the slightly more girl-oriented La Avispa, but there was no such district then, no Tripadvisor, no Google. You had to know someone who knew. At La Avispa, a painting on the entrance wall showed a woman slapping tortillas near a wood fire. "Tortillera," the label underneath it said; that *tortillera* meant lesbian was something you just had to know. Finding each other meant overhearing your own secret language. Other expectations changed inside these spaces. The code of conduct was strict at Déjà Vu. When Shari's girlfriend Bonnie flew in from the States, they were so elated to see each other that they didn't want to separate even during a trip to the bathroom; they were instantly dragged out of the club for entering a stall together. "No one goes into stalls together except to do drugs or have sex," the bouncer barked at Shari when she protested. "But we were just—" It didn't matter. The authorities never stopped looking for reasons to shut the place down, so the rules were the rules. We left and were welcomed back the next week to dance with our people in the dark. Some weekends we took buses to the Caribbean coast and found each other on the black sand beaches of Cajuita. On Mondays I returned to my classroom, feeling clear about who I was and why I was there.

Being queer and abroad means learning the rules. It means taking stock of one's ability to quickly drop one persona and embody another. In "The Return," Putsata Reang explores how layered the act of code-switching can become while traveling. Her calculations activate the minute she lands in Phnom Penh: If the customs official takes her for a Khmer living abroad, he will expect a bribe; if the cab driver takes her for a Khmer national, he might treat her with less respect. Putsata performs these identity scans on automatic, considering which hat to wear, before she sees their connection to the mission of her trip: to officially come out to her family in Cambodia, knowing it was easier to let them believe she was straight. It would be easier if she *were* straight. Feigning straightness is, of course, a necessary skill in many places of the world. Sometimes, easily passing as straight creates problems of its own. In Senegal, Nicole Shawan Junior spends days discussing faith—but never their sexuality—with their guide, a "spiritual" Muslim; when he sends a friend request on Instagram, Nicole accepts without pausing to consider their queer life on full display. A hasty internet search reveals multiple warnings to gay travelers in a potentially hostile environment. Nicole braces for a pounding on the door while deleting rainbow-flag posts in a panic. It is not only actual confrontation that terrifies. Even imagining what might happen to a person for being gay in the wrong place, among the wrong people, can squeeze a heart.

For others, moving undetected through the world is not an option. Queer travel might mean correcting, confusing, or explaining oneself to others—or avoidance of those things. Daisy Hernández arrives in Miami with her nonbinary partner, whom her elderly father takes for a man. Her father keeps referring to them as her "husband." Daisy doesn't even know where to start in explaining nonbinary identity to him. He is old, from another time and place. Should Daisy correct him or let it go?

Denne Michele Norris does something New Yorkers don't usually do: She buys a car. She straps her nervous chihuahua mix, Hughes, into the back seat and sets off to visit her mother in Ohio without making a plan for a bathroom stop. But as a gender-nonconforming Black woman with a dog who hates to be left alone, a rest stop in a conservative state means considering every choice, calculating all the things that might go wrong.

For Calvin Gimpelevich, who first traveled to Berlin at the beginning of his gender transition, a second trip a decade later illuminates how disembodied his first experience of Berlin had been. This time, Calvin becomes fascinated by Berlin's omnipresent memorials and how symbols of the past take on alternate meanings: A public installation of concrete stelae memorializes the Holocaust while also serving as a popular make out spot; Hitler's office is now the site of a restaurant specializing in Peking duck.

Depending on where you're going, travel can become the reopening of a closet door. In "Romantics," Garrard Conley escapes a fundamentalist upbringing and conversion therapy only to find himself back in the closet as a Peace Corps volunteer in Ukraine. Raluca Albu spends much of her trip to Russia angry about its homophobic laws, wanting to explode her gayness all over the place and make everyone just deal with it, but she can't even hold her girlfriend's hand. Andrew Ellis Evans's "My Cohort" explores the revolving closet door that he and his "cohort" spend their lives pushing through as husband-and-husband world travelers: in when it's necessary, out when it's safe, but having a lot of fun along the way.

Code-switching can feel like a superpower. Sometimes it's fun to have a secret. It's not always terrible to spend the day cooperating with heterosexual expectations and then lock your hotel room door and have especially gay sex with the person you have chosen to be with in the face of it all.

———————◆———————

Today we find each other on the internet with ease. It is hard to remember, now, how inescapably we were bound to our physical communities and how this linked queerness to travel in an essential way. To be queer before the internet, in the great majority of cases, meant that at some point you had to leave the place you knew. Reading was one way to do so; queer literature, if you could find it, was a prized portal to another possible world. You needed to make the right friends and stand in front of their bookshelves. You had to live near a very good bookstore, or in a big city, or have a cool high school English teacher willing to risk the repercussions of assigning or recommending queer books. Eventually, if you wanted to be free in both body and mind, you had to physically *go somewhere*: a bar, a club, a rest stop, a music festival, a parade, a specialized bookshop; San Francisco, Provincetown, Key West, Northampton. In the pursuit of recognition or comfort or community, you'd enter an unfamiliar culture and learn its rules. You had to do this with your body. There were risks, but there were also rewards.

There is no way for me to disentangle my travel history from my queer worldview. I've long searched out gay spaces everywhere I go. Only when I was away from home—far away, but for a measured period of time—did I allow myself to fall in love with a girl. I could test what I was willing to risk. No matter how hard I fell, an end date was already on the calendar—so I found out what it was like to fall hard and fast. I learned a lot from risking a lot. Perhaps such recklessness with the heart is a rite of passage, as Zoë Sprankle explores in "For a While, This was True." Zoë drops everything to join a girl in New York for Pride, knowing this girl will break her. She abandons her friends, tastes her first flakes of MDMA, and wakes up with a rainbow tattoo. After the up comes the down, and it's as bad as they say. But she would never warn a younger woman against being heedless with her heart. We invite things to play out, sometimes without considering the costs at all, because the journey, good and bad, is worth it.

I met the woman I would marry on one of my greatest adventures: circumnavigating the globe as a professor on Semester at Sea. By the time we set sail for our first port in Hawaii, I understood the straight-seeming administrator was flirting with me. By the second port of Japan we were a couple. Before we knew each other's phone numbers we traveled around the world together on a ship. Even in the darkest days of our divorce, I could close my eyes and reinhabit a whirlwind romance around the world. Falling asleep in one country and waking up in another. Dates in Saigon, Istanbul, Dubrovnik, Alexandria. Making out on a futon in Miyajima and in the back of a taxi in Hong Kong. Our first fight erupted in Granada, Spain. When I read Alexander Chee's "Mirador," I recalled how she and I argued in a hotel room overlooking the Alhambra, how I was mad to be ruining my memories of this city by having a fight, and with a view like this. Alex, too, recalls accompanying a long-ago boyfriend to Granada, where he is ultimately lied to, betrayed. Looking back on his time in Granada, Alex realizes he also had a secret, that despite the betrayal, he would always be able to remember his weeks in Granada with fondness, the pleasure of cold red wine in his mouth, walking the smooth river stones "like the backs of fish." Savoring the good moments, cherishing the experience that was only his.

Though we divorced, my former wife and I still travel occasionally with our three kids. I will always smile at the memory of traveling with our toddler son in Croatia, where we befriended a mother with a son his age. As our son tossed a beach ball with his new friend in the street, the child's mother looked us over intently, trying to figure us out. We were two women, both playing the role of mother actively. This happened a lot. "Yes, this is our son," we clarified. "We're married," we said, always wagging a finger between us when we said it so as to be clear we meant married to each other and not to men who were not there. A while later, she asked me about my pregnant belly.

"Did you get pregnant on purpose?" she asked.

This was a new one. I was more accustomed to questions about the technology we'd used to get pregnant, how long it had taken. I laughed. "I am forty years old and married to a woman," I reminded her. "I don't think it gets more 'on purpose' than this." Traveling while queer comes with laughs.

Let's not forget adventure. When I landed on *Edge of the World* as a title, I liked it as a nod to the long-standing spirit of adventure in travel writing, and also as a provocation. *Edge of the World* is meant to raise questions around the centering of one's own culture, while I hope the contents undermine the idea of cultural centrality. *Edge of the World* also speaks to queer origins on the edge of society and how our edge—the savvy cool of rule breakers with our outsider status—accompanies us as we move through the world and when we write about our lives. We *are* the edge of the world. Here are a few of our stories; there are many more to be told. I hope the conversation will travel.

# My Cohort

## ANDREW ELLIS EVANS

I t's one thing for two guys to click in bed. Quite another to make it on the road.

For six weeks I'd been sharing a single bed with a hot scientist in the middle of England. Was it too soon for Paris? I wondered. Could our grad school pair-bonding survive a foreign dimension?

And both of us Leos.

I remember that first drink in a dark and sagging pub, where I confessed to this handsome Zimbabwean zoologist that I dreamt of writing for *National Geographic*, which meant I intended to travel incessantly. He chuckled at my lack of ambition—journalism? As a serious conservationist, he was committed to saving the world's rarest species from extinction.

I was new to meeting men in bars, so I thought this was the best moment to put all my cards on the table, starting with the fact that I don't drink, which caused Brian to spill his beer. I then explained how I had spent two years as a Mormon missionary in eastern Ukraine.

He wondered if the whole thing was a setup. Was I trying to convert him—an agnostic scientist? We miscommunicated like that for several hours, rehearsing for marriage. Then we went looking for dinner. It took many more awkward hours before we landed on the rug in my room and confirmed that this was in fact, our first date.

Sometimes travel is like that. The best destination takes a path of discovery. Every relationship is its own journey. I always knew that I wanted a sidekick in life, and despite my college years undergoing conversion therapy in Utah, my male body and brain still only wanted to make love, purchase property, and spoil dogs with a he/him. I imagined a male lover who also loved to travel, because travel is kind of my life. Going to Paris was a litmus test for lifelong same-sex partnerhood: Could our fresh and budding romance survive a long weekend in France?

I purchased Eurostar tickets. I overplanned an itinerary with a list of my favorite must-sees. Brian quietly rejected my list, just like he ignored the gothic glory of Notre Dame; he was far more interested in the native sparrows hopping on the dusty ground. Then he wanted to go to Les Tuileries and ride the Ferris wheel, even though I explained that only cheesy tourists did that.

"But *we are cheesy tourists*," he said, and kissed me at the top of the Ferris wheel.

Brian showed me a different side to my City of Light, and we came out like never before. Two young men sharing a rickety metal bed on the sixth floor of a cheap walk-up hotel on *la rue des Mauvais-Garçons*—the street of naughty boys. Two gay men exploring the shadowy alleys of the Marais, pretending not to care that we were holding hands out on the street. Clutching hands in the Louvre, gawking beneath the exquisite *Jeune homme nu assis au bord de la mer*. Feeling braver and braver until one sunny afternoon, we kissed on the Pont Neuf—the oldest standing bridge in Paris.

"Oh my god, Barb! Did you just see that?" I recognized the sound of Midwestern shock. "Those two boys were kissin' on the bridge!" Heads turned. I felt the shame of my homeland staring back at me in the Seine.

We travel because we're foreigners back home. We flee the less comfortable places we come from, shaking away social expectations like excess luggage. We wander far in mind and body just to come out. My British friend Guy left England for Berlin and its tall German men. My friend Alex left his Bavarian village for the freedom-loving Americans. I fled the intolerant U.S. of A. to come out slowly in the European Union, where I met actual refugees: queer people from all over the world who faced violence, prison, or death back home.

After we got engaged, Brian took me to his native Zimbabwe, where I was instructed not to show any public affection. We backed right back into the closet, talking to one another like college chums. I did better when it was just us—out in the bush, as they say in Zimbabwe—when we parked at night and hunkered silently in his car, listening to the mighty elephants of Hwange smashing the trees all around us; when we got soaked under the roaring rainbow mist of Victoria Falls. We hiked for three days in Mozambique without ever seeing another human.

After Brian showed me the beauty of Africa, I wanted to share the places in my heart, too. So I took him to eastern Ukraine in late December ... by bus. We ate Christmas dinner at a McDonald's in Kyiv. We argued in Warsaw, and I wept in the biting cold, missing my family that no longer wanted me around for the holidays.

Brian made it clear that as a tropical-born human, anywhere that dipped down to double digits below zero was out-of-bounds. So I joined him for a full season of fieldwork, scuba diving in the

Caribbean. We drove our little dinghy all over the Virgin Islands, sometimes camping on deserted beaches. One night, I scrawled our names in the sand and drew a big heart around it. The next day we continued to hopscotch around so many islands. On our way back to port that evening, a rescue boat nearly swamped us, asking for ID. Our neighbor had reported us missing. They had found my heart in the sand, half erased by the waves, and my raggedy shorts, which I'd abandoned under a coconut palm. From this they deduced we had drowned. A search party had been looking for our bodies since dawn. Meanwhile, we had been eating cheeseburgers at a beach bar.

I remember moving back to England and finding it difficult to wear shoes again. The whiplash from the tropics to the drizzle and grayness of Old Blighty was tough on my psyche. I managed by writing my first book—a travel guide to Ukraine. After Brian submitted his thesis, we took the night ferry to Dublin, then rode our janky student bikes across the whole of Ireland, mending flat tires every few miles it seemed. In Connemara, we berthed in a creepy mountain hostel, then woke up in the flashlight beam of a fellow hosteler checking to see if he'd seen right, if it was actually two men in the one bed.

We started staying in hotels, which spawned its own comedy. Cheerful cards welcoming Mr. and Mrs. Evans to the jacuzzi suite. The glance from a Latin American hotelier when two men ask for *una cama matrimonial*. Or in Delhi, when the staff rushed in to dismantle our king-size bed and replace it with two dormitory-style singles, shoved into opposite corners of the room. *Our sincerest apologies for the confusion, sir. We did not realize it was two men inhabiting the room, sir.* They laughed awkwardly and Brian did not want any fuss, so we slept in separate beds. In New Zealand, the rugby-watching host of our bed-and-breakfast told us that seeing as we were two men, the room was no longer available. No big deal, said Brian, and we drove on to the next town.

Sometimes I forget that some people don't like us. Some people even want us dead. But I got so tired of lying. Trying to balance work life with home life. If I use male pronouns in Spanish, I am corrected—*you mean esposa!*—only for me to insist that yes, I meant to say that I am married to *un hombre*. Legally. *Mira*, his name is my emergency contact on my passport. *Sí sí*, we fuck.

I wish that was a box on immigration forms.

Given our different-colored passports, Brian and I reached that critical crossroads faced by every international couple: which country to settle in? London was simply unaffordable, and my student visa was ending. Back in Zimbabwe, gays were getting beaten up in the street or thrown in jail.

We looked for a place where two men could live together and pursue their careers, which is how we ended up in Washington, DC, at the peak of the Bush administration. I had a couple hundred dollars in my checking account. Even with my new degree, I struggled to find a job. At that time, my über-Mormon family was out of the picture.

But help arrived. The queers showed up. Word spread around the gayborhood, and next thing, a lesbian with cornrows arrived with extra pots and pans and dishes she no longer needed, outfitting our first kitchen. She asked me for a résumé and got me a temp writing gig for one of her nonprofits, which covered our groceries for a few months. A gay pastor we met at a dinner party took it upon himself to furnish our apartment with donated furniture from his largely LGBTQ+ congregation. Within months we felt surrounded by a vast team of strangers who cared. Turns out large cities are rife with queer people running away from rejection and isolation. Year by year, we expanded our family of friends from all over the world, and day by day, we built a life together in the capital of the freest nation on earth.

My new work spun me around the world many times over, and all the while, Brian stayed back in the U.S. I got a nearby assignment to Bermuda—just a ninety-minute flight—but Brian could not leave the country and risk canceling his pending work visa.

Once he got the visa, we resumed traveling as a couple, but every time we flew back to our home airport of Washington Dulles, we became two solo males from two different nations in two different lines sent to two different sides of a one-way door. Sometimes hours passed as I waited for my husband to run the gauntlet of the U.S. immigration before he emerged, sad-faced and exhausted by the mindless questioning.

When the District of Columbia changed the law to allow same-sex couples to marry, we rushed to the courthouse for a license. We did not plan a big wedding, because we felt there was no time—at any moment, the law might get overturned. That June we gathered some friends and family on the tallest rooftop in the capital of the United States and became husbands on paper.

The next morning, on the way to the airport, I surprised Brian with our honeymoon destination—Bermuda—because he'd missed going with me all those years before. He loved the pink sand beaches. We loved diving the colorful reefs. We managed not to kill each other while sharing a scooter. On our way back home, passing U.S. immigration in Bermuda, the officer waved us up together, asked if we lived together, then asked why we had one red and one blue passport. We explained that we were recently married.

"Huh." The agent spoke with a New Jersey accent. "You're my first. Congrats. Welcome home." He handed us our passports and ushered us through.

My husband's path to a green card was long and expensive and boring. We lived in the shadow of constant uncertainty as to whether we could ever settle down permanently, never knowing when our status might change and we would have to move. I was working for *National Geographic* by then, and when I could, I dragged Brian along on my work trips—to Queensland, the Galápagos, Greenland. I joined him in his field work in Panama, collecting poison dart frogs in the jungle.

On our first trip to India we saw thirteen tigers. We walked up the steps to a Hindu temple where a smiling swami marked our foreheads and blessed us. We sat on the old stone floor and watched the pink sun set over the immense tropical forest. Then Brian ran off to explore a cave full of bats.

The second time I brought Brian to India, we flew into Calcutta, which overwhelmed him. I love India—my grandparents lived and worked there back in the sixties, and I was raised on enchanting stories of Kerala and Kashmir. I love the colors and the screaming peacocks. The rhyming couplets on their hand-painted road signs. Brian felt differently about the pollution and poverty that assaults you on the Ganges.

Trying to get into the vibe, I joined an outdoor yoga class on the foredeck of our river cruise. As I posed and sweated out all my bad vibes, we floated up the sacred river. At the very end of the class, seated in half lotus and my eyes closed in deepish meditation, I inhaled a gulp of the most putrid air full of rot and death and maggoty flesh. I gagged but kept my eyes closed. *Mind over matter.*

After class, Brian summoned me over to show me the pictures on his camera. How our riverboat had pierced right through a raft of around sixty bloated cow carcasses. A floating bovine mortuary that I had inhaled with deep breathing.

As we glided over the languid Ganges, watching the sun fall lower and lower in the lavender sky, my husband pulled me in for a kiss, then said, "Honey, never bring me to India again."

Travel is personal. Every person experiences the world differently. Some of us seek bookshops; others want bullfights. Brian wants to look under rocks for reptiles. I want to sip an almond latte in a transitioning neighborhood. India pushes me way outside myself, which is the gift that travel offers. India inspires me to live differently. Over the years I have watched the increased visibility of India's immense queer community.

The more I wander, the more I confront the wonderful complexity of human gender and sexuality. We are everywhere, we are legion, but we are also all very different. Like the aunties in Tahiti they call rae-rae—trans women in a Polynesian society that recognizes māhū, the middle. Or the mob of gender expression at carnival in Brazil. The hyper-homosocial Middle East. The macho trans men of Mexico.

We always spot our kind when we travel—even in the Vatican—but the comfort of finding the other *others* in the world is offset by the constant question: Where do we need to avoid this week? Hungary has turned sour on the gays. Most of Poland doesn't want us around. Jamaica's a big fat no if you're homo. Russia's a pass ever since Putin outlawed the LGBTQ+ movement as an extremist organization.

I felt weird about going to Saudi Arabia—as a gay man—venturing into a kingdom where gay men are hung off the backs of trucks. In public. Standing Sharia law dictates men like me are to be stoned to death. What the hell?

I went anyway. As a traveler, I believe that an open door is better than a wall of misunderstanding. Saudi Arabia was strange and upsetting. Strangely beautiful and sophisticated. Upsetting insomuch as the women were literally blotted out all around me, as if I were strolling through some gender-edited LARPing. Some of the Saudi men I saw were stunning, and my gaydar periodically pinged like a family group text, but to even acknowledge another gay like me could run the risk of serious criminal accusations.

I was in Accra on the day when the Ghanaian parliament criminalized LGBTQ+ expression in any form. That was uncomfortable. Gay sex in Ghana gets you three years in prison, and if I pin a rainbow flag to my backpack, then I face five years for promoting LGBTQ+ rights. So—the idea of being queer is a bigger threat than actually being queer.

If you've never had to flee your homeland or community because of your sexuality, then it's hard to appreciate the gut-wrenching insecurity it brings. One learns to never get too comfortable in a place. Bad or good, the winds can change. Brian and I spent a decade in an immigration limbo undefined by governments and, therefore, delaying a lot of major life decisions.

Then it was 2015. Less than thirty seconds after NPR announced *Obergefell*, Brian was on the phone with INS. "Catch up. We're legally married. I should be a naturalized citizen already. Make it happen." Brian tapped his watch. The agent refreshed her newsfeed and read the headlines while Brian spelled out his last name over the phone. A few months later—after a bit more paperwork—Brian was sworn in as a citizen of the United States of America.

Brian thought it was perfectly normal that his citizenship ceremony be held at the National Archives. He stood six feet away from the original Declaration of Independence and the U.S. Constitution and swore allegiance to a nation that was founded on the concepts of liberty and human equality. As the U.S. Marine band played something loud and patriotic, I looked around at the other new citizens and realized that Brian and I fell amongst the token queer couples, handpicked for a press-friendly citizenship ceremony, followed by a reception, courtesy of the U.S. government. Thanks, Barack Obama.

But it's not always like that in America. Things change quickly. Maybe there's a Pride sale at Target, but they're beating up trans kids in the middle schools and waging war on us from the pulpit and blaming us for the latest natural disaster. The tide of culture flows back on us. They still want us in the margins.

My dear neighbor who is sweet and Southern Baptist just cannot bring herself to call Brian my husband. Instead, she always asks, "How's your cohort?"

*My cohort?* Ah, yes—my cohort. My friend. Partner. My fellow traveler. He's been my traveling companion for the past twenty-something years. Since we were practically kids. Taking the train to Paris. Camping in Mozambique. Dive bums foraging mangoes. Fishing for our supper. Waking up on the beach. Moving all our possessions from Newark to Brooklyn on the New York subway. Pounding the pavements of Rome in search of homoerotic statuary and silky gelato. Skinny-dipping in African rivers. Hiking far to see rare flowers. Making our way in the world, side by side. For better or worse.

I remember evacuating my parasitized gut on the dusty curb of the Agra-Delhi highway while my cohort joined a crowd of Indian schoolchildren who laughed at me, this pitiful foreigner, heaving red-faced on the ground. Brian assured me later that he was laughing *with* me—and not because he had tried to talk me out of drinking the watermelon juice at the hotel. Despite his allergy to cold, he joined me in the Antarctic, just to see the penguins. I lured him up to Alaska in February, where we huddled with a sled dog in a tent. In Greenland we watched a polar bear devour a seal on an ice floe under the midnight sun.

For whatever my life may be worth, I have loved a man all over the world. I have woken up next to him on all seven continents. He is my constant. He is my opposite pole. My dive buddy in dark seas. The man who holds my hand when the plane bumps too hard. The man who followed me across the ocean, around the world, and across a lifetime.

# A Journey Through Motherhood and the Motherland

**NICOLE SHAWAN JUNIOR**

## Dakar Towards Lake Retba, Senegal.

**N**ew construction dust filled my mouth, salt from the Atlantic Ocean my nose. I stood at the sidewalk's edge, BOMA Lifestyle Hotel at my back, and assessed Route de N'gor. A head-wrapped and heat-exposed woman rested her chin in a palm as she rode a horse-drawn cart. Two boys—both stick-thin and shoulders-slumped—manned a rickety rickshaw. A taxi driver gripped a battered steering wheel and squinted through his sun-cracked windshield, while a foreboding SUV with blackened windows weaved precariously around a goat. I spotted my driver, whom I'd be meeting for the first time, parked four traffic lanes and a concrete divider across from me, and stepped off the curb.

I trotted across the street with a pep I hadn't felt in more than a year, exhilarated by the promise of a new adventure—one I desperately needed—and the strangeness of jaywalking between livestock and motor vehicles. The driver's small sedan was new but needed a wash. Like most things in Dakar, it was coated in sand breeze-delivered from the nearby seashore and the far-off Sahara.

I opened the passenger door and stuck my head in. Kendrick Lamar bumped from the sound system. "Oh! This is the vibe?" I gestured my chin at the radio before climbing in. "You a hip-hop fan?"

"Tupac forever," my guide twisted his fingers into a W.

I shook my head and decided not to take the bait. I wouldn't engage in the classic Pac versus Biggie debate every hip-hop head of a certain age has had at least a dozen times. Instead, I introduced myself and learned his name was Babacar.

I couldn't figure out where my seatbelt was. Babacar reached across my lap to hand me the strap. "Here you go," he grinned and buckled me in with teeth that gleamed like stars against skin black as a new moon. A tingling sensation orbited my stomach. It had been too long since I had been touched.

We crawled past Dakar's collision of coastline, construction, and concrete buildings. Horns trumpeted, jackhammers drummed, and a man's silky voice sang Quran verses over a loudspeaker. In the distance, the mammoth African Renaissance Monument hovered; the sun gleamed on its bronze. At its center, a kufi-donning man embraced a woman with wind-whipped hair in one arm and, in the other, held a child whose finger guided an onlooker's gaze to the ocean.

The African Renaissance Monument is the highest sculpture in the world, its orientation overlooking the Atlantic intended to symbolize unity between Black populations in continental Africa and those of the Diaspora in the Americas. I stared at the bronze father, his chiseled chest, and the boy who sat on his bicep. I wondered if any statue of such national significance could ever depict two women holding their son. I wondered if any Senegalese monument would reflect the reality of my family.

## Portland, Oregon.

I snapped my laptop shut, rolled up my yoga mat, and tucked it behind the aqua reading chair. Senegal was not yet on my mind; I had come to the West Coast to write, stringing together two back-to-back residencies, but once in Portland my thoughts turned more towards the situation of my marriage. My morning practice ran later than usual, later than preferred. By the time the online class ended, Portland's sky was already a crisp blue. Car engines grumbled, and a garbage truck's rattle crept into the spacious studio apartment I had lived in for the past three weeks and would continue to live in for one more. There was a lot to be done during that time.

I hotfooted across hardwood towards clouds pluming across Morgan Parker, Destiny Birdsong, and the spines of other books by Tin House writers that filled the wooden bookshelf. Next to my bed and atop a small chest of drawers were my portable speaker, mala beads, and a boat burner that held a frankincense and sandalwood resin stick. The stick's tip smoked. I smudged its smoldering end into the boat's flat plank beside a brass peace sign adornment. Despite the incense's deadened cherry, sweetness clung to the air like spun sugar.

I poured water into African violets and golden pothos pots in the kitchen, chomped back a bowl of Kashi shredded wheat, then sat across from the front door to pull on my sneakers. Through stained glass I looked out onto Northwest Thurman. The street, like my temporary residence, was alive with nature's things. For a fleeting moment—though not the first or last—I thought, *This is the life I want for myself.*

With my navy Northface finally on, I grabbed my headphones. The late hour meant listening to song sparrows during my walk would be impossible. I'd listen to music instead. Mary J. Blige's *Good Morning Gorgeous* had just dropped and I couldn't get enough of the album from beginning to end. I pressed play and dropped my phone into my coat's oversized pocket.

This was my first trip to the Pacific Northwest. I'd arrived in early February, leaving for the first of my two residencies as a whiteout covered the East Coast in snow and a hailstorm rocked my home. In Portland, I developed a practice of walking every morning just before sunrise, not because I had steps to count or anywhere to be, but because of the trees.

From the oval buds of large red sunset maples to the umbrella-shaped cascara clusters, the trees spoke to me. The towering ponderosa pine spoke the loudest. It commanded my touch, its call taking the form of itchy palms. On that morning's walk, my hands longed to find calm in its soft, north-facing moss, but I felt silly touching trees without the cover of dawn's dark. Instead, I stood about a foot away and stared.

Mary sang through my headphones, "This isn't love. This is roulette. I just want back what I put into this. And then, I'll keep movin'." Though Chanel and I had only recently reached the one-year marriage mark, the tree, Mary, and many other signs confirmed a need I couldn't ignore: I had to keep it moving. Yet something about my marriage felt stuck. Leaving the marriage was something I had meditated on every morning since I arrived in Portland. Should I stay and endure or leave and plot an authentic path?

The answer wasn't a simple one. Not with Chanel being six months pregnant with our son.

## Dakar Towards Lake Retba, Senegal.

As American hip-hop bumped in our car, a clash of traditional garb and Western street fashion held my attention. Older men wore grand boubous with long pants, while younger men sported Yankee fitteds and NBA jerseys. Some women wore vibrant head wraps or braids adorned by cowrie shells, and others rocked European-stylized wigs and weaves that draped whip-long down their backs. My heart sank at the sight of a KFC amid open-air markets, fabric shops, and local fare restaurants. The place—the problems—I tried to escape, it seemed, wouldn't let me go. "Can you play some Senegalese music?" I asked Babacar. He fiddled with his phone.

A haunting voice claimed the car.

"This is my favorite musician," Babacar said softly. "Souleymane Faye."

After each verse, Babacar loosely translated the lyrics. "God guides everyone somewhere. And there is where you want to guide yourself... When God loves you, you just know it. Because he puts you out of trouble each time." I nodded and gave gratitude silently; Maferefun Egun, I thought. My ancestors sent signs through people, animals, numbers, and songs. I heard the message loud and clear: I was, for some reason, where I needed to be.

Much like the tension in my throat, traffic was thick throughout Dakar. Finally, on a highway headed northeast, the speed picked up. Dakar's basketball arena, communities of half-built concrete houses, and a grand mosque passed by like kaleidoscope images. I turned my head away from the passing land and toward Babacar. "You're Muslim?" I asked. It was a safe guess; Senegal is an Islamic country.

"Yes. Mouride." My eyebrows bunched into a question mark. "Do you know about Sufi?"

"Oh! Yes." I eyed the pack of cigarettes in his cup holder. The Sufi, I thought, were highly religious—purists of the Islamic faith.

"I'm no longer devout. I think I'm spiritual now," he tapped the wheel.

I could relate. Though raised by Catholic and Southern Baptist parents, I claimed neither. Instead, I practiced various cosmologies rooted in ancient Africa, namely Kemet and Benin.

Babacar and I spent the rest of the drive playing our favorite songs and discussing our spiritual journeys, including the dreams and synchronicities that led me to Senegal. My legs were stiff when we made it to Lake Retba. Babacar opened my door long enough for me to stretch and step out. My neck craned back to look him in the eyes. "Got'damn! How tall are you?"

"I don't know American sizes," he said. "Maybe 6'4"."

"Nah," I sized him up. "Gotta be 6'7". 6'5", at least."

We headed from the sandy parking lot towards a vendor's village on the water. My nose twitched at the fishy malodor, and my lips pursed at the sight of the murky green water. I'd expected it to be bright fuchsia. "Is this Lac Rose? Shouldn't it be . . . pink?"

"Climate change," he shrugged.

I wondered, then, at the point of visiting such a site, of driving for almost three hours due to Dakar's traffic. Babacar must have noticed the disappointment dampening my lips. "It's important we bring people to the lake. It has a history. And, these people," he gestured to the vendors alongside our path, waving us into shacks housing their Pink Lake–memorializing merchandise, "only have this. This is how they feed their families." His gaze returned to mine. "If we stop bringing the tourists, what will *they* do?"

I considered his words, their sentiment, our spiritual conversation, and the Senegalese music he played on the ride up. I liked this man. It seemed he was more than a handsome face. I was beginning to see a beautiful being.

## Dakar, Senegal. Dreamscape & Conversation in Curaçao and New Orleans.

Though I had studied abroad in South Africa twenty years earlier, spent a week camping on a white sand beach in Mozambique, and aspired to visit every African country—Benin had long been next on my bucket list—Senegal had not been on my radar. I had never set foot in the country or researched it online. Yet, in a dream I had mere months after my divorce proceedings began, I followed Dakar's coastline with my eyes from a sedan's passenger seat as my driver cruised along the city's main road.

Several months later, while celebrating my mother's birthday in Curaçao, the husband of a couple she met randomly recommended I go to Dakar. The husband said, "You'd love it!" even though I hadn't said more than "Hi" to him and his wife.

Weeks after returning from the vacation with my mom, I prepared for a work trip to New Orleans. I'd be there in late November. I contacted a college friend to ask if we could see each other during my forty-eight-hour stay. She wrote back: "Omg the soft opening for my restaurant @dakarnola is on the 17th!! It's invite only and you have to come!!" Unbeknownst to me, she had quit her longstanding dental career to open a restaurant: Dakar NOLA.

The signs kept coming until I was called into action. An acquaintance tagged me on Twitter about a writing residency. She didn't know me well, but the residency she recommended was in Popenguine, Senegal's fisherman village. I applied for the residency that very day. Sitting in my new apartment, a canopy of trees just outside my window, I pulled my feet from the floor and crossed my legs on the mustard couch. Octavia E. Tuxfur, my tuxedo cat, swiped at a fabric mouse on the hardwood. L.A. Blacks, my black cat, rested on a mudcloth bench. Smoke from a burning stick of sandalwood plumed across the split-leaf philodendron, succulents, and prayer plants adorning my altar room. A new message landed in my inbox. It hadn't been a day since I applied, but the message began, "Congratulations!" I was invited to join the writing residency.

Days before its start date, though, the residency was canceled. In an email, the executive director explained that it may be offered later that year and wanted to know if I'd consider joining then. I thought about the already paid-for flight and the time I had taken off from work. I asked the executive director for a refund. She said I'd receive it eventually, but the residency could not return my tuition payment just yet. I had nowhere to stay and hardly any money left after paying for airfare and residency fees. I had no meal plan—the residency was supposed to cover my every meal and excursion—and no plan at all.

After receiving the email, I went to my altar room, lit the white candle on my Boveda and sat on the floor before it. I pressed the Egun. Should I cancel my trip? Should I go to Senegal another time? I listened and, later, confirmed what I had heard by discerning messages the ancestors sent through angel numbers. The Egun had said yes, I must go to Dakar.

The point of the trip had always been about getting to Senegal. I was an arts administrator and literary artist who'd experienced several residencies. I would curate this one on my own.

## Portland, Oregon.

A foot away from the ponderosa pine, I knew I wanted more. I wanted more than a marriage based on obligation. I wanted our child to experience more than two parents sticking it out "for his sake." I wanted more than a bland relationship. My marriage was passionless; my wife, I had come to realize, was a stranger. I was losing myself to a misery of my choosing.

I'd made the mistake of sticking with unhappy relationships and career choices before.

In my twenties and thirties, I spent years in relationships I knew should've ended by the third date. Though I had spent a lifetime aspiring—and took out a mortgage worth of debt—to become a lawyer, two years into my decade-long legal career, I began smoking a pack and a half of cigarettes—sometimes two packs—a day and suffered daily heart palpitations. Misery was the hag that rode my back. But now I was over forty years old and knew better than to choose fear again, no matter how bumpy the road less traveled appeared.

Standing before the Talking Tree, I began to see the life I wanted. I wanted out of South Philly. I needed a neighborhood with trees and hiking trails. Unlike our laminate-floored and dimly lit townhome, the space I saw myself living in had natural hardwood floors, lots of light, and many plants. I heard my son laughing, listening to classic hip-hop, and chattering nonstop, a far cry from the constant bickering his parents had fallen into.

John Legend's "Everything"—the ringtone reserved for my wife—interrupted the tree talk. Chanel was calling with a weekly update from our OB appointment. I pulled the phone from my pocket.

"How'd it go?"

"Everything went well. His heart's strong. He's growing. Check your texts."

I opened my messages, then clicked on the grainy image. "Boy's got your noggin on him," I joked, trying to clear the tension so thick that it crossed a country to connect us.

"Yeah," she said without a trace of friendliness. "The placenta moved. Now we won't need a C-section—"

"No shit! So, we can do a natural birth. With a midwife?"

"Yeah. We should talk about what needs to happen in your room and where we want to keep the crib."

My stomach cliff-jumped. My wife and I spoke no more than twice a week—once after every doctor's appointment and *maybe* once more if something else came up, like a conversation about couples therapy or coparenting. Now, despite the dozens of discussions about separation and divorce, she wanted to make plans for my return to our marriage's wasteland.

"I don't think I want to re-sign the lease," I said.

"What?"

"I don't think it's best for Mikhail for us to live together."

"No. We discussed this. I want you here. The best thing is for Mikhail to have two parents. Together."

"Two parents who don't talk about anything other than divorce and coparenting? Who don't even laugh?"

"I need you here."

I arrived at a quaint café. Through its window, I watched customers line its counter and sit at tables.

"All right," I conceded, despite the pit burning in my stomach.

"Promise me you won't change your mind," she said.

My skin grew hot. Anxiety clawed like a desert cat across my chest. What should I do? Follow the trees or reassure my wife? I hedged like a gray-barked maple. "Aight," I nodded. I had no way of knowing how crushing the punishment for a broken promise could be.

## Gorée Island, Senegal.

The top of the boat was hot. I sat at its edge, watching the sea lap and wave, a distance from the canopy-covered passengers seated in its center. Behind us, sunbaked backs, ocean-washed sheep, and stilled pirogues manned by Lébou lined Dakar's coastline. Each fisherman became small enough to squeeze within my fingers' pinch as the ferry sailed from the mainland. Three women surrounded me and Babacar. Crunched around us, their sleeves of pink, purple, and red flapped. Each one's eyes pierced my own. "Sister, you come to my shop," "Look at these beads, my sister. You want to buy," and "Sister, come see me. I have nice things for you," they sang. I smiled, shrugged, and faced my open palms to the sky. The calls of these new vendors mirrored those we'd met at Lac Rose the day before.

"Maybe," I diverted eye contact. I didn't have money to spend frivolously. A costly custody battle and the transatlantic trip to Senegal had depleted my bank account; I counted on credit cards to carry me through. My neck craned and stretched, as I took in the choppy ocean waters, the frothing sea's top. I thought about the water's depth, the sunken secrets, and the bones buried at its bottom. Babacar spoke in Wolof to the women. His laughter broke my wonder. "What's so funny?" I asked.

"They asked if you're my wife."

I shook my head and let out a snort.

"Why not?" one of the women asked, smiling.

I admired the beauty of her dark skin against the rich fabric. "I'm already married," I huffed.

Twenty minutes after we set foot onto the ferry from Dakar's port, an island came into clear view. Mammoth stone walls lined its golden sands. Children jumped off rock formations into the Atlantic's water. Bodies thronged along the stone walkways just beyond the harbor. Finally, we arrived at the one place I was determined to visit during my first trip to West Africa— Gorée Island.

Used as a prominent port for exporting ivory, peanuts, and people, Gorée Island was a centerpiece of Western Africa's slave trade. It is estimated that twenty million captured, kidnapped, and enslaved Africans from myriad tribes across Benin, Togo, Nigeria, Ghana, the Gambia, Senegal, and elsewhere in Africa were processed, chained, and bound within its watery boundaries from the fifteenth to nineteenth centuries. A tiny island that could be walked in mere hours was the largest slave-trading center on the African coast.

I tried to follow close behind Babacar as we descended the steep stairs to the boat's main deck, but the horde of ferry riders swallowed me whole. At 6'7"— or 6'5"—Babacar's lean frame commanded space. He looked over his shoulder and, seeing me struggling to keep up from a distance, stood staff straight in the middle of the boat as flesh parted around him. Arm extended towards me, "Nicole," he said my name, letting the *i* linger on his tongue like a long *e*.

I bounced between bodies and grabbed his hand, melting within the warmth of his calloused palm. We walked the boat's width and stepped across the sliver of space between it and the deck. I hadn't realized until then how much I longed for my hand to be held, how much, after a year of battle in Philadelphia's Family Court, I wanted to be supported.

We passed a string of shack-styled restaurants, strolled along a lava stone path, and crossed French colonial homes painted marigold, salmon, and carnelian with windows shuttered in teal. Babacar hooked a left and led us into a squat, stony building. Inside a cramped room, we paid our fares, mine slightly higher than his because I was a foreigner. I wondered about the classification, the othering I felt, and the price I paid—the same as the loads of white tourists who wandered about—even though it was likely *my* ancestors who had been chained on this island born of black volcanic rock.

Inside the House of Slaves, our guide—a young Senegalese man with locs dangling from his head and a dashiki on his back—led us through every stony cell. Despite the breeze, the cramped spaces were pungent, plagued by a past too vile to be sanitized by sea-salted air. With clipped detail and a cavalier voice, our Gorée guide described the purpose of each cell. I wondered when he'd become desensitized to his home's history; I wondered if he'd ever been sensitive to it in the first place.

As Babacar snapped photos of me, our Gorée guide noted where chained men were kept, where they were beaten, and with what instruments. The guide led me to the rocky quarters for women. He knelt and placed his hand by a rounded dip in the ground. It was there where rebellious women were forced to put their pregnant bellies when slave traders bludgeoned their backs as punishment. He described how stolen African women impregnated by Europeans were shipped to Europe, where they and their babies would live as indentured servants. "I'm Black, Creole, German, and French," Chanel had once said.

I thought about my stolen son.

It had been a year since I saw him. No, not *him*—his grainy image, captured while in my wife's belly and sent via text while I was away, writing on an island near Seattle.

## Kirkland, Seattle, USA.

By the time I reached my second residency on Whidbey Island, off the Seattle coast, I'd already broken my promise to my wife. We'd been fighting on the phone. Every call ended in argument. Peaceful conversation was possible via text message, but we kept it strictly to OB visits. I was more certain now than ever that living together was an awful decision. No amount of breathwork, yoga, meditation, or walking to and along the bay brought ease around the topic—and I'd done them all daily between writing.

I called my wife and came clean.

No, I wouldn't stay in our home past the lease's end in July. Yes, I would live within fifteen minutes of her, no matter where she lived in Philly. Yes, I'd be there around the clock to care for our child and her. But I needed a place of my own to retreat to. I needed to be somewhere where I could cultivate the full spectrum of my personhood.

She listened and agreed.

A few days later, I emailed her "[i]n the spirit of being communicative, clear, and love-centered." In my message, I confirmed,

I'll be moving out of 1449 S Bouvier St, Philadelphia, PA 19146 when our lease is up on July 31, 2022. You've stated that you'd prefer for us to live together for another year, and while I'd love to be in the same household as Mikhail, our communication has deteriorated to a point where I don't think it'll be healthy for Mikhail, or us. When we restart therapy in April, I'd like to talk about/develop a co-parenting plan and schedule for parents who live with each other for the first couple of months of the child's life, and who then transition to living near (not with) one another. Of course, if you decide to leave 1449 S. Bouvier Street before July 31st, I ask that you let me know your new Philadelphia address so I can secure housing in proximity to you and Mikhail . . . I believe this is the best course of action for us to co-parent and support Mikhail's personal, spiritual, intellectual, and emotional development.

My legal training prompted the email. Chanel, also a lawyer, responded with one line: "Understood. Thanks for letting me know. I'm on board."

A week later, I left the island and traveled to a Lake Washington neighborhood where I'd booked an Airbnb for my last days in the Pacific Northwest. My Uber left me on a pristine street uphill from the lake and a few miles from Seattle-Tacoma International Airport. I pulled my luggage from the trunk and slammed the back door shut, eyeing my surroundings in the driver's taillights.

The land had once been home to the Tahb-tah-byook Native Americans of the Duwamish people until English settlers arrived with diseases, eliminating a majority of the local Indigenous population. Houses with white planks, manicured lawns, and detached garages surrounded me. I hoisted a bag onto a shoulder and rolled the other to my short-term home's entrance. A middle-aged white man approached as I eyed the door for a lockbox. "Are you in the right place?" he asked.

I ignored him, even as he followed me to the door and watched me plug in the code to open the lockbox. I pulled my bags into the house's narrow foyer and slammed it shut with the man just beyond the threshold, wishing I'd rented a place in Seattle.

The question of place and its rightness had been on my mind before the man policed my movement. It lingered for months. Though I knew I had to get back to nature and far from South Philly, I had no place lined up to move to, no money saved for a security deposit, and no car to get around in. But I did have faith.

Days after I arrived at the Airbnb, I awoke to an uncommon predawn call from my wife. Nervous she was in labor, I quickly answered. "You okay?"

She paused.

"Yes, I'm okay," she finally exhaled. "I'm sorry, but I don't want to move forward with the second-parent adoption."

Newly awakened, my brain churned. "Have you filed for divorce?" I asked. Considering the months of conversation around it, it seemed a fair question and a strong possibility.

Another pause.

"No," she responded.

I didn't believe her, but it didn't matter. Arguing with my now seven-month-pregnant wife when we'd already decided our romantic relationship was not working seemed foolish and pointless. I steadied myself for what I knew would be a long road with an unknown destination. "This seems like an issue for family court," I resigned.

### Gorée Island, Senegal.

At the Door of No Return, Babacar finally spoke. "It's a shame what they've done to us. We're divided because of them, yet they come here. And for what? What could they possibly want to see?"

I gazed at the dozens of white tourists—European and American alike—who snapped photos and cut between us, their shoulders sharp into our chests, as we tried to glimpse the Atlantic Ocean—the last sight enslaved Africans would see before being dragged onto boats or jumping to their deaths.

"They paint Africa as this unsanitary and unsafe place. But, look, this is where they come to vacation." I sucked my teeth. We discussed the need to get more Black people to Senegal, particularly Black Americans. "I'm going to bring more. Aşe O!" I promised him, my eyes cast on the sea, my shoulder pressed against the threshold of the Door of No Return.

"Insha Allah," he nodded, standing next to me. "Insha Allah, Nicole."

Outside the House of Slaves, Babacar grabbed my hand. We ditched our guide and climbed steps of rock to see a cannon left by the French. We sat with two local artists, and drank tea made for us while we discussed Muslim and Christian relations. "Here, Muslims and Christians live together in peace," one of the artists said in Wolof before Babacar translated.

We visited an artist's underground home in a dark bunker built by the French during the Second World War. There we met the artist's wife and children. My nose suffocated in the heat and stink. His son was years older than mine but a child no less. An ache cut across my chest, and I squeezed Babacar's hand. The thought of this family living on pallets under the gleam of a single fluorescent light was devastating. As I stood in the dark crawlway, wondering about my son, what his room looked like and whether he'd ever see the nursery I created for him, Babacar stooped next to me and never once let go of my hand. That night, I invited him to my bed.

## Philadelphia Family Court, Pennsylvania, USA.

The Philadelphia Family Court sits squarely on a congested corner along Broad Street, Philly's central artery. Its elevators, hallways, and waiting rooms are as packed as the surrounding streets. My attorneys and I waited in a glass-faced office for our emergency hearing to be called. While waiting, we reviewed the questions the head attorney on my team would ask, the evidence she would try to move into the record, and the mounds of contracts, affidavits, pictures, emails, and text messages that would help prove our case. But nothing could have prepared me for what was to come.

The case was called. My attorneys and I followed Chanel and her attorney into the courtroom. The judge sat spectacled on his throne, hovering over us litigants and lawyers. Because I filed the emergency petition to establish legal parentage of our child, I was the first to testify.

On the record, I described the start of our relationship, how Chanel and I, both writers, met at a 2019 writers' retreat in Los Angeles, where she lived. How, there, we began to date. How we flew between coasts to see one another at least once a month. How months later, during the beginning of a global pandemic, I unexpectedly moved to LA to be nearer to her. I described our aspirations to create a family. Before either of us proposed to the other, we'd begun dreaming aloud about our future child. How after I proposed to her in Napa and she proposed to me in Waikiki, we called on our queer friends to share with us how they created their families.

Chanel's friend Greg and his husband hired a Guatemalan surrogate to carry their children. Her friend Angel and her wife got pregnant through artificial insemination after several failed attempts with in vitro fertilization (IVF) and other methods in Mexico and at home in the States. My best friend Connie and her wife Rahel got pregnant after many attempts and a miscarriage following artificial insemination. Connie had heard good things about a fertility treatment center called RMA, which was based in Philadelphia—the city Chanel and I considered relocating to to be closer to both our moms while raising our future child.

As my attorney asked questions, I described the research I'd conducted about RMA. I learned RMA had fertility clinics in Philly and LA. The LA clinic was so close to where Chanel and I lived that we could walk to it in under ten minutes. Upon this discovery, we booked an appointment for an in-person consultation. We headed to the clinic, newlyweds giggling beneath our masks, ready to begin the work of creating a queer family unit. At RMA's LA office, we both underwent testing and had blood work drawn, even though I wouldn't carry or use my eggs for our child. Once it was determined that we were free of sexually transmitted diseases and Chanel did not have any medical issues other than age to prevent a viable pregnancy, we were cleared to continue our IVF journey.

Angel and Connie warned us about the lack of Black sperm donors, but we were still excited to begin our search. We logged on to an online sperm bank they both recommended and adjusted the filters to our needs: a Black sperm donor was the only real requirement. Angel and Connie had been right. The number of Black sperm donors was paltry in comparison to the white donors, but we clicked on each photo, all taken of the donors during childhood. One by one, we scrolled through the profiles, noting the donor's ancestry, passions, hobbies, height, and the celebrity to whom the cryobank likened each donor's physical features. None of the donors excited us. They were largely uninspiring, nonartistic, or too short. That is, until we landed on Donor 5787.

Donor 5787 loves to laugh and enjoys the simple things in life. He is spontaneous and likes trying new things. He plays soccer with his friends and creates videos in his free time. Although he is studying accounting in college, he aspires to be a filmmaker. He is kind and friendly and although quiet at first, he opens up easily. He always flashes us a bright, cheerful smile each time he comes in. Our staff consider him very attractive with his nice brown eyes, dark skin, and a tall slim build.... He has a strong jawline and chiseled cheekbones that add to this donor's attractiveness. He looks like rapper Meek Mill.

*Ancestry*: Black

*Ethnic Background*: African (Benin)

*Interests*: Soccer, Videography

*Pregnancy Reported*: No

*CMV Status*: Positive

*Age Range at Donation*: 18–22

*Astrological Sign*: Sagittarius

*Favorite Subject*: Arts, Natural Science, Technology

*Religion*: Christian (Catholic)

*Favorite Pet*: Dog

*Personal Goals*: Financial Security, God/Religion, Marriage/Family, Success, To Be Happy, To Help People, Travel

*Talents/Hobbies*: Soccer, Videography

"He's cute," Chanel lit up, digging her shoulder into mine as we sat side by side to share a single laptop screen. Even though Chanel would carry and I would have no biological connection to our child, we both wanted to see me in the person we made. "And he looks like you, and Meek Mill if these people can be believed."

"Yo, he's a filmmaker, too," I acknowledged. Chanel was a screenwriter, and it was cool to see that they shared this passion.

He was the one: a Black artist, like both of us, who was also a Sagittarius with roots in Benin, like me. Chanel and I were excited and called it kismet. I thanked the ancestors, including her dad, for sending the perfect donor our way.

## Somone, Senegal.

The road from Dakar's rowdy center to La Petite-Côte, in the south of Senegal, took four hours to complete, though without traffic it should have taken less than ninety minutes. No longer clocking a watch, I enjoyed the unpredictability of Senegal's travel time. It meant more time with Babacar and less attention to what was happening in my world. On the highway, we bumped the music we loved, from Senegal's Souleymane Faye to Brooklyn's Jay-Z. We ignored throngs of foot vendors who tried to sell us everything from pamplemousse to pillows. We trickled in and out from between busses packed with people and barely fit for the road.

Babacar beamed. He squeezed my hand and stretched his smile as we discussed the possibilities of a transatlantic romance. To our right, he pointed out a beautiful building made of white and green tiles. Its roof topped the highway we traversed. "This is Camberene, a holy Muslim city. There, in the building, its leader is buried. Seydina Limamou Laye. Behind his grave is the city's cemetery." I gawked at Limamou Laye's gravesite: a colossal building fit for many dwellers but only housing one man.

"Can we go in?" I asked.

He eyed me over. I wore a sleeveless jumpsuit that revealed two tattooed arms from shoulders to wrists.

He pulled my hand to his lips and kissed my fingers. "Next time you come, I'll bring you. Insha Allah. But you must wear a dress and cover your arms and hair."

"To enter the city?"

"Yes," he smiled. "It's tradition."

Almost forty miles south of Dakar, a gathering of baobab trees sandwiched our stretch of the highway. "We're almost there," Babacar said smilelessly. "The baobab welcome us here." My stomach churned at the thought of us separating. Intimacy was something my wife and I lost well before our final decision to separate.

"I'm going to miss you," Babacar said as his thumb stroked my knuckles.

"Me too," I admitted. "You should come up at the end of the week."

"I'll do that," he paused. "Do you have Instagram?"

Much like the road we traversed, our days together had been jam-packed. I rarely went on the internet, and as with time, I gave no thought to social media. Charged by our in-person connection, I hadn't even considered connecting with Babacar online. But the thought that we could stay connected, that I could see how he'd spend his next several days, fueled me. "Of course," I responded and gave him my Instagram handle.

In my villa, away from Babacar, I unpacked my suitcase, stripped into a bathing suit, and took my laptop with me to sit by the pool. It had been days since I last logged in to my email, though I often did a cursory review of incoming mail on my phone to scan for correspondence from the family law firm I retained.

There was no new news. I switched from email to Instagram and saw a new follower alert: Babacar. I followed him back and studied every photo on his page. There weren't many, but a few posts about family, Senegal tourism, music, and politics. I closed out the window and moved to the pool's edge.

Later that night, my phone pinged and the screen glowed. The notification showed an incoming DM from Babacar. I opened his message. I anticipated him telling me how much I was missed, what he was up to, or asking about how I spent my afternoon. Instead, the words sprang from the screen: "Nicole, are you a lesbian?"

I gasped. My body buzzed, protons and electrons colliding. Despite all we shared, Babacar and I hadn't discussed past lovers, sexuality, or queerness. He knew I was married and divorcing, but I hadn't mentioned my spouse was a woman, and he hadn't questioned me about my divorce. I didn't ask him what he thought about queerness. Because I'd made my travel plans when the possibility of a romantic tryst hadn't remotely crossed my mind, I hadn't researched how queerness was perceived in Islamic Senegal, nor considered how a Muslim man in Senegal might view my life as documented on Instagram. So caught up in our romance, I didn't consider that Instagram would out me, that I didn't want to be out, or that being out might be dangerous.

I hadn't even considered stealthiness as a strategy for safety. Hiding my queerness did not require effort if I was traveling alone. I had the privilege of being femme and straight-presenting. It wasn't like my wife would be with me.

But there she was now, in rainbow emojis and queer content spread across my Instagram feed.

## Philadelphia Family Court, Pennsylvania, USA.

My testimony lasted for about an hour. Still under direct examination, I continued to describe our IVF journey for the judge. I told the court that once we moved to Philly, I administered fertility medications to Chanel's abdomen daily until she had enough mature eggs to be retrieved. I waited for Chanel in a parking lot with her mom as the fertility doctor extracted more than twenty eggs from her ovaries.

At home, we awaited word for the number of viable eggs. Then, after arranging for the cryobank to send RMA our sperm, we waited some more to know how many eggs were fertilized. Four. We embarked on another series of shots to prepare her for the placement of one in her uterus. Again, I brought Chanel to the treatment facility and waited for her during the procedure. At home, we waited some more. Finally, we learned we were pregnant.

But, still, we had work to do.

Every morning between 7:00 and 7:30 a.m., I administered progesterone shots into Chanel's buttocks, alternating the side each day, to help prevent miscarriage. Each day massaging the area I pricked to keep hard, swollen, painful lumps from forming. This carried on for months.

We attended weekly blood draws, fertility clinic visits, and obstetrician visits. I drove Chanel to prenatal yoga classes and registered us for classes on what to expect during birth and how to care for infants. We researched and hired a doula. After signing contracts for the fertility clinic and affidavits for second-parent adoption, our doula's contract was the final one we signed.

We spent approximately $40,000 on sperm, IVF treatments, medications, retaining a law firm to complete the second-parent adoption, and a doula. We split every large expense down the middle and attended every class and appointment together. I bought our baby clothes, Pampers in bulk, items for his nursery, and books that I read to him in vitro. But by the beginning of 2023, when Chanel was five months pregnant, things shifted between us.

As our families entered our shared life, we lost trust in one another. Chanel thought my father and stepmother treated her poorly during a visit—which they did—but I resented her for suggesting that I should cut my father out of my life. After a surprise birthday party I threw for her, I shared with Chanel that her brother had crossed a few lines, and I thought he was a gaslighter. Chanel took offense. We found ourselves at an unexpected impasse. Our communication dwindled, and it grew contentious on the rare occasion we did talk. I moved my stuff and myself into the guest bedroom without warning. "Things aren't working," I said when I made the last trip from our second-floor bedroom to the basement. Chanel agreed.

We spent the next month sleeping in different bedrooms but sharing most meals. While eating, we'd watch an old episode of *RuPaul's Drag Race*, a new episode of *Ready to Love*, or some other brainless show. We talked about the possibility of repairing our marriage as well as of divorce and coparenting. "What do you think about trying to work on things?" she asked.

"With a therapist? I'm game. But we should also be prepared to discuss how to divorce and coparent with love at the center."

"A radical queer love," she joked.

"A radical queer love," I deadpanned. "What does that look like to you?"

We would live together for the first year of our son's life, though we'd continue to sleep in separate rooms. We'd arrange for both our moms to come to Philly and help. My mom lived two hours away in Brooklyn, but Chanel's mom lived much closer in a Philly suburb. We ideated that the room we planned to make our nursery, the one directly up the hall from our marital bedroom, would instead be mine. We'd incorporate a nursery in Chanel's room. The basement bedroom into which I moved would return to being our in-law suite.

But then, in February, I left for two months of residencies. In the fresh environment of the Pacific Northwest, without the strain of relationship dysfunction and with the time to pour into my spiritual and emotional wellness, I meditated. During those morning meditation sessions, lying on my back or sitting cross-legged, the same questions pierced my consciousness: *Do you want this marriage? What's best for your child?*

I wanted to raise my son in a household of love. I wanted out of my marriage.

While eating dinner with writers at my second residency, someone remarked that writing residencies birthed two things: new work and divorces. Everyone laughed, including me. But damn if her statement wasn't true to the bone.

Chanel's testimony corroborated all of the facts about our pregnancy I'd testified to, but she added some things I had not seen coming. Not from a mile, not even from five feet. When asked why she no longer considered me our child's parent, she responded, "I changed my mind." Later, she said I could not be our child's parent because I was "toxic" and "abusive." When pressed by the judge, she offered no examples to support her claim. Then, when pressed further, her tune changed. She said she never intended for me to be our child's parent, despite all the contracts and affidavits we jointly signed, and that she did not know what any of those documents meant. She testified under oath that she did not understand a single contract we signed despite taking a year's worth of contract law before graduating from law school. Despite her fifteen years as a lawyer.

Under the penalty of perjury, she lied and lied again.

## Somone, Senegal.

I abandoned my phone for the superior research device of my laptop. I typed "gays in Senegal" into Google's home page and skimmed the search results with dread. "Rise of homophobia in Senegal forcing LGBTQ people into the shadows," read one news article. "For homosexuals in Senegal, a life prevented," read another, and my hands balled into fists as I took in its subheader: "People here are not trying to understand. You are homosexual: you are banned, typed, handed over to the police." Wikipedia confirmed that "Same-sex sexual activity is illegal in Senegal." Indeed, homosexuality was seen as an offense against Allah. My head pounded; my breath quickened. The man whom I made love to for days on end was far from a devout Muslim, but still, I knew he held tight to his faith.

Panic consumed me.

Babacar knew my whereabouts and that I didn't have a car to make an escape. I was alone in a foreign land. I wasn't only vulnerable; I was an easy target. I didn't even know how to call the police. Was 911 worldwide? Even if I did call, Senegalese homes rarely have actual addresses but rely on geographical coordinates instead. I was in the middle of a rural village. How long would it take the police to come? Would they even bother to show up? Would the dispatcher understand English? I didn't know Wolof or French. I was stuck in the sticks with only household utensils to defend myself.

I spent the night fighting with a precarious internet connection. Whenever my Wi-Fi returned, I deleted rainbow emojis from my IG bio and posts. I archived pictures of queer friends and past loves. I removed from my website every mention of my queerness, including the many articles I'd written that touched on my nonbinary, queer identity, even if remotely.

With a spotty internet connection, it took hours to erase myself.

For those hours, I stayed awake, afraid to close my eyes, worried that Babacar and a pitchfork-carrying gang would arrive at my doorstep, climb its guard walls, and violate me—by rape or murder.

While purging the internet of my queerness, I cried and lamented my decision to travel, my decision to leave my wife, and my decision to marry in the first place. At home, my queerness rendered me childless. In Senegal, my queerness was a crime that rendered me exposed to violence and criminality.

### Philadelphia, Pennsylvania, USA.

Nothing happened to Chanel for lying on the record, like no one hunted me in Senegal for being queer. Not one man climbed over the wall, kicked in a glass door, put a knife in my belly. I wouldn't give anyone a reason to. I opened my phone and returned to Babacar's message, *Nicole, are you a lesbian?* "No," I thumbed. "Why would you ask that?" I feigned confusion.

I wish I could say I was more courageous. That I claimed my queerness in whole or part under all circumstances. But I didn't. I wanted to make it home. I wanted to see my family. I wanted to meet my son.

After two weeks in Senegal, my flight landed at JFK ahead of schedule. I opened my cell to a text from Babacar, "Did you make it?"

I smiled at the care, at having someone other than my mom concerned about whether I reached my destination after a long trip. The last time I'd traded travel texts with someone other than her was a year before, with my wife. "Just landed at JFK. Now, headed to get my car for the drive to Philly."

For the next few weeks, Babacar and I video-called one another through WhatsApp at least once daily. We sent text messages with pictures of our time together and songs that made us think of each other; we traded voice notes that professed our love. "I wish you could come to the States," I pressed the arrow to send the voice note his way. "I know, La Lune. It's not that easy for Senegalese."

I stiffened, surprised by the endearment—the very one I called my son since we learned he existed. *La Lune. The Moon.* My Moon-child. Mr. Moon.

Though I had been safe at home, I hadn't revisited the conversation about my queerness with Babacar.

"Do you have time for a call tonight?"

"Of course," he replied.

On our call, I fumbled through the words. "You know, I'm married. I'm, I'm . . ."

"Yes, you divorce?"

"Yes, yes. But, I've got something to tell you." I paused.

"You can tell me anything. It don't matter, La Lune. I got you."

"I'm married to, um, divorcing, a woman."

Babacar was silent. "But," he asked, flummoxed, "why you lie?"

I shared with Babacar the circumstances of my divorce, my choice to walk away from my marriage when Chanel was seven months pregnant, Chanel's decision to cut me out of our son's life, the custody dispute we were currently in, the suffering that led me to Senegal, the fact that I had not met or held or seen a picture of our then nine-month-old son. He listened without interjecting. When I finished telling him about the legal proceedings and where the case stood, he sighed.

"That is your child, Nicole. God sent him to you both. It doesn't matter how he got here. He came to you both. Keep fighting for him. No matter what, you will be with him. Insha Allah."

I bawled like a baby. Like my own, I do not know. I do not know when my Moonchild cries, for how long, or why. I do not know the sounds of Mr. Moon's wails or joy. But Babacar listened. "It's okay, La Lune. It will work out. Trust in God. Trust him."

## Somone, Senegal.

Separated by an ocean and a five-hour time difference, the whirlwind romance Babacar and I established ended almost as fast as it started. But we continued to reach out to one another once or twice every couple of months, staying caught up via video calls. Finally, a year after we met, I returned to Senegal, and we saw each other once again. Under a full moon and outside a thatched-roof hut, we drank whiskey and listened to music from one of our cell phone's speakers.

"I have a son on the way," he said.

I smacked his thigh. "Get outta here! When?"

"Soon," he swallowed. "I didn't know it. The mother and I were only together two times. She sent her family to tell me four days ago."

"What?" my mouth widened; a laugh rode an exhale. "No shit?"

"Yes. I have responsibilities now." He raised an eyebrow and took a drag from his cigarette. "What about you? How's your son?"

I had developments to report. A few weeks earlier the Pennsylvania Superior Court had issued a nine-judge unanimous ruling in my favor. In response, Chanel filed an appeal requesting that the state Supreme Court hear the case. But now, instead of dread, I felt optimism. My attorneys were working on our response. I caught Babacar up and sucked the whiskey down straight, only to chase it with a swig of Coke.

He followed my move and threw his glass back. "What I tell you? God knows what he's doing. Your son is yours."

"I know," I smiled. "God is good."

"All the time."

I thought back to the years before, the dreams about Dakar, the conversation in Curaçao, the friend in New Orleans, the Dakar residency that never was. The Egun's messages came at a time when I questioned why God hated me so much that he'd take my son away. Now, sitting under a starlit sky, drinking whiskey with a beautiful Mouride, talking about his soon-to-be son, my ex-wife, our child, and the appellate court's precedent-setting, unanimous decision affirming that I was his parent, I was awestruck at the course of my life. The journey of one year. The joy I hadn't thought possible before crossing the Atlantic with only my faith.

"I think I'll see him soon," I said.

"You will, Nicole. You must believe it." Babacar smacked his glass's bottom against the rickety table and leaned in close. Our eyes locked, and I took another swig of the brown liquor, enjoying the trail of fire it burned down my throat and chest. "Insha Allah!" he said.

Once the feeling returned to my tongue, I affirmed, "Aşe O, my friend! Aşe O."

# Mirador

### ALEXANDER CHEE

It was summer 2005, and I was in Spain, and I told myself I was in love.

M., as we may as well call him, my boyfriend at the time, was taking classes in an immersion school there. He had been hired by a private college in New York to teach French, and then, after he accepted the job, was asked if he could also teach Spanish. He said yes and began looking for immersion programs.

This was his first job after finishing his Ph.D. in comparative literature—he was a scholar in medieval French literature, with a specialty in sodomy—specifically, the history of the idea of pleasure during sex. It was something he always had the presence of mind to joke about—part of what I liked about him. He chose Granada because it has many excellent immersion schools (for reasons I've never understood) and because he had always wanted to go to the city of the poet Federico García Lorca.

M. loved poets, wrote poetry, sometimes wrote me poems, and his favorite poets all seemed to have met violent or tragic deaths, including Lorca. The day we visited Lorca's house in Granada, we found the whole of it kept much as it was when he was there. I noticed the roses in the vases were almost gone, ready to be replaced, while roses bloomed outside. I imagined the poet had planted them, or at least tended them, but I didn't want to ask in case it wasn't true. I can still see the shrug as the tour guide said, "Yes, he was the son of a wealthy man," a detail I wrote down in my notebook, along with how we all then looked at the beautiful wooden desk that seemed like a boat. I didn't know why the guide said that and still don't. Just as I don't know why a book of his poems on the desk that day was open to "Poet in New York"—his other city. Lorca's murder had made him Granada's presiding ghost. If his body had vanished at the hands of fascist murderers, he was everywhere there now, his face and words on mugs, T-shirts, restaurant menus and graffiti nearly anywhere you looked.

Unlike M., I already spoke Spanish. I needed to go to Paris and London to research my second novel, so we planned a summer trip across Europe to combine our aims, beginning with me in London and Paris, where he would join me, then Granada, beginning in July and concluding in late August.

We were still getting to know each other then, boyfriends in a literary mode. Our love was just seven months old and built out of romantic email after romantic email, romantic trip after romantic trip, until here we were. I was increasingly aware, though, that just a month before, I had been buying phone cards in Paris to call him from the glass phone booths still everywhere then, and the urgency to talk to him faltered now that we were together. And so I was at once happy, sure I was in the most fulfilling relationship of my life, and also sure that I didn't know him well enough—that I was even making a mistake, the size of which was as yet uncertain because it was still happening.

The street to our apartment in Granada that summer ran roughly parallel to the Rio Darro, a trickle for many years now, really, and, that summer, always full of stray cats and dogs and the occasional ducks, which during the worst of the sun hid in the shrubs, a bright seam of green foliage in the dusty city that hid what water remained.

M. had chosen our apartment because it was opposite the Alhambra, the magnificent historic Moorish palace on the hill across from our neighborhood, the Albaicín. The Darro ran between us. Our roof patio was opposite a simple mirador with a fountain, where there always seemed to be people playing guitar and smoking marijuana, with whom we exchanged waves. The apartment was simple and clean, its magnificence concentrated in the patio view of the palace and the city. Each room was on a different floor off a spiral staircase, the apartment as winding as the hill it was on. We left and returned by climbing a series of winding footpaths and side streets, and if I was confused, at night, I was always able to follow the guitar music home.

I had never been to Spain. We had come by train, leaving for Madrid from Paris in a Trenhotel, an antique overnight train, spending a night in Madrid before going to Granada on another train. I remember best the six hours of olive trees and little else, the landscape sere and sparse. I counted the people I saw in between: a gang of six men on horseback with guns and, separately, a single man on a tractor.

We arrived and did our first shopping at Corte Inglés, pure tourists; after all of those olive trees, we bought a bottle of flor de aceite, a raw green cold-pressed Andalusian olive oil that impressed us as being as smoky as our favorite whiskies. We made a first dinner of bacalao sautéed in butter and leeks with brown rice and lentils and a salad of beautiful green tomatoes and manchego dressed with the olive oil and some sea salt bought in Paris.

M.'s days at the school began early and were long, and left to my own devices, I would write for a few hours and then walk through the side streets, where I mapped the ancient cathedrals, most of which had been mosques before the expulsion of the Muslims, and then had the traditional breakfast of bread with tomate, a fresh tomato purée on toast, and olive oil. In Granada, there are usually two kinds of olive oil on the tables to put on, it seemed, anything you ate, but especially for this.

My Spanish was a Mexican Spanish learned during a summer immersion program twenty years earlier, and I knew Spaniards condescended to it. As I practiced speaking again, I listened for the differences and adapted accordingly. It was the first time in a long time that I had no direct obligations—I was there just for the fun of it. So I busied myself with finding the best of the cheap wines sold at the candy shops, seeing flamenco performances, eating churros late at night, ordering a salt-baked fish and watching as the waiter cracked it open and filleted it tableside. And I wandered the Alhambra in awe at the tile, the gardens, the lushness made possible by the ancient waterworks left behind by the exiled Muslim engineers.

We became obsessed with a panadería that sold bread made with whole wheat grown locally, staffed by the most expressionless girl ever, a paragon of the Granadian phenomenon of mala follá, a famous expression of local exhausted disinterest that doesn't even rise to the level of contempt, and which, once we learned about it, we looked for everywhere. I practiced asserting myself with the same flatness at an ancient taberna we favored, where, under the smoked ham hocks hanging over the bar in rows, the hooves facing the ceiling, I would order quickly, in my best casual quick Spanish. A moment's hesitation and the bartender's eyes would flick away to whoever was ready.

At first we imagined this practiced detachment was a legacy of Franco and of socialism—a reluctance to participate in capitalism? But why was it Granadian exclusively? Why would their disappointment be greater than that of all of Spain? We never found the answer.

It is hard to think about him at this distance, easy to think about Spain.

I would be right about the mistake he was. What I would learn in the year we were together after this, but did not know then, was that there was someone M. was pretending to be with me—someone content to be monogamous.

For example, easily the biggest attraction besides the Alhambra in Granada is the hammam, the baths. M. went, but I never did, which seemed innocent to me until it did not. And there was the night he came home late from a gathering with friends from the program. He was drunk and fell asleep quickly. I found his clothes in another room—something he had never done before. It was as if he wanted to hide what had happened in them. But this didn't matter enough yet, not enough to put a stop to it.

I liked M. I was having my first summer in Spain, and he was good in bed, funny at dinner, smart about books. Enjoying that was not a mistake. Hiding himself from me was. When I eventually discovered the truth, I was more offended that he wouldn't tell me. He thought I wanted monogamy more than him, and I didn't. And I couldn't forgive that I didn't get to choose.

Some things I remember very clearly from that summer: learning to love the feel of cold red wine in my mouth on a hot day. The beautiful boy on the bus the whole way to the beach at Carboneras from Granada, who was burning the back of the rubber and vinyl seat with a lighter, but slowly, never enough to catch fire, who stopped only to take pictures of himself on his phone. The man putting saccharin in his fresh orange juice. And the streets paved with stones taken from the river, smooth and shining in the dark, like the backs of fish.

M. can keep his secrets, I told myself then. I have this. That was my bargain. I still think it is a good one.

# The Return

PUTSATA REANG

**1.**

From high above, ten thousand feet and approaching Po-chentong Airport in Cambodia's capital, Phnom Penh, the Tonlé Sap River is a liver on the landscape, splayed in the center of a nation that has struggled to find its calm. It's ringed by rinds of green land, tropical trees and shrubs that camouflage busy fishing villages thronged along its banks. Apart from its sheer size—it's enormous whether you're looking from high up or up front, straight on—it stands out for a simple, stunning stunt that only four rivers in the world pull off: It reverses course each year, going the opposite way it came. Which is a matter of hydraulics and nature's will. But for a queer writer returning to her geograph-ical beginnings, it's a matter of meaning.

It's here, and only here, the place I come from, where I meet myself most fully in the landscape. The children's book author Dr. Rudine Sims Bishop says books are a window that allows us a glimpse into the lives and experiences of others *or* a mirror re-flecting parts of ourselves back to us. I think it's places. Places do that, too. We travel to see ourselves from the outside, at a remove, to locate ourselves in the landscape, and if we're lucky, we return to where we started better for having slung ourselves into a new environment, for travel often demands us to question where and how we belong.

But this particular trip to Cambodia was different. Though I was born there, I had spent my entire life in the U.S., where I studied journalism in college and where, at age thirty, I crossed back over the Pacific Ocean to live and work in my homeland as a journalist. That move to the motherland was not my first time home but rather one in a string of crossings started when I was fifteen years old. But what made this particular trip different from those prior visits was that I was going home changed in two fundamental ways: I was completely out of the closet that July 2023, by way of a memoir that launched the previous year detailing my conflict with my mom over being gay, and I was returning as a tourist rather than a resident, as someone who was meant to move on. I was nervous about how these two ways of being and seeing my country would interact with the land I so deeply loved—a land I was forced to flee fifty years earlier. Every return since then has been another chance to practice leaving, by choice rather than necessity.

My family fled our country in 1975 when the Communist Khmer Rouge regime captured Cambodia on a navy vessel insufficiently stocked with food and water. The boat was built for a crew of roughly thirty men, and on that day, three hundred refugees were crammed on board. The ship had no destination when it set out across the Gulf of Thailand and veered into the Pacific Ocean. The only purpose was to leave.

Ten days into that journey, my one-year-old body—hidden in the sling of my mother's sarong—stopped feeding, stopped crying, then stopped moving. The captain ordered my mother to throw me overboard. "The corpse," he said, "will contaminate the others."

But she refused. And within that refusal, the rest of my story spins. Eventually, that origin story would come to overshadow this particular trip home with an onslaught of complicated emotions.

I spent my life trying to repay my mother for saving my life, trying to be worthy of her rescue. I wanted to be the perfect Cambodian daughter—an effort that included getting good grades, going to college, galloping into a journalism career. It did not include coming out as gay. When I finally did shake off my shame and tell the truth of me, my siblings surrounded me with the kind of ardent love that comes from shared trauma, the kind we carried in our bones, the kind that comes from being cleaved from home.

But it was our mother's reaction I feared most. She cast me off with an immense anguish in her voice that made me wonder whether she wished she'd done it sooner, on that boat, before I had the chance to blemish our family's reputation. She called me ungrateful, disloyal, disrespectful, and stopped talking to me for months. I had spent my life trying to win my mother's heart and suddenly lost it in three simple words I couldn't take back: I am gay.

Now our story was out, on bookshelves, in classrooms, in clubs, and I found myself traveling across the U.S. to spread a single message: Be who you are. Since the book's release, my mother and I took slow, tentative steps back to each other, and now we were about to travel together with our family back to where our story began.

I couldn't have known then, before boarding my flight in Seattle that July, that this trip would expose cracks not obvious on the outside—both in my country and myself. And those cracks would lead me to a different kind of reckoning than merely coming out to my family and community in America; it would be a reckoning, whether I wanted it or not, of what it means to be a queer Khmer refugee come home.

On that July night, peering out the window of the Airbus A321neo, the Tonlé Sap was mere silhouette, the surface shimmery and sauced with a mix of moonglow and the jet's landing lights as the wing tipped us toward Phnom Penh. I both wanted to take this trip and didn't want to. When my five siblings chose Cambodia as the destination for our annual summer reunion in 2023, I stayed unusually quiet.

I was excited that my entire family—including my two older siblings who had never returned since our leaving—would be together in our country for the first time in nearly fifty years, and I was excited for my ten nieces and nephews, who would see, in the plainest and loveliest terms, one half of who they are. But something in my gut twinged at the thought of my own journey to Cambodia, an emotion I couldn't yet name. I thought I was nervous about the elections that summer of 2023, because elections in Cambodia often meant protests, and protests had a way of devolving into bloodbaths—violence not only sanctioned but ordered by the country's authoritarian ruler. It wasn't fully that. I thought I was worried that Cambodia might have changed so much, from what I'd heard from friends who had recently visited, that I might not recognize it, that I might be disappointed. It wasn't completely that either.

It took a long time for me to understand I was riddled with anxiety about turning backwards to face the person I once was, or, rather, the person I thought I could make myself be, all those years ago when I followed my journalism career to Cambodia.

It had been more than a decade since I had lived in Phnom Penh and loved a man I thought I'd marry. We had an apartment, a housekeeper, books banked along the walls. Having a husband made sense in the context of my country, where girls are raised to follow a single path of getting married and raising babies. Back then, as a resident of Cambodia, the pressures to marry a man were magnified by a cavalcade of pushy aunties, who regularly registered their discontent that I was in my thirties and not yet married.

It was 2005 when I moved to Cambodia, and it seemed impossible to find a woman to date in Phnom Penh, both because the pool of expats consisted largely of bachelors and because my conservative Khmer culture made even considering being with a woman, much less a Khmer woman, feel untenable, untouchable, unfathomable. In the U.S., my American culture became a ballast against my Khmer culture when I came out as gay; Pride parades, Pride flags posted on businesses, and the legalization of gay marriage reinforced who I was. But in Cambodia I encountered no parades or posted flags, no cultural counterbalance that made my queerness feel okay.

Being gay in Cambodia wasn't illegal, but all my life I had tried to tread carefully around my culture. Cambodian gender roles were rigidly fixed. To be born a boy was cause for celebration; to be born a girl was considered a burden. As a girl, you were meant for one thing only: to grow up, get married, have kids, and exist to serve your husband. My mother insisted that my sisters and I learn how to cook, telling us, "One day, when you have a husband, you have to have a hot meal ready for him." She said "husband," not "wife," and I sensed the inevitability of her words.

To be gay in Cambodia would be a betrayal and an unforgivable moral offense in the eyes of my relatives and my people, disrupting a centuries-old cultural order in which gender roles are distinctly delineated. To fail at being a girl was to also fail one's family. I could fail in this way in America, where having a career was encouraged for girls, and, for a little while, that career gave me cover for my gayness. But to fail in this way in Cambodia felt too disrespectful to me. So, I did what I have always been good at: I adapted to my surroundings. I found a man to marry.

But identities, like rivers, reverse course, too, and we find our truest selves in the turbulent churn. I later left the man, the country, and my beloved if pushy aunties and relatives, and I flew back across the Pacific Ocean to America for good. It was spring of 2015. Two years later, I finally did get married—to a woman.

Now, I was about to return to my homeland to face a past still barbed with the kind of rough-hewn pain cut from years spent bending away from who you are. Since leaving Cambodia for good in 2015, I finally accepted the fact of my existence, let myself be who I was meant to be. I didn't know if the fundamental way I had changed—embracing my own queerness—would be acceptable to my relatives, my country, or even myself.

I also didn't know just how thin of a line exists between courage and cowardice, and how hard it would be to make myself repeat the same three words that made me lose my mother's love. Or that for all the ways I had changed, my country had transformed, too, in ways that I both could and couldn't accept. And maybe that was the lesson; people and places are in constant flux, spinning into and out of different drafts of ourselves, and sometimes the best we can do is not lose ourselves completely in the revolutions.

**2.**

When the wheels of the plane screeched to a stop at Pochentong Airport just past 11 p.m., a familiar surge of anxiety gripped my ribs. Getting through Customs was a delicate dance for Khmer *pordadeh*, or Khmers from abroad. The Cambodian customs officials know many of us Khmer from the diaspora return, flush with cash strapped to our chests in sling bags to distribute to our relatives; the officials operate with an expectation that they, too, will get a disbursement from the cash bags.

"Younger sister, can you spare some change for cookies and drinks?" a customs officer would invariably say to me while holding my passport hostage in his hand.

More than a decade prior, when I lived in Cambodia and traveled frequently around the region, I learned to say in Khmer, "No. I only have credit cards," and I was left alone.

But experience has a way of imprinting memories on us that come back when we meet those moments once more.

Yet this time, there was something different. To my surprise, the customs officer didn't ask me for anything. He stamped my passport and waved me off. Had the corruption I'd been accustomed to when I lived and worked in Cambodia as a journalist ended? I was skeptical, but I liked this new stress-free way of entering my country.

Dragging my suitcase out of the terminal to hail a cab, I entered the familiar sauna of Southeast Asia, a hot blast of air hitting me like a heat lamp on high suddenly flicked on. There are only two types of air in Cambodia: the refreshing cold air of an air-conditioned building or car, or the thick, slippery, oppressive air outside. My pores responded automatically, unleashing a flash round of sweat that soaked me.

At Pochentong Airport, as at other airports in the region, the hustle hits as hard as the humidity.

"Miss, where you go? I have taxi," men called out from seemingly all directions. Only a few took me for being Khmer, beckoning me in my mother tongue.

"Bong srey, doe nah? Khyum minh taxi."

I chose an older man, thin and lithe as he helped load my luggage into the trunk. He asked, in Khmer, if I was "Khmer," and I didn't lie.

"Jah, khyum mao be Amerique," I replied. "Yes, I'm from America." And so began the code-switching I'd become accustomed to as a Khmer from abroad, the daily decision-making of whether to speak in English or in my native tongue, based on how I thought I might be treated. In America when I was growing up, my mother often feigned not being able to speak English in certain circumstances, which was a half-truth. She didn't speak English well, but she could communicate fine enough. I noticed how she pretended not to speak English when she wanted to observe rather than participate, or when she thought she might get away with something, like illegally sneaking durian fruit across the border from Canada.

In Cambodia, I used language in strategic ways, too. I sometimes feigned not being able to speak Khmer if I thought I needed to command a certain kind of treatment—namely respect—as a Khmer woman. Communicating in English established authority in the context of the hierarchical culture of Cambodia, and I deployed it to position myself as an equal to Khmer men.

On this cab ride, the driver was quiet and kind. I detected no threat, so I spoke in Khmer as his 1990s model Toyota Camry careered out of the airport parking lot and swerved east toward town.

The ride from Pochentong Airport to the center of Phnom Penh carried us past the Royal University de Phnom Penh with its mid-century modern concrete structures emphasizing arches and modernist angles and circular stairways—the handiwork of famed Khmer architect Vann Molyvann. We drove past beer halls advertising cheap Angkor draught and BBQ, and storefronts selling SIM cards and shrimp puffs and countless motorcycle repair shops. These were all familiar markers in my memory.

When we passed the turnoff to Olympic Market and the neighborhood where I once lived with my then-boyfriend, I felt my heart pinch, realizing in that moment how far I had traveled away from that past self when I tried to convince myself I could be happy with a man, not yet letting myself recognize the distinction between "could be happy" and "am happy." We had met just as he arrived at the international media organization I was preparing to leave; I was on my way to Afghanistan to work for the same organization, and he was starting a new program to train Khmer journalists how to cover the imminent Khmer Rouge tribunal, where surviving leaders of the genocidal regime would take the stand. We loved each other hard and recklessly in those two months before my departure to Kabul, and by the following summer when I returned to Phnom Penh, we moved into our apartment near Olympic Market.

From the taxi window, my eyes took in the turns my memories still held. There goes the narrow side street lined with sundry small shops and cafés where we bought batteries and baked goods. There goes the corner where we stood, waiting for tuk-tuks to take us across town to our favorite restaurants on the riverside.

There goes a past I didn't know I'd still find painful to remember for the way I ended that relationship. And here came the first ghost of myself among many scattered across this land I'd meet in the coming days and weeks.

But then my gaze got long, extending upward on shadows and outlines I didn't recall seeing before; Phnom Penh had grown up, literally. The closer we got to town, the more I saw a changed landscape: multistory office buildings rising vertically on the cityscape and living quarters stacked like Lego blocks having risen out of what had been before vacant land. It wasn't just the vertical skyline; what struck me even more was that I couldn't read the words on the sides of these buildings. They were not in English. And they were not in Khmer. The signs featured the feathered calligraphy of Mandarin.

"It's everywhere," the taxi driver said, as if reading my thoughts. He spoke into the rearview mirror, watching me watch the city I once called home. "Everything is Chinese now."

In that moment, I didn't grasp the extent of what he meant, and I wouldn't find out until the accumulation of days and experiences on this trip started stacking up.

Just before midnight I checked into the Royal Gate Residence & Hotel, a modest colonial-era building, white and bright with outrageously heavy teak doors, on the south side of the Royal Palace near the bank of the Tonlé Sap River. Half of my family, including my parents, stayed there, too, while the other half billeted at the more deluxe Royal Palace Resort Hotel a few blocks away. My older sister Sinaro and brother Sophea marveled at how plush accommodations in Cambodia cost the same or less than one-star hotels in America.

My first morning back in Cambodia, I was awakened predawn by the chanting of Theravada Buddhist monks from the nearby Wat Botum, the pagoda my relatives visited during major holidays because it was said the monks at Wat Botum were especially adept at bestowing fortuitous blessings on devotees. When I lived there, one of my aunties, so intent on finding me a husband, once dispatched to Wat Botum for the express purpose of asking the monks for a special prayer so that I might soon find a match. I politely thanked her when she told me. I couldn't have predicted that months later I would meet the man who became my boyfriend.

The monks' moderated morning invocations calmed me, singular and steady in tone and tenor the way a heart beats when the body is at peace. I split the blinds to a provocation of bright light that shot into the room, barging in like nosy neighbors, pushing past you before you have a chance to say no.

That early in the morning, I expected working men would be shoulder to shoulder in the noodle stalls slurping *hieu tiev* and washing it down with coffee thick as motor oil, its potency mitigated with condensed milk. I went to find my parents first, thinking they might like a bowl of noodles, too.

There was something about a steaming bowl of *hieu tiev* in the morning that plants you precisely in place. The hot broth in hot weather is said to be healing. And the hunt for the best *hieu tiev* shop has always been a point of pride among Khmers. My niece, Lydia, born and raised in Nebraska, joined our search, excited to dive headlong into the local cuisine.

In the hotel lobby, I searched for a newspaper to take along, but the only thing clamped inside a wooden dowel on the newspaper rack was the *Sin Chew Daily*. The voice of the airport taxi driver drifted back to me: "Everywhere is Chinese now." I considered asking the front desk staff why only a Chinese newspaper was available, but then I heard my mother call to me from the hotel entrance and was reminded of the morning's priority. Once we stepped outside of the hotel's air-conditioned lobby into the sultry air, it only took a half-block walk to find noodles. But what we found was not *hieu tiev*. Instead, the noodle shop only offered Vietnamese pho noodles. When the waiter, short and trim with a look of disinterest etched on his face, arrived at our table, my dad asked bluntly, "Do you have *hieu tiev*?"

"No, sir," the waiter said. "This is a pho noodle shop."

"But you're Khmer," my father intoned. "Isn't the shop owner Khmer? Why aren't you serving Khmer noodles?" My father smirked, dismissively, and the waiter just shrugged and walked away.

Lydia and I ordered the Vietnamese pho, prepared by a Khmer chef, while my parents decided to hold out for Cambodian noodle soup that they were certain they could find somewhere else. They didn't succeed. Not that day, nor the next. I later learned from my relatives that many of the city's *hieu tiev* shops had been replaced by pho noodle shops—another startling transformation in Cambodia. The Vietnamese have been historic enemies of the Khmers; so why were the Khmers now cooking Vietnamese cuisine in our own country?

When I lived in Phnom Penh, no one wanted to eat pho. There was exactly one pho noodle shop, in the tourist part of the Sisowath Quay on the waterfront. Its customers were tourists and expats, and the shop was relentlessly full of people speaking a variety of foreign languages. The owner sold her bowl of pho noodles for quadruple the price of a bowl of Khmer noodles. My people clearly caught on.

Suddenly, the Khmer hustle felt hostile. I felt offended that such a ubiquitous part of my culture could get so summarily supplanted by another culture via one of my favorite foods in the name of turning a profit. But I couldn't judge. In a country where a majority of residents still earn less than $1 a day, hustle was synonymous with survival.

That afternoon, Ma texted my siblings and me to meet in the lobby of our hotel: Our first outing together was to visit some of our city cousins and their family-run coffee shop on the outskirts of Phnom Penh.

Reaksay, my cousin's husband, drove me in his Hilux pickup truck while my siblings loaded up into tuk-tuks, "for the experience," they said, even though I tried to tell them it would be hot and dusty and, depending on the driver, maybe a little hair-raising. Riding in Reaksay's car, as he lurched and swerved through Phnom Penh's rush-hour traffic, I confronted an upsetting fact: that even as some families were able to climb the tricky and slippery social and economic rungs of our nation, a relentless disappointment still loomed among so many people.

I'd asked him about all the new buildings I had seen between the airport and the city center, and how they seemed to suggest luxury and a country suddenly speeding away from its dark history of genocide and racing toward capitalism. I asked him about the Vietnamese pho noodle shops and the comment the taxi driver had made about the Chinese being "everywhere."

"They are," Reaksay said. "Our country has swung fully toward China. Our leaders don't care about equality and human rights. The 'big people' only care about money."

As Reaksay moved his hands on the wheel, I noticed that his finger lacked the purple ink that I had seen on nearly everyone else's fingers, from the hotel staff to the families walking on the riverfront promenade—evidence of having voted in the recent elections.

Before I could ask Reaksay why he didn't vote, he told me about the ongoing corruption that made it near impossible to be a business owner and turn a profit when corrupt government officials kept finding new ways of imposing bogus fines and fees on businesses that could be easily erased with the right amount of bribe money.

"The elections are a joke," Reaksay said. "I didn't vote because I can't vote for a man who allows this kind of corruption to continue and is the mastermind behind so much of it." He added, "On the surface, Cambodia looks like it has made progress. But the people are being pinched by corruption. The small people are unhappy. And if you speak up, you better watch your back."

I thought about the customs official at the airport who didn't ask me for bribe money to enter my own country. Surface-level change. I thought about the new buildings I saw with signage in Chinese languages that hinted at deeper economic and political dysfunction. And I thought about how odd it was that for the first time in years, there were no public protests, which had become common, in advance of Cambodia's July 23 elections. In the intervening years since I had last been in Cambodia, Hun Sen's regime had effectively banned all opposition parties via a Supreme Court decision that made it illegal to operate an opposition political party within the country; and the prime minister succeeded in shuttering the nation's last independent English-language newspaper, the *Cambodian Daily*, by having its Ministry of Trade and Commerce levy a multimillion-dollar fine that put the newspaper out of business. In the weeks and months before my family's arrival in Cambodia, Hun Sen ordered remaining opposition party leaders to be jailed, along with journalists and human rights workers. Among those the prime minister imprisoned the year before my family visited in June 2022 was Theary Seng, a Michigan-raised human rights lawyer organizing for human rights and democratic reform in Cambodia.

I had met Theary in the fall of 2005 when I first relocated to Cambodia as a journalist. She invited me to a house party at her modest but beautiful flat overlooking the Tonlé Sap on Phnom Penh's Sisowath Quay. When I entered the room, I was thrilled to see it filled with Khmers from the diaspora, like me, from countries such as France, Australia, even Germany, and, of course, America—all of us there to help our homeland in whatever ways we could. Back then, there was a robust media with two English-language daily newspapers and dozens of Khmer-language newspapers, along with independent radio stations and a burgeoning online news ecosystem. There were opposition parties at national elections, and I spoke openly to my relatives about political corruption.

"You can't do that anymore, bong srei," Reaksay said. "They'll throw you in jail, American citizen or not."

I wanted to continue my conversation with Reaksay, but he turned the pickup down a dirt road and sped toward a housing development containing multiple blocks of row houses, where he lurched to a stop at a corner. Several of my cousins, including Reaksay's wife, dashed out from their coffee shop to greet me, pressing a delicious iced latte in my hand as they pulled me inside. Minutes later two tuk-tuks pulled up, and I watched my siblings step out of the carriages one by one, wild-haired and wiping grit from their eyes with *kramas* but smiling enormously from the thrill of riding in a three-wheeled open cart.

When a few hours lapsed spent laughing and sampling different drinks and fielding get-to-know-you questions from my relatives, specifically to Sinaro and Sophea, who were meeting our
relatives for the first time, my family loaded back up into cars and
tuk-tuks and returned to their hotels. I stayed. It had been nearly
a decade since I last saw these relatives; they insisted I stay so that
we could continue catching up. Another cousin nearby was waiting to receive me for dinner—it had been decided. One of many
traditions I missed when I moved back to the U.S. was the insis-
tence on sharing a meal together, followed by the only acceptable
response: "Yes, thank you." We set off for my cousin Davin's.

The walk from one development to the next involved crossing
a part of 60 Metre Road with motorbikes and trucks six across in
a chaotic blur of honking and passing. One of my younger cousins
took my hand, expertly guiding me step by slow and steady step
across the expanse.

Once safely across the road, we walked down a long, newly
paved driveway, past street vendors selling snacks, and entered
a complex of row houses where families gathered to eat on tiled
ground floors. Residents shouted out my cousins' names and
waved and my cousins shouted back.

"Our cousin is here from America," one of my cousins hollered
across my shoulder. "We brought her to see how nice it is to live
out here."

At the entrance to Davin's house, I kicked off my shoes where
they joined a large pile of flip-flops, tennis shoes, and dress shoes.
A round table was already covered with plates of food. One cousin
opened a case of Angkor beer and tossed the cans into a cooler.
And soon, a parade of even more dishes emerged from a tiny
kitchen at the back of the house: stir-fried cockle shells in a tam-

arind sauce, roasted eggplant with minced pork, curried river lobster and garlic-stir-fried morning glory. In case I was still hungry, another cousin made fried hot and sour fish while her husband dispatched to the market to get a specialty—fish carpaccio preserved in banana leaves.

When I finished one beer, a cousin snapped open a new can and pressed it in my palm, and after three, when I insisted I'd had enough, they all insisted back, "One more! Come on, Put—we'll drink one more all together."

I relaxed into the evening as we bantered and laughed and told stories straight toward midnight. I had worried that the Khmer language I'd acquired in my thirties would be lost, but it came back quickly, and when I stumbled or paused and couldn't find a word, one or more of my cousins would step in and find the right word for me.

Khmer was a language I'd always loved, with its singsong sounds that popped from person to person. And though I didn't feel fully at home inside my mother tongue, language and food were the two bridges that inevitably connected both parts of who I am: Cambodian and American. It was there, that night with my cousins, that I felt most myself as a Khmer woman and at the same time, uneasy in the fact of my queerness as my cousins' banter turned toward how they had met their husbands and built their businesses. They worked together, they said, saving enough money collectively to help each other buy homes and cars, and pulling their husbands into their coffee shop business and side hustles selling bird's nests harvested from swifts and exported to a predominantly Chinese clientele. They were solidly rooted in Cambodia's middle class.

As I emptied more cans of beer, I kept wanting to update them on my life, too. Which is to say, I wanted to tell them I was gay.

I would be telling them what they already knew. The rumor that I'd married a woman had reached my cousins' ears the year before, likely spread through my relatives in America. But it still felt important to tell them directly. I had come out to my entire family in the U.S., and not being out officially to my relatives in Cambodia felt like I was still hovering at the threshold of the closet, not fully in or out. I've never liked middle realms.

Even as I wanted my relatives to know I'm gay, I was terrified of how they might react. To be rejected in America, where I had the support of my siblings and so many friends and a culture of embracing authenticity to fall back on, was one thing. But to be rejected by my relatives in my own country felt like it might be a loss too deep to bear after wanting for so long to be the perfect Cambodian daughter.

I hadn't come to Cambodia specifically to come out to my relatives, but I had wanted to put an end to years of enduring the question, "Put, when are you going to find a husband?" I wanted my relatives in Cambodia to accept me fully. I wanted the thing I have always wanted regardless of where I physically was: I wanted to belong.

On the plane trip from Seattle to Phnom Penh, I had practiced it in my head.

I debated what word I would use for "gay" because the only one I knew was a derogatory term I'd heard used in Cambodia, including by my relatives: *kateuy*. The only thing I knew how to say was I love women, and I was prepared to say just that.

All night at Davin's house, I wavered between relaxing into the rhythms of our conversations and anxious about wanting to declare who I am. But as we kept talking, the courage I had to come out drained away, supplanted by a cowardice that kept me caged in my own silence. I wanted someone to ask me that annoying question, "When will you find a husband?" even if they already knew there was no husband. But my cousins never asked about my relationship status, maybe because they knew the answer or maybe because it didn't matter. I'll never know because I chose to stay quiet, to postpone my fear of being rejected, and instead let my cousins crack open one last can of Angkor as we raised a toast together to prosperity and a long, happy life.

---

In the morning, my family boarded a bus to transport all twenty-three of us to the rice-growing province of Takéo to visit my parents' villages. Making travel arrangements for a group our size wasn't difficult; Cambodia is built for tourism, for big groups visiting the famed Angkor Wat temples and the Killing Fields—two main tourist attractions that spoke to Cambodia's intractable juxtaposition. I sat with one of my nephews toward the back of our bus and watched him watch the land unfurl in great green, hopeful swaths, knuckled with hills and groves of palm trees like pinbones stitching this landscape together, giving it structure. We watched fractioned fields pass by in quick sequence, and he pointed at water buffaloes grazing in the distance.

Some of my nieces and nephews gazed wide-eyed out the windows while others napped or passed snacks of beef jerky and bags of lychee up and down the bus aisle. My siblings chatted excitedly, nervously, and merrily as they watched entire families of five or six zip along dusty roads stacked onto a single motorbike as other motorbike drivers balanced plastic jugs eight feet tall with a single strap to the backs of their seats. I watched with wonder, too, seeing my country with new eyes. I thought what tourists must think—that Khmer people are so skilled, determined, resourceful—and I felt proud.

At Smong village, where my mother is from, my mother's oldest sister, Om Oeurn, a lifelong rice farmer whose husband died in the genocide, received us with a banquet of food befitting a wedding. Om Oeurn's daughters had made some of my favorites: chicken curry, tamarind leaf and pork bone soup, steamed river prawns with lemon pepper salt and lemongrass-marinated pork ribs.

My older sister and brother choked back tears as they met multiple aunts and uncles and cousins for the very first time. My nieces and nephews gathered around a cousin their age who cracked coconuts with a machete and passed them to each of my nieces and nephews with a straw. My parents sat regally on colorful plastic chairs at a round table, quietly taking it all in.

After lunch, several cousins corralled their motorbikes and drove us to the village pagoda, where monks waited to give us blessings and my mother pressed her offerings of cash into a gold-plated dish, bowing with her hands clasped in prayers. As we prostrated before the monk, I glanced up to the walls above where a photograph of my grandfather, yellowing in its frame, hung high amid photographs of other villagers who had donated significant sums to the pagoda.

There, at the pagoda that had been there for centuries, where generations of my ancestors on my mother's side had worshipped, I was reminded of such old ways of being. My heartbeats slowed to match the chanting of the monks, an even flow of instructions about living and acting with virtue and collecting karma with good deeds. We bowed three times at the end of a prayer. The smoke from lit incense sticks curled into the air, creating a smoke screen around a massive golden Buddha surrounded by garlands of marigold. When the monks finished their prayers, my family walked to our family stupa in the shade of a tamarind tree, flanked by village children who had surrounded us from all sides. The stupa, a steeple-shaped mausoleum the size of a child's playhouse, with an arched entrance and roof decorated at each corner by an ornamental *kveay* in the shape of a chicken's tail for good luck and a single blossoming lotus bud spire at the apex, held the bones and ashes of my maternal grandmother and her parents and a photograph of their family.

No longer in a trance by the monks' chanting, I let out a long breath, feeling my body collapse in on itself as my shoulders and head drooped toward my chest and my heart pounded a series of panicked beats.

The last time I was here I had a boyfriend. We shared a home, and a future that matched the lives of all the other Khmer women in my life. To be gay in this place steeped in history and heritage felt like a profound betrayal, and in that moment, the fact of who I am felt completely wrong.

I thought about the monks' chantings about karma and felt my chest tighten, worried that by being gay, I had ruined all my karma—for me and my family. I thought about what it means to be gay in my homeland and how perhaps I might always feel the push and pull of my queerness depending on where I travel. I understood how profoundly I did not belong there, in the pagoda, at the stupa, in my mother's village, perhaps even in my homeland. A deep grief I hadn't expected ambushed me. I felt the sensation of a hole in my heart, shot through with shame and the painful realization that perhaps I would remain transient in the territory of my beginnings, meant to only visit for a time before moving on. It was one more reminder that I was a traveler here where I once imagined I might always remain.

### 3.

Our itinerary for the following days suggested that we were, indeed, a tour group: Sihanoukville, a beach town on the southern coast of Cambodia where I was born; nearby Ream, where my family last lived before we fled the war; and finally Siem Reap to visit the Angkor Wat ruins.

Of all the stops we made, it was the leg of the trip to the coast that put into stark relief just how much China had taken over Cambodia. Our bus cruised down brand-new highways, which the bus driver explained were built with Chinese investment dollars. At new rest stops along the way, travelers could buy snacks and boba tea and use restrooms with Western-style toilets. Only a decade before, what counted as a rest stop was an unmarked spot on the side of the road where a woman sat on a raised platform next to three pots of soups and stir-fries available for purchase, a row of latrines with squat-style toilets nearby.

As we approached Sihanoukville my heart raced with anticipation. But this landscape had also changed. What I remembered as a beautiful beachside town now had an ominous feel; Sihanoukville was dotted with unfinished, moss-covered buildings, some lacking even roofs and windows, like a collection of skeletons slumped across the landscape.

"Why are these buildings half finished and abandoned?" I asked the driver.

"These are Chinese buildings," he replied. "Chinese investors came and started building new casinos before Covid. But then Covid came and the government cracked down on gambling, and the Chinese investors ran out of money and just left."

I couldn't believe my eyes, nor his explanation, so when we finally arrived to our seaside hotel, which was also hauntingly vacant except for our family, I logged in to the hotel's Wi-Fi and Googled "abandoned buildings in Sihanoukville." The bus driver was right. Across Sihanoukville, some 360 buildings were left unfinished while another 170 were completed but remained abandoned. They were called "ghost buildings."

I felt a curious creepiness slink down my flank, as if a dark spell had been cast across this country. This ghost town feeling was all too familiar. In 1975 the Khmer Rouge entered Cambodia and forcibly evacuated the country's citizens into rural concentration camps, leaving urban spaces and the structures within them completely abandoned. Taken together, the vacant and dilapidated buildings of Sihanoukville reminded me eerily of those evacuated cities during the genocide—inescapable ghosts of an unreconciled past.

That afternoon, after my nieces and nephews spent a few hours swimming and playing in the hotel swimming pool, we loaded the bus again to travel several kilometers south of Sihanoukville to visit Ream Naval Base. We wanted to see the spot where my family once had a home. But as we got near the base, we were greeted with walls made of sheet metal that ringed the base, which the bus driver explained was also being taken over by the Chinese, whose government paid for a wide-scale expansion. He said the Chinese planned to take over the base as their own naval station. Four months after my family left Cambodia, Chinese warships began docking at the very same port from which my family fled the war.

My family stayed only two nights in Sihanoukville before returning to Phnom Penh, and on the two-hour bus ride back to the capital, my head swam circles in a specific sense of loss. When I lived there in my thirties, my country held so much hope. China's influence was tempered by the West, whose promotion of democracy meant opposition parties had room and rights to operate and at least attempt to curb the ruling party's worst impulses for social and economic development; journalists openly criticized the government on air and in print in dozens of radio stations and newspapers; and countless local and nongovernmental organizations worked to protect forests and farm fields against encroaching development. All of these things were no more, and the loss weighed on my conscience like a stone that could sink me if I didn't find a way to let it go. Back in Phnom Penh, I went to find Ming Pheaktra, my favorite aunt. She would talk me down from the edge of my own anguish about my homeland.

———————◆———————

Ming is the wife of an uncle on my mother's side of the family, and when he abandoned his kids, I abandoned my ties to him and clung to Ming and her young son and daughter. They lived in a shack directly across from the city's open sewer, where rats the size of cats snuck in through the rafters and bit their toes as they slept. Her street was known as Sewer Street.

Now her son and daughter were grown. The son, my cousin Daros, drove me to see his mother, who was no longer living on Sewer Street, but in a two-story walk-up nearby she had saved up to buy.

"Put! Put! Come in!" Ming shouted as she waved me into her house, set in the middle of the block of a middle-class neighborhood. Immediately, she raced to her kitchen and emerged with cut pineapple and watermelon and a fresh coconut with the top hacked off and a straw jammed in so I could rehydrate. There was more; Ming made multiple trips between her kitchen and the front family room, where she brought out bags of corn on the cob and banana sticky rice and cookies in the shape of long tubes with chocolate drizzled on top.

Ming was my best friend for the nearly decade I spent living in Cambodia. She figures prominently in my memoir as the relative who helped me obtain a Khmer passport and who sat with me for long evenings on the riverfront, drinking Angkor draught and eating peanuts in bars full of foreigners as we talked family and politics.

Another ghost of my past came rushing back as I met with Ming. She knew me when I dated two different men: the first, a fling, and the second, a few years later, the man I thought I might marry. When I broke up with the boyfriend, it was Ming who came up with shenanigans to try to set me up with Khmer bachelors she knew. It was Ming who first suggested I marry the boyfriend, whom she met multiple times and then secretly called my mom to tell her the exciting news that I'd met a handsome, kind man. And it was Ming who eventually dragged me out of a much smaller studio apartment I moved into after the boyfriend and I broke up to shake me out of my depression. She took me to the river, "so the breeze can wash your sadness away," she said.

Now I was here, in her home, with her grown daughter and son and their spouses, who I saw every day when I lived in Phnom Penh. And when they asked me about my life in America after I left Cambodia, I felt the words forming in my mouth, but my teeth clamped shut, caging in my intentions, refusing to let the sentence escape: *I love women.* If I was going to come clean with anyone, I wanted it to be Ming. But still, I was afraid. There were the rules of the culture. The prayers at the pagoda. The centuries of customs that seemed to shroud Cambodia in a protective layer, and to come out as "gay" within that space still felt like I might disappoint my relatives. And if I disappointed my relatives there, I worried I would be too ashamed to ever return to Cambodia again.

Instead, I said I was teaching in America and I lived near two of my sisters in Seattle and we lived less than a four-hour drive from our parents. I told her I still traveled a lot, and then I quickly shifted the conversation to my cousins and how they found their careers: Daros worked for an architect and construction firm while his older sister, Sreyda, taught English at a school nearby.

Ming had one grandchild, the two-year-old son of Daros and his wife, and I asked how many more she wanted.

"As many as they will give me!" Ming said, exuberant at the thought of a growing family.

Soon enough, Ming and I began to talk about the current political situation in Cambodia, how she wasn't hopeful there would be much change. The prime minister, one week after being voted in for another term, decided instead to install his eldest son to take his place and continue the family's dynasty and corrupt rule.

Ming told me how she had scrimped and saved enough money working as a loan shark at the biggest casino in town so that when she saw this house for sale, she sprang into action and negotiated a good price and paid in cash.

"I'm going to save more money and add one more story and make an apartment," Ming said, speaking in quick, clipped phrases as if her excitement could not be contained in full sentences. "And when I build the apartment, that will be for you, Put.

That will be your house when you return and live here, so you can live above me and write your books."

Up until then, I hadn't considered ever returning to Phnom Penh to live again. But underneath her offer, I understood what Ming was trying to say, which is the same thing she told me the day I got my Khmer passport: "You are Khmer. Your home is here."

I wanted to tell her I did once feel my home was here, and didn't anymore. That the version of who I was now, the version that fought to belong to this place and claim Cambodia as mine, no longer fit. And that was okay. Everyone wants their own spot, and I was quickly realizing that mine, as a queer Cambodian refugee, was in my other home, America.

### 4.

On one of our last evenings in Phnom Penh, my siblings and I went to one of my old haunts on the Sisowath Quay, along the Tonlé Sap, where we sipped lychee martinis and dug our forks into pork chops and steaks with mashed potatoes. You can learn a lot by sitting in one place and watching. I sat closest to the window.

As my siblings and I processed what this trip home meant for all of us, every now and then I glanced out the window. I saw little children hawking bootlegged copies of my best friend's book, *First They Killed My Father*, Loung Ung's story of surviving the Khmer Rouge genocide as a little girl. I saw another familiar scene: a shriveled white man in blue jeans and a barely buttoned short-sleeve Hawaiian shirt, walking arm in arm with an inappropriately aged Khmer girl in heels and a skimpy dress along the riverfront.

As a Phnom Penh resident, I used to glare at these white men, hoping my gaze would burn holes into their consciences. I donated to nongovernmental organizations that helped sex-trafficked Khmer girls learn trade skills so they could enter livelihoods that didn't involve exploitation. I warned my young female cousins from poverty-stricken families in the village who wanted to work in the garment factories in Phnom Penh to be aware of and avoid the pimps who recruited from among the factory girls.

But on this night, seeing the old white man with the too-young Khmer girl, I looked away. When you live in a place, you want to change it. You work to make it better. When you're a tourist, you make a mental note of the wrongness and move on. Only later, when I was back in my own bed and in my own home 7,500 miles away, did I finally feel the bruise that moment left: "What happened to my heart?" I wondered. I felt hollow and ashamed for not feeling more angry and disgusted at being confronted again with the grossly unequal power dynamics of white men and Khmer girls. I felt a stabbing guilt that as a tourist, I was no longer compelled to care.

But in that moment, on the riverside with my siblings, I was distracted by another ghost coming into view. I thought of the man I nearly married, how we used to meet our friends for drinks and dinner in this very restaurant and how we often sat in this exact corner where my siblings and I now sat. How I loved him but not enough. How I had left him, and my country, and a past self that needed to exist in a more honest way than she did in Cambodia.

As my mind wandered and my siblings reflected on their experiences in our homeland, I caught a reflection in the window and glanced out to see a drag queen in a sequined dress, high heels, and a feather boa around her long broad neck sashay along the sidewalk outside. She walked like she belonged exactly on this street, exactly in this country, and I wondered whether the fact of her existence was a surface-level change or something deeper, something better for my country—a transformation I could support and be proud of.

My country had evolved in ways I could not recognize, and so had I. Traveling helped me see I still have residual shame about being gay; it took launching myself out of the context of America and plunging back into the context of my motherland to see this, to know I have not yet reached the outer frontier of my own reckoning, even though I had written a memoir about being a queer Cambodian refugee. Healing happens in the churn of our returning.

———————◆———————

On our last day together in Phnom Penh, before parts of our family flew back to the U.S., we took a river cruise on the Tonlé Sap, climbing aboard a vessel outfitted for parties. On the upper deck tables and chairs were set up between palm plants strung with lights. My mom chose a seat on the lower deck, alone on a faux leather sofa. When she didn't join the rest of us on the upper deck, I descended and took a seat across from her.

"Don't you want to see the view?" I asked. "Feel the breeze?"

"I know what this river looks like," my mother said. "This was my life, a long time ago, along this river."

It hadn't occurred to me that being there, on that boat, on a river where she—newly married and newly relocated from the village to Phnom Penh—once bought fish from Cham fishermen to prepare for her new husband, would cause memories of another version of herself to come flooding back. I wondered which of my mother's ghosts had found her.

I left my mom there alone in her reverie, and I hopped up the stairs to join my siblings and in-laws and nieces and nephews. Eventually, Mom clambered up the stairs, too. We clinked glasses of Angkor beer and snapped photos of the fishing villages and the sun dropping beneath Phnom Penh's skyline.

We hadn't intended to take that river cruise on the Tonlé Sap, but it was suggested by one of my sisters as a fun group activity—the last we'd do together. We started on a boat nearly fifty years ago, my family and I. It felt improbable and right to end on one, too. This time, no one was running from war. By the fall, the river will reverse course again. I'll have returned to my life in the U.S. and back to my life's current preoccupation—traveling across my America with a single message: Be who you are.

The movement of the river is the movement of the country is the movement of the human soul. There is sometimes pressure to go one way, and you do, and eventually you learn to relax until the timing of the earth's own rhythms force you back the other way. Blame it on hydraulics, gravity, or greater gears at work.

Here I was on my last day in Cambodia, on the Tonlé Sap, a river that does the only thing it knows how to do: It goes with the flow until the waters rise once more, and it goes backwards again from the way it came.

# Romantics

**GARRARD CONLEY**

**M**y seat was not enclosed within a compartment; instead, it nestled in an open alcove that faced another identical alcove, both flanked by thin, adjoining walls. Its proximity to the central aisle meant I could sense each passerby's movement through the train car. An immediate intimacy sprung up between all of us. There was an elderly man holding a half-eaten yolk in his farmer's hands, and beside him a toddler, a grandson perhaps, chewing with comic attentiveness. The man smiled at the boy's clumsiness, picking at the stray pieces with infinite patience. In the man's smile you could see that the boy could do no wrong. I turned away from the pair to watch the passing landscape, so similar to the flat fields I'd known all my life in the Arkansas Delta, yet framed now in the warped glass beside this casual display of love, the fields were no longer oppressive; they were full of possibility.

The smell in our area was strong, but when I tried to crack the window, the man stopped me by shouting a word I finally understood by the way he pointed to his neck meant *draft*. The train began picking up speed. The attendant brought the pair a silver tray with two glasses of black tea. The glasses were also encased in silver; the silver sprouted from the encasement to make up an ornate handle. It was the kind of precious detail I was on the lookout for at the age of twenty-one, fresh out of college and free for the first time from the influence of a childhood I felt I'd barely survived. When I left to use the restroom, I spotted a samovar in another tiny alcove and thought of Dostoyevsky.

By the time I returned to my seat, the man and child were gone, but the smell was not.

———————————————

I didn't have a chance to see the town of Radyvyliv before we arrived. I was nervous, and I kept looking down at the instructions Peace Corps had sent me about where I was supposed to meet Alla Vasilyvna, director of the school where I was to teach for the two and a half years of my service in Ukraine. The attendant appeared in the aisle and led me to the train door, where a tall woman covered almost entirely in what looked like real fur beckoned me with open arms.

"I thought you might not be real," Alla said, leading me down the icy steps with her strong grip. "When they said they would send someone, I thought they might send a runt. Why does our tiny Radyvyliv deserve anything else? But here you are, a healthy boy! A little thin, but healthy."

It was dark now. The dark was familiar, but even in my tiny hometown, our streets had been mostly lit. "Thank you," was all I could manage.

A snow flurry began the minute we stepped off the platform, and as we passed through the tiny square with its bright green benches and its statue of a famous poet whose name I had already forgotten, I hoped there would be a fire where we were headed.

"Tell me your impressions of Ukraine thus far."

I told her about the man and the boy, the samovar, Dostoyevsky. I tried to explain why it was all so touching, but I could see from her frown that this wasn't the answer she wanted.

"An ugly old farmer and some tea," she said. "Do they not have those in America?"

We drew closer to the giant statue. The man was frozen mid-stride, hands outstretched as if offering his genius to the world, his mustachioed face imposing, impenetrable.

"Ah, yes," Alla said. "Impressive, is it not? After the Soviet Union fell, we replaced Stalin with Shevchenko, the great Romantic poet of the Cossacks."

"He doesn't look very Romantic."

"Even our new statues are very Soviet in design. Some of us still enjoy the style even if we do not enjoy the legacy."

I knew from my training that Western Ukraine had maintained its independent traditions even under Soviet rule, that their resistance often took the form of folk songs, rich embroidery, and a language distinct from Russian, with its own verbs and nouns. I also knew that all high school teachers were once forced to report any religious activity within their student body to headquarters in Kyiv, that they were often stationed outside Orthodox churches with clipboards meant to record the name of every person who did not practice atheism. I asked Alla if what I'd been told was correct.

"Yes, we all did that. It was a strange time, but we didn't know any better. My husband was on cleanup for Chernobyl, for instance. No one told us a thing. He died very suddenly, and I didn't know why for many years, until one day the papers printed the truth."

I didn't know what to say to this. People where I was from were often blunt, but never this blunt. Finally, after a long moment of awkward silence, I said, "My parents tried to cure me of being who I am. They tried to make me believe a lie."

"What do you mean, cure?"

"It's just that they didn't like me ... being me." Peace Corps had warned me against sharing anything about my sexuality. A few months before I was to leave, I was surprised to find a personal note in my application materials instructing me to return to the closet for the duration of my service.

"You're a fine young boy," Alla said. "You'll stay in our newly independent Ukraine where we like boys like you."

A half-truth, I knew, but I was eager to believe.

◆───────◆

When we arrived at the house, Alla took my coat and gloves and scolded me for not wearing the proper number of layers. She ushered me into a parlor where my host family had been awaiting my arrival. The father was not yet home, but there on a large flower-print sofa sat mother, son, and daughter. Ruslana, Sasha, Oksana: commonplace names I still found exotic. As I stood nodding at the introductions, I thought how funny it was that an American had shown up to this place with visions of Dostoyevsky, for here was a room that looked like my grandmother's house, but in place of the old wood-framed television stood a new flat-screen. Mentioning Dostoyevsky in connection with samovars was like saying flowers reminded you of Wordsworth.

Alla wasted no time leading me to the spread of traditional foods. I'd never seen so much food in my life. I had recently learned the word *smorgasbord*, but this went thoroughly beyond that word.

I was glad to find the room sweltering, a fire baking our backs as we took our seats at the table. Ruslana and Oksana sat near the stove with nervous smiles as Sasha, seated at the head of the table in place of his father, though he could have been no older than thirteen, declared that he had gathered all the mushrooms for the gravy.

I tried to keep my face clear of emotion. "In a forest?" I said, thinking maybe his English was poor, that he might have meant to say "bought" instead of "gathered."

"Yes," Sasha said. "I'll show you the forest tomorrow. It is a great forest. One of the best."

In orientation we had been told that handpicked mushrooms were to be avoided at all costs. Radiation might persist in the region; there had been birth defects found in those living near the Chernobyl blast zone. However, the family seated before me seemed perfectly healthy. Besides, wouldn't Peace Corps be overly cautious with Americans, who were always so worried about everyone in the world but themselves?

"You're thinking we might die together tonight," Sasha said in perfect English. Perfectly serious. I watched to see if the others would reprimand him, but no one did. He laughed, and I laughed with him.

"Peace Corps sent us instructions," Alla said, not meeting my eyes. "You Americans know nothing of real danger."

I tried to fill my embarrassment with words. "Well, that seems very Romantic," I said, to which Sasha made a face. I had wanted to say, *This is like something out of Shevchenko*, despite never having read any Shevchenko, but I couldn't even remember the poet's name.

All throughout the meal I was worried about the mushrooms, but I was more worried about my stupid comment.

When the host father finally arrived and offered me three shots of vodka, I swallowed them greedily. By the end of the meal I thought I could understand what the television was saying, but soon I realized they had switched the channel to an English one.

---

It took only a few months to learn enough of the language to get by. My students and fellow faculty members seemed impressed by my ability, which had come about through sheer survival. Except for the classroom and my nightly conversations with the family, there were simply no opportunities to speak English. Complex emotions were beyond me, but almost everything I could touch had a name.

I wasn't too surprised to soon discover that my proficiency was an illusion.

"They lie to you, you know," Sasha told me one night. "They want to make you feel proud because they're proud an American has taken the time to learn their rare language."

"It is a beautiful language."

"Everyone says that. Everyone says that, and then no one really learns it."

---

About a year into my stay, a man named Sergei requested private English tutoring, and though Peace Corps forbade our receiving payment for such services, we worked out a deal where he could supply me eggs from his father's chicken farm in exchange for one hour of conversation. He was Alla's cousin, a man I had heard mentioned in passing many times, his name dropped casually into conversation to suggest status and wealth.

On our first evening together, Sergei picked me up at the house. He insisted I not walk, though the street outside was too small for regular traffic and too muddy to justify driving a good car on it. Sergei idled his very expensive-looking Mercedes sedan in the driveway. He wore a too-big suit with pinstripes, his hair slicked to one side. He was handsome in a way I found intoxicatingly sleezy, though I corrected myself almost at once, thinking it was only my American bias at work. I caught a strong scent of mint and tobacco as I slid in beside him.

When he put his hand on my headrest to back up, these scents were replaced by the odor of his unwashed armpit. I found it hard to concentrate on anything else.

"I know, no bribes," he said. "But I bought you some flowers."

To my astonishment there was a bouquet of flowers whose stems were buckled into the back seat, the kind of ultrablue flowers that seem spray-painted. I reached. He reached. Our fingers touched on the crinkled plastic. He put his hand on my headrest again to gift me his scent. I pressed my nose to the flowers to find some relief from my sudden desire, but the flowers were odorless.

"We can do anything," Sergei said, "as long as we speak English."

In this small village it was rare to see a car in the streets, much less a Mercedes. I felt even more out of place than usual. A few of my younger students began running alongside the car, screaming and pointing and laughing. Their mockery had become familiar to me by now, a kindness I had not recognized as kindness at first, but sitting beside Sergei in his car made the experience feel alien again.

"They still aren't used to seeing men like me," he said.

"We could have walked."

"Screw them," he said, accelerating so rapidly I thought we might fling mud on the children. "A past modal, yes? 'Could have walked.'"

We reached the highway at the far edge of town, a road I hadn't yet visited. The tiny vans most people used, marshrutkas, were always too crowded. You had to push to get on, and I didn't like the idea of pushing some old babusya out of the way so I could travel a few kilometers to another village.

Sergei wanted to max out the speedometer. These highways weren't made for speed, yet he seemed to have memorized where the potholes were, so my head hit the roof only one or two times. I was scared, but in a detached way I've come to associate with being abroad. Somehow death only seems possible at home.

After a few minutes of this, we came to a sudden stop in a gas station parking lot.

"I'll piss," he said. "They have great coffee here."

I waited as he exited the vehicle. I closed my eyes for a moment and began to deliberately slow my breathing. Before I could get a handle on things, a loud tap startled me.

"Come inside," Sergei said. "Real Ukrainian men piss together."

I was a real Ukrainian man now. I followed him to a set of restrooms behind the register. I don't know what I'd been expecting, but the gas station was like any other gas station in Arkansas, only this one was nicer.

There were no stalls, so I took the urinal farthest from the door. To my surprise, Sergei sidled up beside me, unzipping with a loud flourish and releasing a fart and a sigh. I pretended to piss, turning my shoulder from him to shield myself, but Sergei put a hand on my shoulder and turned me almost to face him. I kept my eyes on the backsplash but felt the edges of my vision drifting. He held himself there longer than seemed necessary, and when I finally looked down, he was shaking himself, half hard. If Sergei was a real Ukrainian man, I was eager to meet more of them. He didn't glance up at my stare, though I knew he could feel it.

The moment passed. Soon we were sitting in the coffee shop annex as though nothing had happened. Nothing did happen, I told myself. I leaned back in my chair to hide the swelling in my jeans.

Sergei took a deep breath, staring earnestly into my eyes. I don't know what I was waiting for him to say, but it certainly wasn't, "Do you follow Jesus?"

I set down my Styrofoam cup to hide my surprise. I waited, long enough for him to catch something of my history. "My father's a pastor."

"Wonderful!" he said, nearly spilling his coffee. "I work with some men in Texas to build a church here, in our town."

I almost didn't want to ask. "What kind of church?"

"A Baptist church. Your father is Baptist?"

"Yes."

"How lucky we met. What are the chances? I mean, what are the chances?"

---

It hadn't been all that difficult to head back into the closet for this teaching post. I'd tasted only a small dose of sexual freedom thus far in my life, a few college flings but nothing that drew me out of my self-loathing long enough to appreciate what the future could hold. Identity is a trap, I told myself. And I was right in the way only twentysomethings who read Judith Butler for the first time can be right. That is, technically right. Not emotionally right. To be emotionally right you must be very wrong in some fundamental, theoretical ways. You must live with contradiction, enjoy paradox. At twenty-one, I believed I could think my way out of the problem of the closet. The closet was completely irrelevant. The difference I felt each day as I walked through this village was unimportant, an impediment to seeing the bigger world.

Queerness had made my world small, impossible. Queerness was the closet.

All of that changed after meeting Sergei. I felt my desire for him pressing against the edges of my daily life. He was everything wrong about the place I had escaped. He was a corporate suit, a show-off, a charmer, polite in the most chauvinistic sense, and, worst of all, an Evangelical. To seek out Sergei was to seek out my past, to wish to merge two very different lives into one, when all I thought I wanted was to escape my past. I began to find it more difficult to evade questions of marriage, of girlfriends. My students' curiosity about my former life irked me. I showed them where on the map I was from but mentioned nothing of my father, nothing of my life there. I felt I was clearly a fake. I even made up a girlfriend to stop their incessant questioning, but soon I found having a girlfriend only led to more questions, namely those concerning her physical attributes. I feigned modesty and anger on her behalf in order to evade any realistic depiction of a living human being, but when I was forced to imagine someone, I thought of my college friend Amber. Soon, however, I felt I was being unfair to her memory by suggesting that an intimate relationship had existed between us when everything had been strictly platonic, so I tried switching it up a few times, adding other women I had known in college to the portrait I was making of this girlfriend, so that anyone attempting to sketch her likeness would have seen one of Picasso's cubist women staring back at them.

Sergei was the only person I told about my Baptist background, and even then he couldn't have guessed the extent of my involvement, or of my tumultuous break from it, how I had stormed out of the conversion therapy facility and created a rift in my family.

As I said, none of this had seemed so difficult until Sergei and I began meeting once a week. At eight o'clock every Wednesday evening, he'd pick me up from my host family's house on that narrow muddy street in his conspicuous car. Always he carried with him a box of chocolates or a bouquet of artificially bright flowers. Always I left with a dozen eggs from his father's chicken farm. We sat together on his bedroom divan during most of our lessons, the middle cushion sinking us close together, knees touching. His bedroom, not to mention his house, was grander than any others in Radyvyliv. After living such a Spartan lifestyle, subsisting on two hundred American dollars a month, hanging out with Sergei was the height of luxury.

"I know what we'll do," Sergei said one day, swatting aside our small talk. "I'll teach you more Ukrainian."

Our conversation lasted five minutes in his language before he pulled me to him and held me in a strong embrace. He kissed me on the cheek.

"You speak like a real Ukrainian," he said.

I pulled away, not sure how to react.

"It's all a lie," I said, thinking back to my conversation with Sasha. "You just say that because you're happy an American took the time to learn it."

"Who said this to you?"

"My host brother."

"Screw him, and screw you for repeating it." Sergei crossed his arms over his chest, truly upset. He wouldn't look at me.

"I don't know how to describe emotions beyond happy, sad, tired. I don't know how to talk about philosophy. He's not wrong."

"Philosophy? You want to talk about philosophy? Why? Talk about what's real. What's true. Jesus in the parables speaks of sheep, shepherds. You don't need any more than that."

"I'm sorry," I said. "Let's continue."

"No. I offered you a favor, and you mocked it."

We ended our lesson after five uncomfortable minutes of silence. I stood in the doorway waiting for the eggs, but Sergei bent down to retrieve something unexpected. He held out one giant egg that was about the size of a premature infant.

"I was hoping to surprise you," he said, his voice softening. "It's an ostrich egg, from the farm."

"You have ostriches?" I said, cradling the egg like a real baby, swaddling it with my scarf, not sure how to hold it.

"I thought maybe this was something you wouldn't have where you're from."

At the time, I thought that was the nicest thing anyone could ever give me.

---

I waited a few days before I worked up the nerve to fry the egg. I thought about scrambling it, but I wanted to see what the runny yolk looked like when it popped under my fork. In the end I couldn't eat it. As I was scraping the remains into the trash, Sasha walked in. I felt like another wasteful American. I knew Sergei would ask about it, and that I would lie.

I began planning ahead for our conversations each Wednesday. When I learned something new about the country, usually from my students, I couldn't wait to share it with him.

I wanted him to see the effort I was making. But Sergei wasn't interested in his own country. He was interested in mine. He wanted to know everything about my father, everything about my past mission work. He wanted Ukraine to be just like the South, just like Arkansas and Texas and all those other places where *God* wasn't a dirty word.

"My parents were forced to be atheists," he told me. "Soviets wanted to abolish our country's religion. So as you can see, we need a better model."

I agreed with him every step of the way, nodding along with biblical notions for which I no longer held any convictions. I don't know what about him made me seek his approval. Probably it was as simple as unresolved trauma, but I suspect it had more to do with him being the only romantic prospect in town. Celibacy, like the closet, was more confining than I'd first believed. Then there was that special something about him, a naivete I had savored in the Christian friends of my youth. I'd almost forgotten that. How you could talk openly about love and joy and the beauty of heaven, all without the slightest trace of sarcasm. Though Christianity in my home church had taken on many noxious forms, it had also provided me an outlet for a kind of Romantic expression that was deemed holy because it was all part of God's creation. I think I still believed that the romance could make up for all the rest.

---◆---

A few months and several wasted ostrich eggs later, I found myself face-to-face with the ostriches themselves.

"Their feathers will heal soon," Sergei said, gesturing to the alarming bald patches I'd noticed on many of the birds' bodies. From time to time one of those fuzzy little heads would whip around and pluck a large tuft of feathers from its side with a disturbingly loud pop.

"Do ostriches molt?" I said.

"Molt?"

"Shed hair. Naturally."

"No, this is a question of climate," Sergei said, as though that explained it. He led me away from the ostriches rather abruptly so we could have a look at the peafowl, which were similarly depressing without their fanned tails. The farm was bigger than I'd expected, far more automated than anything I'd seen thus far in the country. Sergei's tour had led me through a complicated set of conveyors designed to clean and sort the chicken eggs, with dozens of gloved and capped workers nodding sternly as we entered each part of the factory.

"This place is half mine, and one day it will be all mine," he said. "In the meantime, I've been saving. Soon I'll have enough money to build the church." "What about the men in Texas?" I was put out once again by the conversation's turn. "Shouldn't they be paying for some of it?"

"I live in Ukraine. I work in Ukraine. I want a church in Ukraine. I'm the one who needs to take the most responsibility."

"Yes, but don't you think that's a little unfair? I mean, money works differently here than it does in Texas."

"I've prayed a long time on this, and God has sent me His answer. You will talk to your father, and he will pray for us."

———◆———

Sometimes I found it easy to mold Sergei into the boyfriend I needed him to be. Our talks could be surprisingly sweet. We spoke of our ambitions: how I wanted to be a writer, how he wanted to take what his father had given him and make it so much bigger. He encouraged me. I encouraged him. The romantic gestures were never explained, and though they might have been the result of conditioning, for I had seen many of my students gift roses to their female teachers, I thought he could tell that they meant something different to someone like me. I had never received a rose from any of my male students, for example, and when girls handed me a present before class, it was usually a liquor-infused box of candies, somehow deemed more appropriate for my sex.

Touch was different in this country. I understood that. On my Christmas trip home, I'd been shocked by the amount of space between people, shocked and annoyed. Personal space seemed like a statement America was continually making: *Everyone but me is disgusting*. When I returned to Ukraine, I was happy to be back in a place where no one seemed to care how close you came, where intimacy of this sort wasn't forbidden. But Sergei seemed to push even those established norms. He put his arm around me. He drew me to his shoulder, to his chest. He kissed me on the lips, then laughed. Awkwardly, I thought. Hesitantly.

Like it wasn't really funny at all.

But then Sergei would tell me about his plans for the church. He would tell me he listened to some of my father's sermons online, then repeat them almost verbatim to me. He would take me to his farm, and I'd glimpse those eerie bald patches I couldn't look away from.

"Promise me you won't take any photographs inside," Sergei said, leading us toward a giant gray shed at the edge of his father's property.

"My phone can't do that," I said, brandishing my simple flip phone.

Sergei showed me how his phone could do that. He took a photo of the two of us smiling.

"We look good," I said. Thinking: together.

"We do!" Sergei said, adding filters, zooming.

We walked on in silence, clouds patterning the field, the day beautiful and crisp. I didn't ask where he was taking me. He liked to keep the buildings a surprise until we entered. At the time I didn't think anything about his rule against photos. The big-hitting documentaries on the horrors of corporate poultry farming hadn't yet hit the mainstream, and even if they had, I wouldn't have had the bandwidth to stream them. That Sergei didn't even think to worry about confidentiality made me warm to him even more.

"Your girlfriend?" Sergei said. "When will she visit us?"

I came to a stop. "Girlfriend?"

"You can't keep a secret in this town. I was sad you never mentioned her."

"Oh, you know," I said. "Long distance."

I was glad when we finally reached the giant double doors. Sergei reminded me not to take photographs, strangely, I thought, since he knew I didn't have a camera. Inside was as bad as anything I would later see depicted in those documentaries. Cages upon cages, all of them tiny, with oversized birds crammed inside.

Birds dangling by their legs, sweeping by at tremendous speed
to some new horror just out of sight. My eyes watered from the
smell. Even now, sitting at my computer more than a decade later,
I can still smell it. A smell worse than death, more unnatural than
death. I turned away and hurried out, disgusted.

"Wait," Sergei said. "What's wrong with you?"

Nothing could cover up the stench of such cruelty, but Sergei
tried just about everything.

I don't think he understood my reaction at all. Because he had
the car, I had to dine with him at a fancy restaurant one town
over that night. He bought us some of the most expensive wine
I'd ever tasted, some of the best food I'd ever eaten. The whole
time I stared into his handsome face I kept thinking maybe I could
forget what I saw, that this was just how business was done. But
now everything in his personality seemed connected to the terrible vision I'd just witnessed. Most of the farms I'd seen in Ukraine
were sustainable, kind to their animals. Sergei's was different. Was
it any surprise that a man whose model was American Evange-
lism would be capable of such a thing? The whole rotten business
seemed clearer to me now more than ever.

I kept coming back to Sergei's explanation for the ostriches'
missing feathers. Climate? A question of climate? Then don't buy
the foreign bird in the first place.

# La Cubana

**DAISY HERNÁNDEZ**

I like telling people that Hialeah, a city northwest of Miami, is what working-class Havana would be today if the Revolution had never happened in Cuba. Folks work shifts at the local hospitals or at Walmart. They fix cars and toilets, central AC systems and ceiling fans. They drive Uber and Lyft and take classes at the community college. Women don't leave the house without a full face of makeup, not even for a quick car ride to Sedano's to buy a bag of onions, and grown men live with their mothers and drive SUVs or Teslas. Hialeah, which along with Laredo, Texas, has the highest concentration of Latinos of any city in the country, brims with old folks whose children have gone on to study medicine or yoga or to work for the CIA. If you report a missing elderly parent or auntie to the local police, they will actually drive the city streets looking for the vieja. The one time I called 911, paramedics arrived fluent in Cuban Spanish, called my mother "Mami," and assured me that she'd had a panic attack, not a heart attack.

There are gay men in Hialeah. One of them is my cousin, who lives with his husband. Once in a while, I'll spot a woman who might be a lesbian, but it's hard to say. I'm a pansexual with no gaydar. The woman could be a butch or simply a middle-aged Cubana who cut her hair short and is not shy about elbowing her way to the counter at the bakery. While Cuba legalized gay marriage in 2022 and Fidel Castro's own niece, Mariela, has spent more than a decade advocating for pro-LGBTQ+ policies, Hialeah remains entrenched in a culture of "don't ask, don't tell." Family friends and strangers alike ask me about my husband and children, and the one time I shaved my head, my mother's friends looked at me with the most enormously sad eyes and spoke to her in low voices as if I had died. By the time of my next visit, a year later, my hair had grown back, and I looked like a Cuban woman sporting a pixie cut. No one gave me a second glance. I wasn't queer. I wasn't pansexual or bisexual or anything nonhetero. I was just a grown woman visiting her viejos in Hialeah.

No, I did not grow up in Hialeah. I was born and raised in Jersey (a fact about which I am very proud for the sole fact that I like to side with the underdogs in all matters), but my father could not return to Cuba to grow old and die, so the year I turned twenty-nine and finally moved out of their home, he hauled my Colombian mother to South Florida. They knew I was dating women at that point, and over the years they knew that I followed a woman out to California, that we broke up, and that I never brought her home for a formal visit. They knew about the other women and a man who they knew only as *the Mexican* and another man who they only knew as *the Chino*, but to be honest, it helped both my parents and me that traveling to Hialeah took more than five hours by plane from California. They didn't have to see my love life as a lived reality, and I didn't have to see their reactions to my love life.

All of this changed with Frankie. We met in North Carolina, where I was working at the time and where Frankie had relocated decades earlier from Philadelphia. Almost forty by then, I showed up for our first brunch date like a true city girl in a dress and boots, my dark hair flat ironed and perfumed. Frankie, in their early fifties, arrived as if they had stepped out of an REI catalog complete with the requisite puffy vest, the tidy jeans, the chiseled jaw, and the shorn salt-and-pepper hair. Over brunch, we bonded about growing up in the Northeast and navigating all twelve years of Catholic school. Frankie wasn't Latinx but came from a white community where big tight-knit families were the norm, and as we talked about our childhoods, they felt familiar to me. When I shared that I was writing a narrative nonfiction book about a vector-borne disease, they asked about the insect: Do you know the species or genus? Frankie had degrees in botany and sustainable agriculture, and they appreciated the scientific names for bugs, as well as plants and flowers and trees.

Two years later, Frankie and I decided to make the trip to Hialeah. We told friends that we were headed to Florida. It sounded pleasant. It sounded like a trip white folks made, flying to their rental on the Gulf or staying at their grandma's condo, that sort of thing. What I should have said was this: We're leaving the country. We're going to Hialeah, to old-school, working-class, white Cuba, where they vote for Trump and mostly talk in Spanish and make racist comments. It's a city where having a gay kid is a bit of news about which grown women whisper and where if Frankie were not white, I would honestly never take them because the community, my parents included, are indeed that racist.

But I don't say any of that. Instead, sometimes I tell people about my first trip to Hialeah.

———◆———

The bus was called La Cubana. The name flared across the vehicle's flank, and it would have been easy to mistake it for a tour bus except that in the 1980s in Union City, New Jersey, everyone knew La Cubana was how families traveled directly and cheaply for twenty-eight hours to the motherland (a.k.a.: Hialeah and Miami). It was the way my mother, sister, and I made the journey. No, none of us had ever seen Cuba, but the island was my father's patria, and the only way he could get us there was by spending the summers working overtime at the textile factory and shipping us off to his cousins via a bus called La Cubana.

We boarded the bus around Thirty-Second Street, right off Bergenline Avenue, where shops fixed the soles of women's shoes and rolled cigars in back rooms and sold cookies the size of my ten-year-old face. The bus drivers chucked our suitcases into the belly of La Cubana, and we climbed aboard, probably close to thirty of us filling the bus seats. I sat behind my mother and younger sister. A woman took the aisle seat next to me, a gold ring on almost every finger, a slew of gold chains around her neck, her hair perfumed with mousse and jasmine, her eyelids adorned in a startling turquoise. The rest of the women who boarded La Cubana proved to be variations on this woman. Years later when I saw drag queens for the first time, I thought of these women on La Cubana, women in their thirties and forties and fifties with their indulgent faces, their tits spilling out of low-cut blouses, and two-inch heels on their feet for a bus ride that would take almost thirty hours.

My mother was no drag queen. I blamed it on her being Colombian. Although I never asked any of the passengers about their national origins, I felt confident that Mami was the only Colombiana on La Cubana. She wore no makeup except for lipstick in a shade of rose that blended into her pale face. She wore sensible shoes (slip-ons). She did not believe in heels or hips or showing tits. Even now, decades later, I cannot imagine her having sex. But the Cu-

banas on the bus? They were having sex. They were sex. While my
mother would spend this bus ride almost virtually in silence, the
Cubanas spoke like women who were entitled to everything: to
time, to attention, to a destination. "Open the door!" one of the
women hollered. She had forgotten that she'd stuffed her medication in her suitcase and that she would need it by nightfall. She
shared this with all of us on the bus because she apparently believed that whatever happened to one woman here was the business of all the women.

I leaned back in my seat on La Cubana, a wild grin on my face. I
liked these women. They made me laugh. They made me think of
pop songs. They made me want to bury my face in an enormous
pillow. I was ten years old and cisgender, a budding bisexual, pansexual, queer, and I had no language for desire, so I told myself,
*This is marvelous. All these women on La Cubana. They are marvel-
ous.* And it was mostly women. I don't know how the men traveled
to South Florida. It is possible that they were on the bus and simply overshadowed by row after row of women with their infusion
of hairspray and bright red lipsticks.

———————◆———————

Hialeah is not a tourist destination. When you travel there, you
stay with family. Your family pulls out the sofa bed or they find the
cousin who's getting rid of a mattress, and they throw that on the
floor and call it a guest bed. The bulk of the hotels, from what I can
tell, are motels for quickie sex, prostitution, and sex trafficking.
Still, I was not taking Frankie to stay at my parents', and without
a guide on "where to stay with your nonbinary, white partner in
Hialeah," I picked a hotel that didn't have hourly rates and served
a continental breakfast. As we checked in, it occurred to me that

I was forty-two years old and for the first time I would be sleeping in the same city as my parents but not in the same house.

After checking into our room, we hopped into the rental car and drove over to meet my parents. I got behind the wheel, not trusting Frankie to manage the antics of Hialeah drivers who, like those in Miami, don't believe in signaling when they're switching lanes and who consider a yellow light a signal to gun it toward the intersection. We made it to the house safely, and at the front door, I hugged and kissed my mother and auntie. In their seventies, they dressed like twins in cotton tops and the knit pants people now refer to as loungewear. They both had their short hair dyed a bright copper, and in that moment, neither had a poker face. Their faces were tight with anxiety. In fact, they barely looked at me, peering instead over my left shoulder as if they were unsure of who they might find there at my heels. I stepped aside so they could get a good look at Frankie, who hung back shyly, in their cargo shorts and thick T-shirt, a polite smile on their face. Since I had never formally introduced my family to a queer romantic partner before, I half yelled in a fake, cheery voice, "This is Frankie!" as if I had brought home a labradoodle puppy.

My mother gaped. My auntie, too. Frankie said, "Hola," their voice tinged with anxiety. No one moved. We stood there with the door still open behind us as I realized two facts at the same moment: I had not taught Frankie to hug and kiss in lieu of shaking hands, and my mother and auntie had no experience hugging and kissing white people as in white-white, not Latine white. Luckily, Frankie quietly closed the door, and my mother and tía shuffled into the house. I told Frankie, "Let's go say hi to my dad."

My father was in his usual spot on the back porch, settled in his patio chair, a cigar in his right hand and the radio tuned into a local talk station whose sole purpose for the previous eight years had been to trash Obama and convince people like my parents to vote for Trump. Unlike my mother and tía, my father cast his eyes on Frankie and lit up with a smile. The stroke from six years earlier had slowed him down, but he leaned forward and steadied himself on the table with his left hand and got to his feet to shake Frankie's hand. In the moment, I thought, *Oh, good, that went well.* Later I realized my mistake. My father had shaken Frankie's hand because he was reading Frankie as a white man.

No, I had not called my family ahead of time and said, *I'm bringing my partner to visit and they're nonbinary and use the pronoun* they—which in Spanish would still have to be gendered as ellos or ellas because this was in 2016 before anyone had told me that I could use elles or ellx. Yes, I could have phoned my mother and said, *I'm bringing my novia to meet you,* except that Frankie did not want to be described as a girlfriend or boyfriend. I had told my parents once that Frankie was a woman because that was easier for me than schooling them on nonbinary gender identity, but apparently my father had forgotten that he knew anything about Frankie's gender.

We sat on the porch with my father, and I served as the interpreter. My father wanted to know about Frankie's property in rural North Carolina. Frankie wanted to hear about everything that grew in my parents' yard: the avocados, the mangoes, the bananas. They pointed to the roosters foraging in the yard. "Tú gallos?" they asked my father. No, the roosters belonged to the neighbors, but the man kept his yard extremely tidy while my father's overflowed with trees and ferns and anything that managed to grow by itself. It offered the gallos a wild sanctuary. Frankie nodded in approval. They thought all yards should have a touch of the wild.

The next morning, in the hotel room, Frankie was still sound asleep when I noticed their phone light up. One of their brothers had left a message and sent a text message: *Call me.* My stomach clenched. When you have parents in their seventies and eighties the way Frankie and I did, messages like these could mean anything, all of which bruised. I shook Frankie awake, and when they phoned their brother, we learned their mother had died overnight in her sleep at the assisted living facility outside of Philadelphia.

The trip to Hialeah ended within twenty-four hours. We booked a bereavement flight for Frankie and rearranged for extended pet care. I would join them in a few days for a Catholic funeral that would prove to be glorious with more than a hundred people in attendance and one of the grandsons playing the violin and the eulogy even including my relationship with Frankie, which, I suspect, was the first time that particular Catholic church heard the mention of a queer couple.

But all of that came later. After I dropped Frankie off at the airport, my mother wanted to make a trip to the Walmart Superstore, which was on the other side of town. The Walmart in Hialeah might be like every other one in the country, but I suspect it's the only one that has bragging rights to employing the highest number of political refugees in the United States, since everyone who works there seems to be Cuban. I paused in the bakery section. It never failed to surprise me that Walmart sold Cuban bread. For the uninitiated, pan Cubano is a ridiculously delicious fluffy affair with a crisp outer layer, and it can only be rightly purchased at a local bakery in Hialeah where it's made fresh with flour and lard and where customers routinely take home three loaves at a time. But there it was—el pan Cubano at Walmart.

Back home, I didn't ask my family what they thought of Frankie. It had been such a short visit. What was there to say? What was there to ask? But at the dining table, my auntie peeled a mandarin and said, "When I came to this country, at the factory, they warned me about women like that."

"Women like what?"

"Like Frankie."

My auntie had landed in Jersey in the early seventies and worked as a seamstress, and while I knew all about her life, this was the first that I was hearing of anything even remotely nonhetero.

My auntie clicked her tongue. "Sí," she said, "they warned me about women like that. They told me, 'Watch out for her.'"

"Why?" I asked, smiling.

"This woman, she was like Frankie," my auntie said, then paused. "She carried a tool belt on her waist."

I burst into a laugh. "And did you ask if she was gay?"

Tía huffed. "Eso se sabía," she said. Her being gay—that was known.

On the porch, I sat next to my father, who wanted to know if Frankie's flight left on time. Yes, it did. My father did not have anything to tell me about lesbians with tool belts in Jersey's factories, but he did want to talk about my husband. I half laughed. I should have expected the husband reference. In working-class Latinx families, or at least in mine, couples who've been together for years are referred to as spouses even when no marriage has taken place. Papi pulled the cigar out of his mouth and asked, "He's rich, right?"

I didn't know it was possible to frown and laugh at the same time, but that's what happened to my face. I skipped the husband reference and asked, "Why do you think Frankie has money?"

My father shrugged his shoulders and looked at me for the answer, but we both knew what he meant. Papi had grown up in rural Cuba. White men who owned property had money. White men who owned property in the United States had even more money. Frankie was, to my father, a white man. "Está bien," I said about Frankie and their money, by which I meant, *They're fine*, but I liked that the Spanish construction of the sentence allowed me to bypass gendered pronouns.

In bed that night at my parents' house, I thought about how to tell my father that Frankie was not my husband but also not a woman in the way he thought of women, that there were other options when it came to gender. Then I considered the facts, which were these: My father was about to turn eighty. I had been out to him for more than twenty years, and nothing about my life had challenged his ideas about hetero life. In other words, I had managed to reach my forties without the milestones of middle-class lesbian life in the United States. I'd had no wedding, no search for donors, no birth of children, no adoption of children, no lesbian divorce. Did I need to use my relationship as an educational lesson on queer life for an old Cuban who was smoking cigars despite having had a massive stroke?

Nah, I concluded and fell asleep. Later, it occurred to me that my friends had given me pep talks on coming out to my parents when I was in my twenties, but no one had prepared me for talking about queer life when my parents began entering their elder years. My sister, who was younger than me and also my best friend, couldn't help either. In Maryland, she was planning to move in with her boyfriend. She didn't have anything to explain to my parents.

Seven months later, I took Frankie with me to Hialeah again. This time we would be celebrating my father's eightieth birthday, and I skipped the hotel and picked an Airbnb instead, which meant renting what the Cubans call an "efficiency" and what everyone else in English refers to as a furnished studio. I couldn't tell my mother that it was an efficiency because that was usually a long-term rental and she had never heard of a company called Airbnb, so I said, "We're renting un apartamentico," which is the way Colombians talk when they want to make something sound sweet and small.

The Airbnb was actually spacious with a full kitchen because the Cuban woman who owned the house probably couldn't imagine a woman renting a place without a stove and full-sized fridge. Frankie opened the blinds and every window, then started toying with the controls on the air conditioner. They wanted fresh air, which, I had to admit, would have delighted my father, who hated the cost of ACs. I went to bed that night curled up in Frankie's arms, smug in my decision to rent an Airbnb in Hialeah, until the next morning when we woke to the sound of a Cuban mother on the other side of the wall yanking out pots and pans for breakfast and hollering at her children. I actually sniffed the air for the scent of Cuban coffee, which is incredibly sugary, while Frankie groaned, "What time is it?"

It was seven, a normal weekday morning in the life of a family in Hialeah with children readying for school and a great-grandparent in bed probably needing a diaper change. I listened more closely. I could hear a knife on a cutting board. I imagined the Cubana slicing an onion for huevos revueltos or carving through a chunk of ham. I imagined she had a full face of makeup and at least four gold rings, that she was one of the women from La Cubana bus of my childhood. I imagined a great many things because we had not met. She had sent us a code for the keypad to the efficiency, and that had been it.

My sister and her boyfriend did not have to book a local Airbnb efficiency. They were a straight couple and staying at my parents' house. I had friends who would have resented and even denounced the difference in treatment, but not me. I did not want to stay at my parents' home with Frankie. I wanted the privacy, the option to prance around in our underwear and stay up late watching HGTV. As far as I was concerned, my sister and her boyfriend could have the shared bathroom with my seventy-seven-year-old auntie.

The first two days were sweet and full. We convinced my parents to take a short boat cruise for the first time, and so we spent an hour gawking at Miami's celebrity mansions. We drove to a local park for a walk and to Walmart for the necessary shopping. At my parents' dining table, we drank too much Cuban coffee and ate too much bread. We also consumed too many pastries from the local bakery, including ones filled with creamy layers of dulce de leche. These desserts are called señoritas, which means (wait for it) a young, single woman, because, yes, the presumption is that a young, single woman is a virgin and that only a virgin, a woman who has not yet known sex, could be as sweet as this pastry.

One evening, my sister and her boyfriend emerged from the bedroom and announced that they would be marrying at city hall. Tomorrow. They had made the inquiries. They had been talking about it, and we were all gathered now and so they were ready to do it. They would have a party later near their new home in Maryland. I laughed. I was delighted. I whisked my sister to David's Bridal, and Frankie tagged along with the groom to a Hialeah version of Men's Wearhouse for a suit. Ostensibly, we had gathered to celebrate my father's eightieth birthday, but a surprise wedding was way better. A local salon that should have advertised itself as Cinderella's godmother turned my sister into one of the women from La Cubana bus rides. Gone was the sister I knew—the one who, like me and my mother, dressed modestly and wore at most only lipstick. In front of me stood a Hialeah diva complete with thick eyebrows, glittery eyeshadow, and hair swept up and in place with mousse and spray. A high femme.

At city hall, my sister and her soon-to-be-esposo filled out a thin stack of papers and smiled for Frankie, who I had designated as the wedding photographer on account of their talents and their fancy Canon camera. If anyone at city hall gave Frankie and me a second look, I didn't notice. Frankie tried to blend in by sticking with Spanish answers to my questions (sí, no, aquí, vamos), and they even said my name with a lilt as if they spoke Spanish. Afterwards, we ditched the viejos and drove my sister and her new husband to Miami Beach. Frankie photographed them at a local garden and then on the beach before we finished the day with a seafood dinner, where we ate too much and half the waitstaff looked to be gay men.

My father did get his birthday party, and I realized, yet again, that I had not prepared for introductions. I slightly envied my friends who could declare, *This is my novia*, or *This is my wife*. Frankie couldn't help me either. "Why can't you just say, 'This is Frankie'?" they suggested, as if that made any sense, though it was the reason I adored them. They often did point out that I was making a big deal when the answer could be simpler. As it happened, I did not need a plan because three sets of cousins arrived at the same time, streaming into the house in a symphony of hugs and kisses and exclamations, and my sister introduced her new husband and everyone was so taken with the news of the surprise wedding that they didn't even glance at me or Frankie. At least that's what I thought.

In the midst of the hugging and chatter, my father's cousin, a woman in her seventies, asked no one in particular, "Who's the gringo?"

Technically speaking, the word *gringo* means you are talking about a white man. Among my Chicana and Mexican friends, the term comes with a bite so that a gringo is not a white man but more like a *fucking white man*. In Hialeah, among Cubans, however, a gringo is truly just a white guy, not as in white Cuban but as in white-white, a guy who can hop on Ancestry.com and trace his ancestors to the British or the Scottish (or in Frankie's case to the Swedish and Irish). My father's cousin, Margo, was arguably the whitest person in the room with her light skin and red hair, which made it all the more ironic that of everyone in the room, it was she staring at Frankie and asking, "Who's the gringo?"

My mother slipped away, murmuring that we needed forks. My auntie began handing out cups of soda. My sister didn't hear anything as she and her new husband recounted the start of their relationship with our cousin who had been like an older sister to us. I looked at Frankie, who was chatting in English with my cousin's son. Was this the right time to say, *I would like to introduce you to the gringo who you could also call a gringa or maybe gringe or gringx, and their name is Frankie*? And then what? *They are my pareja.* That is the word upon which I was slowly settling: *pareja*.

In Spanish, *pareja* can mean a *romantic couple* but also a *team of two* or a *partner*. One dictionary even insists that *pareja* does not have a translation to English when it means one of a set as in:

*Se me perdió la pareja de este arete.* In English, we would simply say, *I lost one of my earrings*, but I like that in Spanish it has a designation: *la pareja*.

No, I did not make any declaration about Frankie at my father's eightieth birthday party. Instead I led us in singing "Happy Birthday" and began snapping pictures on my iPhone, my almost-bald father surrounded by viejos and teenagers, a wild grin on his face, the candles on fire before him.

When everyone departed in a slow parade of hugs and kisses and promises about future visits, I stepped back into the house to find my father bonding with Frankie. He was trying to tell Frankie that the women in his family talk too much. He was communicating this not in Spanish but instead by snapping his fingers and thumb together. Frankie grinned. "They like to talk," Frankie said to my father. My father nodded, and in English, he asked Frankie, "Drink?"

My father wanted a stiff drink, a whiskey perhaps, and a man to join him.

Frankie, who almost never drinks because alcohol makes them sleepy, understood that my father was inviting them to a social ritual. "Un poquito," they answered.

———◆———

Recently, a colleague teaching a course on mixed-race memoirs told me that most of these books are written by authors whose parents are white and Black (or white and Indigenous; or white and Mexican), and the focus of the memoir is almost exclusively on the BIPOC parent, on the lineage devalued in a country whose institutions still prefer whiteness. However, this attention on the page to the parent of color, while largely ignoring an interrogation of the white parent's experience, actually ends up reinforcing the racial hierarchy by placing the BIPOC parent under the microscope. In these memoirs, the BIPOC parent is the one to be gazed upon, to be turned into a story, to be othered.

This is a danger that every writer faces when authoring stories about how politics slams into the intimate corners of our lives. It is too easy to pivot the narrative toward the person in the story who is not white, not hetero, not cisgender, not Christian, not normative. It is too convenient to forget an interrogation of ourselves as a person with power in these situations.

In Hialeah, when I travel alone and stay at my parents' home, I wake up soaked in social power. I walk the three long blocks to Sedano's Supermarket without worry of a racist comment or a homophobic one hurtling from a passing car, and I wear a T-shirt that clings to my chest because no one is searching my body to answer the question: Is that a woman or a man? At the corner, I rearrange my hair higher and tuck it in place with a claw clip, confident that no one at the supermercado will examine my hair and ask aloud: Is she Black? Inside the supermarket, I know that people will assume I am married to a cisgender man and that I am the mother of at least two children. They will assume I am straight from Cuba or the daughter of Cubans until I open my mouth at the cash register, and then they know I'm something else, nothing bad, just maybe Puerto Rican or the daughter of a Dominican and a Puerto Rican or a third-generation Cuban who didn't learn Spanish with her parents.

In other places, Frankie has the social power. In Texas, Oklahoma, New Mexico, Iceland. Away from major cities, I send Frankie to the front desk at hotels. "Work your white magic," I half joked outside a hotel in a small town in Missouri. I am versed enough in U.S. race politics to know that a white queer in Missouri might get a good room for the night, but that for someone like me, who is usually read as Mexican or South Asian, it would be hard to predict the outcome. I would be assigned a room and wonder if I was near the elevator by chance or by design, and I would tell myself that it did not matter (because it didn't) except that wondering about it was why it did matter.

But this is about our travel to Hialeah, and in Hialeah, even with my Spanglish accent, I am the one with power and privilege and responsibility. I am the one who has a choice, and what I learned about myself over and over again, on every trip, is that I am a coward. When a new family moved in next door to my parents, the woman's father brought his construction crew to gut the house and add a long privacy fence. I was visiting without Frankie, and the man wanted to know everything: Is your dog spayed? Why'd you do that? You could have a good litter! You married? Where's your husband?

I hesitated. It was early in the day, but the sun already towered over us. I was not awake enough to educate anyone, and I was annoyed that this fell to me. I also sensed a pinprick of worry. This family was new to the block. Would they be unkind to my parents if they knew I was queer? Everyone else on the block had known my parents first, and then some of them had figured me out later. I bit my lip and told the neighbor that no, my husband couldn't come on this trip.

———————————

My father continued asking me about my husband. It was one thing to lie to the neighbor at eight o'clock in the morning and another to continue misleading my father, except that I stumbled in my own mind every time I wanted to say in Spanish, *Frankie's not my husband and also not my wife. Let's call Frankie my pareja.* I sighed every time I thought about it. I only saw my parents once or twice a year, but if I am being honest, that had nothing to do with it. My parents had never cut me off or thrown me out of their home for being queer, and I had no reason to expect that they would do that now. But I was a coward. I didn't want to feel any rejection, none of it, not even the disappointed look my mother had given me after I first came out to her in my twenties, a look of such intense sorrow that to this day I can feel the sting of it.

My mother was clear that I had no husband, and when she spoke of Frankie, she used the pronoun *ella*. At her kitchen table one morning, I told my mother, "I don't know what to do about Papi. He thinks Frankie's my husband."

Mami sighed and glanced at the clock. We were waiting on my father, and then the four of us, Frankie included, would be trekking farther south to the Fruit and Spice Park. I don't know what I had thought my mother would say, but I had hoped it would be along the lines of *I'll talk with him. I'll do the work for you.* But my mother is even more conflict averse than I am, and she only shrugged her shoulders in response.

On the road, I filled the hour-long drive with sharing everything that I knew about the park in Spanish and English. It was a Miami-Dade County park, almost forty acres of lush fruit trees, including mangoes and jackfruits. A tram would take us around the property with a tour guide so that my father, who used a cane now, would be comfortable, and luckily for us, a festival that day would let us taste a slew of fresh fruits, including blackberries, lychee, and pomegranates.

The day unfolded as I anticipated. The tram crawled slowly in between banana trees with the guide talking about the varieties of fruit trees at the park. The tram stopped at the jackfruit trees so the guide could pick one from the ground and hold it up for us to admire its heft. The tour ended at the festival, which turned out to be a slew of tents with musicians playing guitars and vendors hawking fresh fruits and juices. My father, who has an aversion to group activities, barked, "I don't want to see anything. I'll wait here." He stood in the shade of a tent, and my mother tucked herself into his shadow while Frankie and I roamed through the festival tasting mora and kiwi that had been harvested from trees in the park. We drank water, too, and a lot of it because Frankie is almost fanatical about hydration, and the temperatures were in the eighties that day. I wasn't surprised when they needed to use the restroom, and I also knew that this park would not have an all-genders bathroom. Still I said, "Go now. It could take us more than an hour to get back home. Do you want me to go with you?"

They frowned. Of course, they didn't want me to go with them. They weren't a child. We'd had this conversation before, but I always offered just in case this time, this one time, they did want an ally. "No, I'm fine," Frankie said, and off they went. I wound back to my parents, who were turning slightly irritable from standing in the heat of the tent's shade. "And Frankie?" my mother asked. "Fue a buscar el baño," I told her.

The crowds waxed and waned around us. Frankie called. They had found the bathroom but lost track of where we were in the festival. I spotted them at a distance and gave them a few landmarks: this vendor, that vendor. When I hung up the phone, my mother decided to take action on the issue of gender and my father. "There's Frankie!" she exclaimed in Spanish, and she began talking to my father about Frankie while emphasizing the female pronouns: "Mira, ELLA viene por allí. The bathroom must have been far for ELLA. But with this heat what are you going to do? ELLA, she went to find the bathrooms, because SHE had to. And it took HER time. Mira, SHE'S walking toward us. Do you see HER? I can see HER. Look, SHE sees us!"

My father's face puzzled at the start of my mother's monologue, and I watched his face as it shifted from confusion to the start of clarity until it settled on embarrassment. When Frankie reached us, my father was practically blushing, and unsure of what to do with his emotions and thoughts, he proclaimed in his old Cuban grandpa way, "Are we going now? I've seen enough."

Papi did not speak to me afterwards about gender. He treated Frankie the same, as if Frankie were indeed a white man. On phone calls, Papi did start referring to Frankie by their name, but sometimes, when I called late in the day and he was tired, he would nod on the WhatsApp video and ask, "How's the husband?"

---

La Cubana. It took me decades to understand that I loved that twenty-eight-hour ride on the Cubana bus precisely because I was steeped in the privileges of a hetero and cisgender childhood. At ten, I was not out to myself as queer, and I was at home in the gender assigned to me. I spent hours in those days brushing my black hair and smearing lip gloss on my mouth. Boys and men existed on the periphery, much like the garden lizards in Hialeah. In fact, the only men in my daily life were my father and our cat. Everyone who mattered was a woman: my mother, her sisters, their friends, my schoolteachers, my friends.

On the Cubana bus, everyone was a woman I recognized, a woman I admired, a woman I longed to be or to have or both. It makes my heart ache now to think about the child on that bus who was queer and out to themselves, the kid who did not want to be so firmly enmeshed in a woman's world for twenty-eight hours from Jersey to Florida, the kid who did not follow the rules of gender conformity in our community. It's hard to admit it, but the unity I felt on that bus was not unity at all. It was a fantasy of unity, a fantasy that required my complicity.

My favorite times on the bus took place at night when the women fell asleep and I could observe the feminine body as a fact and as a fiction. I tiptoed to the back of the bus, past row after row of Cuban women, all of them asleep in their seats, their made-up, middle-aged faces collapsed into dreams, the creases in their eyeshadow subdued in the dark, their eyelashes stiff from mascara, their arms holding a child's head in their laps, the windows in hues of black.

At the end of the aisle, I reached the bathroom, and when I closed the door, a light bulb blared over my head. The room had only a toilet and a roll of toilet paper. There was no mirror, no window, nothing beautiful or sweet or glamorous, only the blunt, hard plastic and what our bodies discarded as the bus careened down the highway past miles of silent farmlands.

# Myth Maker

### GENEVIEVE HUDSON

**M**y new flat is a fourth-floor walk-up. The neighborhood is quiet, mostly families. A far cry from the bright lights and tight corridors of the districts nestled into the city center, teeming with tourists. I settle into my solo night and make myself dinner for one. I fry up cashews in oil, toss a handful of ripped kale into a bowl, and spoon roasted beets on top. I boil black rice left from the previous resident. At the tiny table in my cramped kitchen with its miniature fridge and miniature stove, I hunch over my salad and begin scrolling OkCupid. The claws of loneliness retract.

Normally, when I'm hurting, I seek more of the same pain. I like to push on the bruise. And tonight, I miss my ex-girlfriend. The one who broke my heart in the most ordinary way. She simply no longer loved me.

On OkCupid, I scroll thumbnails of women. I imagine meeting them, taking them on a date to a cool canal café, thrusting us both into an entirely new reality where we know each other's names, accents, maybe the taste of the other's tongue. But I don't want romance. I unglue my eyes from the screen and peer from my window onto the Admiraal de Ruijterweg with its massive block of beige brick buildings lit in the moonlight and tell myself, "I live here now," meaning Amsterdam.

I'm here because I've been granted a creative arts fellowship from the Fulbright program that allows me to reside in the Netherlands, research my ideas, and write fiction. The program awards a small number of fellowships to young scholars and artists every year to engage in self-directed research in a country of their choice for nine fully funded months. This year in the Netherlands, my cohort includes scholars pursuing projects in health care, pension research, and engineering. While they save the world, I'll be queering Dutch fairy tales.

Fairy tales interest me because of how they've shaped the discourse on morality and their instructions for "how to live" in a society. They provide a framework for reinforcing, commenting on, and even disrupting cultural norms. I'll be respinning these foundational myths to represent unmapped, nonheteronormative worldviews using my own subversive, gender-deviant consciousness. Basically, I'll be making them gay.

Or at least that's what my grant application says.

———————◆———————

I start a story about a girl putting her finger in a dike to save the city. *Hahaha.* Too on the nose. I might finish anyway.

———————◆———————

I'm offered the keys to a spare office in a research institute on the outskirts of Amsterdam that specializes in the cultural history of Holland and holds an archive of their myths. To get to my office, I jump on my bicycle, a heavy, step-over, single-speed with a fat steel chain. I still can't pronounce most of the streets I bike down, including my own address. The names catch in my throat and sound like hacking. I jostle down the Witte de Withstraat, clanking over the bricks, stuck in a stream of bike traffic. Better cyclists ding as they rush past, their cool trench coats trailing them. No one here wears athletic gear like in Portland, Oregon, where I've just moved from, but tailored slacks and sophisticated sweaters. I head onto the Kinkerbrug and take a left on Jan Pieter Heijestraat. My cell phone plan has yet to be activated, so I make little maps on pieces of paper that live in my pocket or clench between my palm and the handlebar. I pretend I know where I am.

I've been emailing with a professor at the institute since before my project was accepted by the Fulbright committee. I sought him out because of his expertise in mythmaking, pitched my project to him, and got his support for the grant application. The first day I meet him in real life, he asks me, "What do you mean by Dutch fairy tale? What does it mean to possess a story? Does it ever belong to anyone?"

He dresses in all black. His gray hair recedes on top and grows long in the back where it lands in thinning wisps on his shoulders. I can't stop staring at his impressive handlebar mustache. The way he asks sounds curious, not accusatory. But self-doubt stands up in me and makes room for more. I don't know how to answer him. Panic streaks down my spine. For a moment, I'm sure my whole project is dead on arrival.

I stumble out an answer, and he tours me through the modern concrete building with its dim lights and big windows that filter in a gray sky. We walk through the cafeteria with its microwave and coffee station for Nespresso and tea. I trail him into the library with its low ceiling and rows of metal shelves. His colleagues blink at me with blank stares. He's kind and curious, a professor of legends.

"Do you read Dutch?" he asks me in English.

"I'm learning," I tell him, citing the hours spent on Rosetta Stone, the classes I've enrolled in. The ease and accessibility of Google Translate.

He nods and departs. I'm left at my desk, twirling my thumbs, drawing a blank page in my brain.

---

In preparation for my Netherlands-based research I've been reading Jack Zipes, fairy tale scholar and hero in the field. Zipes refers to fairy tales as "wonder tales," and I like that. He writes: "If there is one 'constant' in the structure and theme of the wonder tale it is transformation, miraculous transformation. Everybody and everything can be transformed in a wonder tale."

I highlight this line in my mind. *Miraculous transformation.* The queer person transforms all their life. We play with presentation. We shape-shift our gender. We come out again and again and again, and each time we do, we go through a small and miraculous transformation. To be queer is to understand the art of this conversion.

---

I do something I have never done. I go to a bar alone. I order a shot of vodka and a bottle of mineral water. I've chosen a typical Dutch bruin café, a classic low-lit pub with dark walls and dark beers. I bring a book by Wayne Koestenbaum, *My 1980s and Other Essays.* I've been on a Koestenbaum kick. And a Susan Sontag kick. I've reread "Notes on Camp" twice since my arrival. I'm hoping their smart sentences will sink into me by osmosis. Will I look up from the page wiser and more aware? I've revisited Emerson, too, because my month of solitude inspired the idea that maybe I'll write my own essay on self-reliance.

People cram into the café. American pop music cranks through the speaker. The groups of friends laughing and drinking and pushing past my table only make my ache more acute. I get real with myself; I'm not making new friends tonight. But it's nice to be somewhere that's not my flat. Not my desk at the institute, where the ancient stories do not stir my imagination in the ways I had hoped.

I put down Koestenbaum and open my notebook. I poise my pen above the page. I imagine the character I'll write into my new myth. I picture them at the end of their story, transformed. I try to visualize their transformation, an image to move toward. A legend I might let live. A final scene. In one Dutch tale I read, a mermaid is turned into a stuffed doll with glass eyes to be gawked at behind a glass cage. The sea she lived in dried up when a dike was installed to encourage industry. Where she used to swim now stands a cheese farm and blond boys play. What I want is another ending. Real eyes. No cage. Undried oceans. Two mermaids in love.

I leave the bar and cycle home. Tourists whoop on the streets. The trams amble by lit up on the inside.

---

"Fairy tales begin with conflict because we all begin our lives with conflict," writes Jack Zipes in another book. "We are all misfit for the world, and somehow, we must fit in, fit in with our environment and with other people." I love this passage, this idea of being misfit for the world. It sounds queer to me, to start with conflict.

And then there's the problem with fitting in. Wanting some place, some person, to fit with. How to do it. Where to begin.

———◆———

Less than sixty miles away is Rotterdam, the city where my grandfather grew up and where his brother Jan still lives at age 101. I go to see my great-uncle and we eat lunch, drink tea, and partake in one small cookie each. His mind remains sharp, and he entertains me with stories of my grandfather as a boy, then a man. Their family was incredibly poor, and my grandfather raised pigeons on the roof for his brothers to eat. Mostly they consumed potatoes, milk when they could get it. He put himself through night school, studying engineering, and during the day, he worked in the shipyards. The hard manual labor gave him abs so chiseled he used to joke that he could break a nail against his stomach.

When my grandfather was in his mid-twenties, around the age I am when I arrive in Amsterdam, he left the Netherlands. He departed from the port of Rotterdam on a boat destined for Puerto Miranda, Venezuela, and sailed for twenty-six days. The farthest he'd ever been from home. He arrived in Venezuela as an engineer for Shell Oil, and there he would meet my grandmother, a nurse from Puerto Rico who tended his broken leg in the company hospital. Together they had four children before emigrating from Venezuela to New York, then South Florida.

After lunch, I explore my grandfather's village. The architecture is preserved, so it's easy to visualize the village alive in another time, my grandfather racing bikes down the alley, snow falling in his hair. Everyone in my mother's family mythologized my grandfather. He has the archetypal immigrant story of being born incredibly poor, moving to America with nothing, and becoming very wealthy. The rags to riches fairy tale. I remember observing him in my grandparents' house in Florida as he made orange juice from the citrus trees in his backyard. Orange juice in Dutch is called sinaasappelsap, translated literally as "not apple juice." Apples, the common fruit in Holland. Oranges, from elsewhere, not theirs. My grandfather wondered at the fruit. He couldn't believe oranges came to life right next to his house. It must have felt like a fairy tale.

I hope his Dutch village will awaken something in me. That I might be visited by an ancestor, feel their presence behind my shoulder like an angel, watching me. That I might open a channel of intuition between myself and my lineage. On one hand, I came to the Netherlands looking to connect with my history through the stories of my grandfather's country. I come from these people. This cold, unsmiling brood. Hardworking and dispassionate. In love with oranges, something that never belonged to them.

I walk along the harbor with its tall ships and gray industrial sky domed above. I try to make my mind very still, still enough to detect my grandfather if he is near and wants to reveal something. I stop on a corner near a bruin café and close my eyes. I empty my thoughts, like I'm praying. The café is deserted but for an old man drinking espresso from a small glass cup. This does not feel like home. No deep recognition greets me.

Disappointment collects in my body. My grandfather's spirit is not here. Maybe he is with his orange trees in Florida on the intercoastal. Maybe he is everywhere and nowhere, like all things.

———◆———

When I was still in Portland, I Googled "queer Amsterdam" and found the trailer for a documentary with the exact title. I watched the trailer and saw androgynous bodies dancing in the night. I imagined myself among them. I imagined the stars of the documentary as my friends.

But now that I'm in Amsterdam, I hardly spot queer people on the street. Do they blend right in? Are they hiding somewhere? I look for them as I spend my days alone at the institute or alone in coffee shops or in museums, wandering, always alone.

The Netherlands was the first country in the world to legalize gay marriage. Rainbow flags hang from many store windows. The city even erected a memorial dedicated to gay people who were killed and persecuted in World War II. The Homomonument lives on as the first commemoration of queer persecution in the world.

But in a tangible, physical way, where are we?

———————◆———————

I'm back on OkCupid a few nights later, and I see her on the screen, Ash—an American living in Amsterdam. Perhaps she catches my eye because she is not my type. In fact, Ash looks kind of like me. Only more obviously boyish. Flannel shirt. Thick-rimmed glasses. I recognize myself and the self I wish to embody and reach for it. I want a friend.

Ash and I meet a few days later at Café Brecht. I wait for her by the bar among vintage armchairs, mismatched lamps, and sturdy brown furniture. Ash walks in with a butch swagger, hair high and tight. She gives off the airs of a particular kind of American expat I will come to recognize as having lived in Europe for a long time. A sort of subdued and refined affect. A slower way of talking and enunciating. The *amazing*s scrubbed from her vocabulary. Leather brogues on her feet.

Ash and I carry our drinks to a table outside so she can smoke. I watch her roll cigarettes as a parade of cyclists ding by on the bike path. For a moment, I wonder if this might be a date after all. What an age-old queer custom of forming friendships on the edges of romance, of wondering what space you will inhabit together— friends or lovers? Maybe both.

Before moving to Amsterdam, Ash worked as a math teacher in Brooklyn. Enamored is an understatement for how she feels about the city. She tells me how livable it is, how affordable, how she discovered a queer subculture unlike anywhere she's been. The epicenter of her community operates from a formerly squatted building in the city center. Every Wednesday queers from around town congregate to get a five-euro vegan meal. What follows is an evening of DJs and dancing or performance art or political talks. Some weeks have themes like "sleepover." The collective that puts on the parties is entirely volunteer run. I'm in luck, because the following night is a meeting at the squat for people interested in volunteering.

"I'm vegan," I tell her, as if it's a sign that I belong.

"You should come," she tells me.

---

I hold a vision in my mind of who I want to be. I see them—this version I have not fully inhabited. Mostly what I see is aesthetic. I see a person long and straight-down. Hipless and flat with soft, simple muscles. I see sinew and boyish charm. I see a chin chiseled into something tougher. I see a girlish spark in boyish eyes. I see a softness you can't scrub off. I see something that isn't here or there, girl or boy, but brighter than those two terms can contain. I see inside of me a more expansive sky. Someone I have not met yet. There are doors in me I haven't opened. When I close my eyes and uncover this future self, they are smiling, looking back as if someone called their name, caught them in the middle of a joke. It's the character transformed at the end of my tale.

———————————

The night after meeting Ash at Café Brecht, I walk through a door marked by spray paint, stickers for queer screamo bands, and Sharpied slogans. The air inside smells stale and yeasty. I train my gaze across the room and take it in. Rattails and asymmetrical haircuts, leather jackets and tough boots. Stickers and handwritten signs on the walls say things like GEEN MENSEN IS ILLEGAL and GEEN BAZEN EN POLITICI, MAAR ZELFBESTUUR EN ANARCHIE! Despite the graffiti and dirty floors, there is a homey quality to the space. The people seem chill and comfortable, lounging on barstools and sofas and at tables pulled out onto what looks like a dance floor. Quiet punk music plays from the speakers, and a tall woman covered in old-school, faded tattoos uncaps beers behind the bar. Above her is a sign that demands phones be kept out of sight and forbids photos of any kind. Another person, short with pink hair and big round glasses, is dishing up lentil soup from a vat and pulling off pieces of bread to add to bowls.

Ash sees me and swaggers over. She's wearing a checkered shirt buttoned up to her neck and a gold chain hangs down from the collar. She sips her Grolsch and throws her arm around me like we go way back. She looks cheery in this worn-down former squat, perfectly in her place.

Ash asks if I want dinner, which I do. She takes me to get some and walks me around the tables introducing me to folks who seem warm but not approachable in the American sense. There is no patina of false nicety like I'm used to, but I detect a genuine curiosity in who I am. I'm new, and people are intrigued.

A queer person with squinting blue eyes and a canvas backpack asks me where in the States I am from. When I say Portland, she says, "It looks like you're from Portland," and I wonder what that means. A sexual energy runs alongside our interaction. To be clocked as an American in Europe is not a compliment. What I hear beneath her words is that I'm not yet like them.

The queers here are from everywhere. I meet people from Holland, France, Italy, Germany, Brazil, Palestine, the United Kingdom, Puerto Rico, Ukraine, Spain, Singapore, Lebanon, Israel, Australia, and so many other countries. We drink cheap beer or sip Club Mates and dip warm bread into lentil soup. Ash tells me that we'll be splitting up into volunteer groups by interest. She's going to join the crew organizing an autonomous festival of radical queer resistance. I want to join the cooking collective. I walk to the sofas and sit among the people who will band together to create the vegan meals for Queer Night. Our team includes an academic, a filmmaker, an activist, a sports trainer, a carpenter, an urban gardener, and me. Other queers will rotate in and out.

I spend the next months of my fellowship at this former squat, with these people. I spend the next five years of my life in Amsterdam. My reasons for staying enter on this evening, among these people and the possibility for transformation, for expansiveness, they seed into me.

———————————

In *Cruising Utopia*, José Esteban Muñoz writes, "Queerness is not yet here. Queerness is an ideality. Put another way, we are not yet queer. We may never touch queerness, but we can feel it as the warm illumination of a horizon imbued with potentiality. We have never been queer, yet queerness exists for us as an ideality that can be distilled from the past and used to imagine a future."

I feel this in my body. This distant imagining, the not-yet-hereness of me. The dream I contain. The transformation story I am writing to my future from my present. My fairy tale. A myth of my own making. One that never existed. Not fully. Not yet.

---

No longer a tomboy and not a boy-boy, I am more myself with each passing week in Amsterdam. My style and clothes begin to shift. I exist in the in-between. No questions asked on Wednesdays. I can be me. Maybe it has to do with a shedding of the Portland self. The one I'd built around the people who knew me. The ex-girlfriend I still miss, but miss less, the old friends I love, but whose fixed idea of me limited who I might become. Without their memories encircling, I'm free to be new. To unshuck. To uncover another, truer thing within.

---

Ash lives with my new friend from the cooking collective—the sports trainer. I bike to Ash's house in Noord so she can buzz cut my hair in her bathroom. Afterwards I feel tough and shorn. The sports trainer and I cycle to the squat to begin cooking duties. Each week someone oversees a different task. This week, I'm in charge of washing and peeling and chopping the food.

The kitchen is large with two huge sinks, three prepping counters, and tall steel shelves. There are no windows, and a thick layer of grease coats every surface no matter how much we scrub it down. Donated cookware stands in stacks or hangs from hooks. Each week a bundle of washed and folded tea towels awaits us.

I'm never sure where they come from or who cleaned them. They appear as if by magic. The occasional mouse runs along the baseboards or darts across the wall, and we uncover evidence of their pellets in the silverware.

I cut endless onions and garlic for a stew. We dance and sing into serving spoons. We laugh and pose for no camera. We cook too much. We create abundance. We taste test and awe. A fight unfurls about the number of garlic cloves the salad dressing requires—if garlic should be added to a meal served before a dance party where kissing is expected to occur.

In my grandfather's country, I am seeking a new self in the margins. In the dim light. In the nighttime. I break bread. And eat vegan meals, and as I cook, I nourish a new me into existence.

At 1 a.m., after more than twelve hours of cooking then cleaning then dancing, I step out of the squat and onto the dark Dutch street. The holy space of queerness and its radical futurism disappears in the wet cool breeze. The collective imagining is replaced with the hetero reality of the city. In the glow of the lanterns, by the Herengracht canal, my boyish clothes do not embody a chic new expression of self but italicize my difference, draw another kind of stare. To those outside the walls, my clothes emphasize what I am not instead of who I am.

———◆———

At the institute I keep a stack of fairy tales on my desk. But the stories don't interest me as much as the life I am now living. On Wednesdays, I leave early to fulfill my cooking duties. One such Wednesday, I've been studying the story of a golden helmet. Then the legend of a wooden shoe. But I'm most intrigued by the tale of the boy who wanted more cheese. He eats an enormous amount of cheese. More and more and more cheese. He is greedy for his cheese. But when he wants to stop eating, he can't. A flock of fairies force more food upon him. They make him consume piles of cheese until he fears he might die from eating, might burst at the stomach seams. He wakes with grass in his mouth, and the fairies are nowhere to be found.

I put these stories aside. It is time to go. I wonder, as I cycle to the Dappermarkt with my grocery list in my fist, if I could be the boy who wants more cheese. I snicker at the thought, because of course I am vegan and not a boy. But this is just a story, and I'm making it up as I go. I could be a boy. I could want cheese.

That evening, we'll be preparing an Italian meal because it's the academic's turn to write the menu and my turn to do the shopping. I pick bulbs of fennel from the stalls, grab jars of fresh olives, and select armfuls of tangerines. The filmmaker waits nearby with their cargo bike, into which I'll load the canvas bags of groceries so we can cycle them across the city to where we'll start preparing and cooking. I hold up a citrus fruit and examine it. Here it is, the "not apple" in my hand. I smile as I consider peeling it open and exposing the pulpy triangles inside, biting in and tasting the burst of juice. Above me, the clouds part, and warmth casts down. The sun shines bright that day. Someone calls my name, and I look back over my shoulder. They've caught me in the middle of a joke. I'm smiling, truly happy, and when I see them, I wave with the fruit in my fist, and I walk toward the sound.

# For a While, This Was True

### ZOË SPRANKLE

---

I was alone with my books in the Boston Public Library when Cameron called and asked me to join her in New York City for Pride. It was already late in the day, but if I could get on a bus and find friends to crash with for the night, I should meet her in the morning for the parade. I'd never been to a Pride event anywhere, and New York Pride would be the mothership of a first time. In between the stacks, I called my friend Max to ask if I could crash with him that night at his Airbnb in New Jersey and then reserved my bus ticket while walking back to my Brookline apartment. I pushed a change of clothes into my backpack and texted Cameron a crooked photo of my tits. Soon I was outside of Boston and on the six-hour bus ride to New York, balancing my laptop on my legs to finish a ten-page essay on *The Handmaid's Tale* for my summer course in utopian and dystopian literature. Like the characters in Margaret Atwood's novel, I wrote, real-life women created heterotopias as a coping response to surviving traumatic situations. According to Michel Foucault, heterotopias were real, yet ambivalent, sometimes ephemeral, spaces that existed as worlds within worlds, like bars or cemeteries or fairs. With the book propped open on my crotch and my fingers typing like wild,

I completed the assignment an hour before its midnight submission deadline and hit Send. When the New York skyline came into view, I was free from Offred and her dystopia altogether. I beheld the skyscrapers set in a fluorescent haze and reminded myself Cameron was somewhere tucked away in that big, tantalizing Tetris puzzle, waiting for me. It was my first time in New York alone. Those few months with her I would become a virgin so many times, over and over again. Turning and turning like a pebble smoothed by the sea.

I arrived at Port Authority at 1 a.m., feeling groggy and wasted off no booze. My mind hadn't made it to the city with me yet. It seemed to be raining. When he was alive, my father used to tell me how his body would reach a place before his brain caught up with him, and there he was with me as rain hit my shoulders, as I dragged my suitcase to the street corner and hailed a cab. All body, no brain. The taxi dropped me off in New Jersey at Max's Airbnb. Max's eyes were sleepy and squinting when he met me at the wrought iron gate. He hugged me firmly for a few moments before leading me up a flight of narrow stairs. Cameron was presumably asleep, staying with her friends in the Financial District. Max set up the pull-out couch for me, but I barely slept; I laid on my back with my eyes on the ceiling and told myself, "It makes sense you're awake. You're in love."

The morning of my first Pride I unintentionally wore all black: black spaghetti strap tank top, black cutoff shorts, and black Vans. In the haste to make my bus in Boston it was what I'd packed. I wouldn't be going back to Max's Airbnb, so I carried my backpack—also black—stuffed with my laptop and *The Handmaid's Tale.* I looked like I was in immediate mourning; so subdued and far from prideful or queer in any way. Max and his boyfriend, Jay, donned rainbow face paint and matching overall shorts with pins exclaiming "Top" and "Bottom." They linked fingers on the subway and kissed at crosswalks and I lingered behind, beaming on their behalf. In a Mexican restaurant near Union Square, the three of us sipped margaritas with tiny rainbow flags that rested on the rims of the glasses. I disliked day drinking, but there I was and there we were in one of the biggest chambers of the city's heart. We kept moving. On the congested streets, now buzzed, I held the straps of my backpack with firm fists, suddenly so aware of all the color and sound circling me. As a little girl I'd been too anxious for large and loud crowds. Amid overstimulation, I'd bury my face into my equally anxious father's pant leg, and he'd take me into a quiet room. With his hands clasped on my shoulders he'd say how sometimes people like me and him couldn't handle that much energy and noise all at once, and that was okay. Instead, we sought refuge in solitude, or maybe the company of one other person. I'd watch his forehead scrunch up as he put on a movie, and under the actor's voices I'd listen as life went on in another room.

I trailed beside Max and Jay down Fourteenth Street texting Cameron, who was taking a while to respond. I periodically looked down at my phone, hot in my hand, waiting for a ping, while the parade went on in my periphery and I bumped shoulders with sweaty strangers. I passed a group of naked women painted head to toe in psychedelic-looking swirls. Near us were drag queens whose faces appeared only slightly dewy from the oppressive heat as if they had no sweat glands whatsoever, packs of older motorcycle butches clad head to toe in leather, and little kids with their mommies and mamas conjuring iridescent orbs from bubble wands. A rare kind of kaleidoscopic beauty it was. Cameron finally texted me to meet her by the stage near Washington Square Park. I told Max and Jay I'd meet up with them later and went to find her. I knew she wasn't mine, but as I meandered through the streets of Manhattan I convinced myself she was.

I spotted her in the crowd and no longer saw or heard any people or life going on around me. That was all in another room now. Just as I reached her and made it to the climax of some internal film, the sound went mute. She picked me up, spun me around. In our ornamental jewelry box we kissed in the crowd, and I let my lips go. She pulled her mouth away from mine and wiped a halo of sweat at her hairline. A little black mole above her upper lip was coated with a sheen. A rainbow had been painted down her arm. I greeted her friends as we crowded together in a port-a-potty to take swigs of warm vodka from a plastic water bottle. Cameron curled her fingers around mine, and my mind finally started to meet up with my body. Even the backpack with its books inside couldn't pull me down.

I'd met Cameron a month prior at a party in Dorchester. A mutual friend had seated the two of us on the lip of a bed in the back room where boys pressed their lips to bongs and bowls and choked back coughs. I noticed the small mole above her lip first. Then how her dark hair curled slightly under her ears just like mine. She was like looking in a mirror. But in the reflection, where I usually saw my most soft and feminine bits, there she was angular, muscular, and proud. Foucault describes mirrors as a certain heterotopia, one of his placeless places. I gave her my number with no hesitation. Our mutual friend raised her eyebrows at me and smirked. Cameron did not linger. I'm certain she evaporated right then and there. It was spring then and would be summer by the time I'd see her again.

On our first date we met for coffee at a café I loved in Brookline. She held eye contact like no one I'd ever known and told me about her ex. How they'd told each other they loved each other on the day they met and how she thought she'd never truly fall out of love with her. I told her about my father, who'd taken his life four years prior, and she listened like no one I'd ever met. She drank her coffee black and in between sips asked me questions about him no one had attempted before. I recommended the two of us grab pad thai at a little place down the block. Her eyes lit up, and I knew I'd succeeded in the manic pixie dream girl way of my words: *Look how spontaneous and impulsive I can be.* Before catching the T to record her radio show down at the college radio station, she kissed me under a tree draped with light-up Christmas balls no one had bothered to take down. It was the first time a girl had kissed me in public. An alarm clock jolted me out of bed and slapped me silly. A cold shower. An espresso shot to the heart. She made her way onto the Green Line, and I crossed the street to go home. "Be my teacher," I thought.

In the center of Washington Square Park, Cameron and I sat on the slippery cool edge of the stone fountain and watched people run through the water like children. Cameron declared she was going in. I stayed back with my books on my back and watched her gallop into the stream. She kicked up cool droplets, misting my hot skin. The rainbow painted on her upper arm bled, and I watched her become a watercolor. She looked back at me, with wet black curls clinging to her cheeks. I kept watching while her friend met her in the stream and kissed her. The people around us cheered for them and their kisses. I told myself not to be jealous. "This is a part of it," I said in my head. "She'll never be yours."

Cameron was dry now, sitting on her friend's bed in the Financial District. I had no idea where my friends were; I'd abandoned them completely and would continue to do this countless times for her, though she would never ask me to. I would starve myself unintentionally and smack my face. I would cry and feel crazy and stupid. I would lose myself and believe the only thing that would return me to a state of bliss was her touch and her touch alone. This would never be true. But for the time being, I shed my backpack and pressed my chin into her shoulder. I watched as she cut open tablets of ecstasy and measured out what looked like tiny bits of mica. She told me to lick the cutting board of scattered crystals, and I did. Before and after her, I'd hesitate to take more than two Advil. The sour chemical dust clung to my tongue and for a moment, my anxiety came in through the cracks of the room. I'd never done drugs until now, and with her, I'd do so many. She gave me a tablet of ecstasy in addition to what I'd just licked up. I looked into her eyes while the powder dissolved down my throat and into my stomach.

Molly is a sweeter and much more innocent name for methylenedioxymethamphetamine in its crystallized form. Molly is a loving and hopeful girl, sneaking into corners of your brain to seduce your ventral striatum and easing any frightening stimuli found in your amygdala. She keeps you up all night like any good lover would. With her it's all beauty and no bloodshed. Not since childhood had I seen lights looking so warm or music sounding so smooth. We were all just silly, stupid souls. In this placeless place I felt in love with the world again.

The music grew louder and I danced with my arms going wild. Bowie was blasting, and I shut my aching eyes closed to see my father swinging me around in my family's old living room in the tiny lavender house by the railroad tracks that shook when the trains went by. Cameron grabbed me by the waist and spun me until I was dizzy. I draped my body across her friends I'd just met. Any anxious thought I had come across my brain perched on a cloud and evaporated as I spotted it. For the first time in my life, everything happened only one moment at a time, not double-exposed with the moment before it or skipped ahead to a future worry. I hadn't taken my Prozac for two weeks. I'd been feeling chock-full of oxytocin love brain chemicals and hormones, something better than prescribed medication. I was convinced Cameron could cure and make every empty part of me whole.

A group of us roamed the streets of the Lower East Side and raced each other from block to block. While Cameron went into a bodega to buy cigarettes I remained on the sidewalk and paced between two light posts because walking felt too good to stop. We slipped into a bar reimagined from an old beauty salon with a deep pink glow. A projection of *Paris Is Burning* moved on an exposed, dark brick wall, and I watched it with my mouth open. Cameron pulled me along, and we descended into an underground speakeasy. I had no idea where we were or where we were going; I just followed. Cameron danced with her leg between mine while icy mango margarita juice dripped down our chins. Everything was sticky, and I wanted to call my mom. Cameron advised against it. I found myself saying out loud, "Thank you, Mama."

By four in the morning Cameron's friends had scattered, and it was just the two of us at a twenty-four-hour tattoo parlor in the West Village. The parlor walls were mirrored, the room reflecting in on itself. So many squares of us. I saw the back of her. Curls tangled, glitter encrusted on her scalp. Her elbow was propped up on a cushioned maroon table while one artist carved a tiny spider into her upper arm. I looked down at my own body and watched a needle pierce red pigment into the base of my middle finger. The tattoo artist poked the needle into the bright orange ink and then in all seriousness turned to me to ask which colors came next. I told him green, then blue, then purple. He warned me finger tattoos fade fast. I told him I didn't care. I closed my eyes and listened to the buzz. A woman in the corner moaned, a thick needle poking out of her lower lip. I caught Cameron's eyes in a mirror. We smiled at each other as my tattoo artist, now finished, swept away the excess pigment from my finger. I was left with six raised dots, like two sets of ellipses. I ran my thumb over the dots and they stung but didn't hurt. I'd wanted this deconstructed rainbow on the edge of my crooked middle finger since I'd accepted I was gay a few months prior. I paid the artist way too much.

If you talk with older lesbians, those who've been around the block and had their guts trampled on and mended, they will tell you that the first girl you fall in love with will not be the one. They will tell you how she'll be manipulative, vacant, and cruel. How you'll abandon yourself on cliffs for her, and once she's left you in the dust you'll realize all along you were terrified of heights and playing brave just for her.

When I meet women who are in the throes of their first queer free fall, I will refrain from telling them this. They'll tell me about their first one, and I'll listen like no one they've ever met. They'll tell me, "She's the one." And I'll believe them. Because she is the one. How could she not be? The one who led them to themselves. Because if queerness is anything, it is not new. It finds you at six or seven, and its shine slowly becomes blunted by a sun-stained, conforming patina. The first girl to find this old painting of you will take a soft brush to your forehead, to the place where your breast meets the bone, and scrub you clean. She'll make a mirror out of you. It will feel effortless at first, all her scraping and claw-ing. You'll convince yourself only she can restore your vibrancy. For a while, this will be true.

Months later, on steps by the Seine River in Paris, we passed *Devotion* by Patti Smith back and forth. Cameron held the book with both hands and recited the story to me in a voice somehow even raspier than my own. She was studying in Europe for the fall semester, and I'd flown 3,400 miles to see her, paying for the flight with some inheritance from my grandmother's homophobic cousin. During my layover I'd nursed a glass of overpriced rosé at an airport bar and wrote in my journal, "Hopefully this trip will solidify that she wants to be with me."

The water made slapping noises while Cameron's mouth moved along with Patti's words. Just above her frizzy curls, a golden car-ousel spun like a child's lazy toy top. We'd been in these kinds of moments before. The magical ones. The convincing ones that made the not-so-good ones seem like misinformed footnotes. There was the candlelit dinner by Moulin Rouge when we aban-doned our table to go fuck in the bathroom. Or when we passed Notre Dame at dusk listening to Jason Robert Brown's *The Last Five Years* between a split pair of earbuds. In the gay district of Paris, we passed through clubs where fully naked men showered in glass chambers, and lesbian bars where women ran their man-icured fingernails up and down our forearms. We sniffed poppers and for brief moments were suspended in a disorienting, stupid kind of euphoria. For a few seconds we looked at each other with big eyes as if it were our first moments on earth. Eve and Eve sur-rounded by ruby-red apples. Grasping at each other's limbs for support and that smooth, good feeling, only before the feeling ruptured and the momentary sensation ran off our bodies like ocean water licked up by hot sun.

In the midst of that magical moment on the Seine, a text alert sounded from Cameron's phone. That singular ping shattered the illusion and suddenly there was no *Devotion*, or lapping water, or golden spinning carousels. The name that appeared on her phone was one that had repeatedly come out of her mouth in Paris, the name of a girl studying in her program. She assured me they were just friends and that she was really just so cool; I would like her if I met her. These were the conditions of loving Cameron, and who was I to quench her freedom? She set the book down on her knee and responded to the girl while I looked out at all that was beautiful and not home.

Memories of our time together would later form into sensory couplets. An image or sound or taste so potent, accompanied by an ambiguous feeling. The tang of tequila on her mouth in New York along with a tender sense of danger in my chest. The smell of French onion soup and the cigarettes she smoked paired with a lustful unsteadiness. Drugs clouded it all. The reason the mirror is a heterotopia and not a utopia, or some kind of sought-after Eden, is that the world within the reflection does not exist. It is a false vista, a concept to keep oneself steady. In some moments our time together seems a hallucination; in others, it remains one of the few inciting incidents of my life. She was the thing that woke me up and brought me into the room.

On our last day in Paris, Cameron slunk out of our rented room early in the morning to catch a train. I woke up alone in a sea of sheets stained bloody from my period. To keep from crying, I relinquished my body to the bed and let it drift in and out of sleep. I couldn't face the disaster we'd left the room. The mess that was now mine. There were wilted rose petals scattered on the floor and tea lights drowning in puddles of their own melted wax. My white lingerie with cutouts all over, like a kindergartner's paper snowflake, hung lifeless over a corner chair, and morning light was seeping in. The room really was so beautiful if you made time to look at it. My hair was matted from sex and neglect, and my head was pounding from the aftermath of booze and Cameron's departure. A hysterical French woman arrived, slamming her fists against the door and wanting me out of her flat. I'd drifted past the checkout time—and, I would learn shortly, my flight departure. I packed faster than I'd ever packed while the proprietor screamed what I can only assume were French profanities. I stuffed the bloodstained sheets into the mini washer under the sink, knowing I'd soon be met with a devastating declaration of character on my Airbnb host reviews. With my bags under my arms, I shouldered past the woman. "Désolée, I'm so sorry, désolée, désolée."

I roamed the Paris Charles de Gaulle Airport, trying to figure out how to get home after my flight took off without me. Outside, a rainbow fanned out over jammed rows of taxis. I took it as a signal from my father that the world would not drop from beneath my feet. The words around me were gibberish. I wasn't thinking about Cameron, or whatever was left of our love. There was no room in me for senses related to feelings, just sounds and sounds and sounds. Once it was clear I was out of options I rebooked my flight for the next day and crossed the airport threshold to a hotel across the street. The receptionist took one look at me and asked if I needed a hug. I usually declined physical affection apart from those I knew intimately, but I nodded and allowed the woman's warm body to take in my own. Her skin was soft and smelled like coconut and shea butter. She pressed her long fingers into the back of my head and stroked me like a newborn. She held me how my father had held me in a room with a movie playing, all to ourselves. How Max had held me at the wrought iron gate. The receptionist pulled away from me and with my hot, red face in her hands she said in a soft voice, "You're going to be okay." She could tell by looking at me I'd travel wherever my heart demanded, even through storms I saw coming. But at the end of it all, I'd find myself in a room of my own making. A warm chamber of my heart, free from conditions or restraint.

# Mother's Day

### DENNE MICHELE NORRIS

I begin with the door that opens to the foyer of my mother's house. I used to think of it as my house, because I lived there, was raised there. In many ways it was purchased for me. I was barely one year old when my father bought this house, and when he chose it, he did so for its expansive backyard and its four bedrooms. Cars drove fast on the busy road out front, but the backyard was fenced in; my parents wouldn't have to worry about me getting out. I could play to my heart's content.

The door to the foyer is a massive plate of glass framed in white wood. Over the glass rests a white curtain made of thin cotton, nearly translucent due to age. As a child whenever I looked at this door, I thought of a bride and her veil. I thought of modesty.

Inside, the foyer is cold. A chill enters my body through my bare feet and travels up my spine. Many years have passed since my feet have touched this foyer floor. I'm transported back to childhood, to running into it and opening the closet, to grabbing my coat and my mother's red peacoat—she expected me to hold it open for her, like a gentleman. I always did. I visualize my father's six pageboy hats stacked on the shelf above the coats. Ours was a busy, lived-in house: the TV always running, the stovetop always burning, my mother on the phone in the kitchen, my father in his office gathering papers for a late-night meeting. My home was never chaotic, but it felt appropriately full, active, perhaps stretched at the seams.

Now the thick wooden, red-painted front door. I turn the key, then swing the door wide, leaving the screen door in front of it closed. I make my way to the living room, where my mother waits in her wheelchair. I step behind it. I wheel her into the foyer because it is a beautiful spring day, the sun gleaming down on us. It is impossible to catch even a sliver of this sun and not feel like the world is inherently a joyful place, that people—all people—make it a better place, not worse. I need some of that joy today, and I think that perhaps my mother does, too.

◆

Two weeks earlier, I'd walked into a Mini Cooper dealership in northern New Jersey on a mission. I was hoping to do something that is unthinkable to many New Yorkers: I wanted to buy a car. While I had no need to rush, I noticed that I kept putting off buying plane tickets for Mother's Day. Online, I researched subcompact SUVs and prices and interest rates and how many miles you might expect a "gently used" car to last. I researched extensively because I had never bought a car, had until very recently never considered the idea of owning a car while living in New York City. It was preposterous, a fool's errand! But recently I'd been longing for a certain sense of freedom that I'd grown up with. I craved knowing that at any moment, I could pack up my shit, strap my dog into my car, and hit the road—without the rigamarole of monitoring airline ticket prices and limiting myself to what I could fit into a carry-on suitcase and a personal item. For many years it was comforting not to feel that freedom, to know leaving

was a greater chore than staying, that movement to a place beyond the city was a challenge, or at least an expense. Suddenly it
was something I felt compelled to pursue.

At my core I am a Midwestern woman. I am accustomed to
open space and to traversing that space in a car. I am built to de-
pend on cars for everything outside of my home. I love the solitude
of being the only person in my car. I love the ability to improvise
my route when there's unexpected traffic or temporary construction. When, as a baby, I was trapped in a fit of crying, my father
drove me around the neighborhood to quiet me down. For many
of my adult years I'd craved stasis—perhaps it was the simple fact
of having ended up in New York City, a place where I had no roots
and had to invest time so I could build some kind of life. Perhaps
it was the toll of living in the city: the constant pull of somewhere
to be, somewhere to be seen. Or perhaps it was the "my-ness" of
it all: I had chosen to come here. I paid my own rent, held down
multiple jobs; no one told me what to do or where to be.

There is also this: In the spring of 2021, my mother's memory
doctor informed my family that she had entered the final stages
of Alzheimer's and would likely only survive another three to five
years. She has long been more nonverbal than not, with little control over her body, and needs constant supervision. I have felt,
since then, an urgency for tackling unfinished endeavors in a race
against time. Since her diagnosis I finished and sold my debut
novel. I came out as a Black woman of transgender experience.
I began to more seriously consider the idea of moving back to
the Midwest—a place I had once structured my entire adulthood
around escaping. Most of all I needed to know I had a direct line to
my mother if she needed me, to remove as many barriers as possible between New York and Ohio, myself and my home.

---

When I signed my first lease in Brooklyn, my roommate and I (best friends from high school) met up with the building manager a few days early. She walked us through the apartment for a second time and then pulled the lease from her purse. She handed us each a pen. Our combined rent was $1,800, which felt, at the time, like a fortune. I had enough money to pay first, last, and security but no substantive plan for making a living beyond reaching out to temp agencies. After she handed us our keys, she left. We sat down on the floor, crossed our legs like we had in school when we were children. I closed my eyes. The apartment was on Fourth Avenue in Park Slope: It was busy, a loud boulevard, but our building was tucked behind another, taller building. It could only be accessed by walking through a gate along an alley at the side of that first building. There was a courtyard in between the buildings that held a grill and a picnic table and was littered with toys. All of this meant a quiet, secluded building, a small oasis in the center of a metropolis.

I closed my eyes, took a deep breath. I listened to the sounds of the city. I imagined myself a year later, two years later, ten years later. What would I look like? Who would I know, and love? For the first time, I felt like I was in control of my life. Thrive or fail, what came next was mine, and mine alone.

---

I told my sister that I was driving my new car to see our mother. "What route are you taking?" she asked over the phone. "Are you driving Route 80, or the turnpike?"

She was doing her big sister thing, making sure I had everything I needed, that I was prepared for this journey. Driving long distances had always been a real thing in my family; it was something we discussed.

"I'm not sure. Probably whichever way the GPS directs me."

She sighed, my lack of intentionality testing her patience. "I know Route 80 was Dad's favorite, but they've really built up the turnpike in the last few years. It has more lanes now. Isn't 80 mostly two lanes the whole way?"

I acknowledged her point about the ease of driving the turnpike, but I feel deeply and personally invested in Route 80. I drove my first long distance in the Honda Civic my father bought for me in high school, with him and my mother in the back seat along Route 80, through the mountains of Pennsylvania. I drove my second long distance in that same Honda Civic on the turnpike, surrounded by giant eighteen-wheelers in my tiny compact car. The turnpike was twisty, even narrower than Route 80, and I was terribly frightened, my hands gripping the steering wheel with all of my strength, my upper back knotted in tension. I sat straight up, at attention, as though I were in school. My father coached me from the passenger's seat, at times leaning close so I could feel his presence. He guided me on when to switch lanes, when it was okay to slow down or speed up. He kept me calm because he was calm, and afterwards, he reminded me that learning to drive through such conditions was a fact of life, a necessary evil. Years later, in the weeks following his death, I returned to graduate school at Sarah Lawrence to study writing, this time driving my father's car. I piloted his car around Westchester County and back and forth between Bronxville and Cleveland for visits home. Over the course of that year, I got to know Route 80 very well.

But it had been twelve years since I'd last traveled along Route 80, and once I found myself at the wheel of a gently used BMW driving through Pennsylvania, mountaintop views far as the eye could see, I found myself dwelling on a few facts. I was thirty-eight years old in the driver's seat of a car that I had purchased. I was now a woman traveling alone across a state that did not feel welcoming to me. I planned this journey because I wanted to return, however briefly, to Ohio and to a house within Ohio where my father died, where my mother *was* dying, where I once felt safe and loved and tethered, as a home should make you feel; where until very recently I'd felt betrayed by the smoke screen of that safety. Because here's the thing about the death of a parent, whether in the past or impending: However universal the experience might be, it rips open the kind of wound that never fully heals. One's sense of safety, of being held and protected, begins, slowly, to shatter. I had struggled to bring myself home, to stay in that house. I often felt that after three days, my skin started crawling, that for some physiological reason I had to leave, had to get back to New York City. I often declined to visit home, feeling that I had to stay in New York.

There's something about this city. I look through the window and listen to the cars and trucks, dogs barking on the street, car doors slamming and people chatting. I get lost in it. I feel myself disappear. It's a security blanket, a way of experiencing the size of the world and the size of myself in it. There's a sense of safety in smallness, a feeling that the worst of all things will pass me by for not noticing me. It's the reason I remained in New York throughout the Covid-19 lockdown, taking walks a few times a week, often the only person on the street. Cleveland is home, but New York City is home, too.

For the first few hours I blasted music, then switched to podcasts, occasionally glancing back at Hughes, my rat terrier chihuahua mix. I brought Hughes to Cleveland whenever I could because my mother, and my sister who cares for her, both love dogs, and it's fun to have him in the house. I passed signs for towns that I'd passed countless times as a boy: the Delaware Water Gap, the small Pennsylvania towns of Conyngham, Breezewood, exits my family preferred for their gas stations and restaurants where we sometimes stopped as family to refuel, to use the restroom, to grab food on the go, to buy kitschy Middle America tchotchkes that would amuse us in the car and end up in the trash once we were home. I couldn't help but think of how different this drive was: I was traveling not for recreation, but to offer relief, to help out. I would arrive, eat something, unpack, and the next morning get to work. Feeding, dressing, doctor's appointments. I would also see firsthand how my mother's illness has advanced in the months since I last visited. I would see the way our house is slowly morphing into a home intended to support aging: new furniture that supports a person who can't hold themselves up appearing in every room, new devices that make getting up and down the stairs easier.

Four hours in I pulled over at a rest area to use the bathroom. Hughes would be ready for a walk. As I unclipped him and attached his leash to his collar, I realized something I'd overlooked in my haste to hit the road. I was driving for eight hours, alone with my dog who exhibits anxiety whenever we are separated. I would almost certainly need to use the restroom, and to my knowledge, pets were not allowed inside the buildings at rest areas.

As I watched Hughes explore the grass, I considered my options. The restroom was in a small brick building surrounded by a field of grass. There was a plaque on the door, honoring some facts of Pennsylvania history. I could leave him in the car for a few minutes with a window cracked. The prospect of his fear at being left alone in a strange car, in a strange place, as he watched me walk into the rest area felt cruel. I couldn't do it. A white couple around retirement age stood near their car a few parking spaces away from me. The husband held a golden retriever by its leash; perhaps I could ask them to watch Hughes for a few minutes. But this, too, felt untenable. They seemed harmless, but they were strangers, white, presumably straight, and we were in the middle of Pennsylvania at a rest stop. It did not seem wise.

I walked Hughes around the building, and we explored the back. There were picnic tables where several adults sat eating sandwiches and a wooded area behind them. Perhaps I could find a secluded spot and pee quickly, no one else the wiser. But no spot felt secluded enough. Cars kept pulling into the rest area. Men jumped out and slammed their doors shut, then jogged into the building to relieve themselves. I felt very much at the mercy of their sizes, and their politics. And besides, peeing beside the road is an especially male thing to do. Presenting more masculine than feminine felt safer for a drive across a swing state, but as a transwoman, I could not bring myself to embody maleness in this way. I was nervous enough just being there.

Finally, it seemed that most of the other cars had left. I simply picked up Hughes and carried him into the men's room with me. I held him the entire time, maneuvering my clothes with one hand, and doing what I've done for as long as I can remember: sitting down (in this case, crouching over the toilet) to pee. We were spotted only once, when I clutched him to my chest and sprinted out of there as a man washed his hands. Outside again, I returned him to the grass just as a band of truckers parked their rigs. I drove off determined to make it home without stopping again.

I would need to come up with a better plan for my return drive.

A few hours later, I pulled into the driveway of my childhood home, of my mother's house, as I most often refer to it now. I rushed into the house holding Hughes. I went straight down to the basement, one of my sisters helping me. Hughes had vomited during the car ride; I needed to give him a bath and wash his car seat, blanket, and puzzle toy. It was a chaotic few minutes as my sister washed out an old basin, handed me his shampoo, and then helped me covertly transport him to the kitchen sink when I realized I needed a faucet to rinse him off. My other sister was upstairs, tending to my mother, getting her ready for bed. She would not have been able to eat for the rest of her visit if she learned that we'd washed my dog in the kitchen sink.

When it was over, my sister and I sat on the couch, catching up about work, about the car, about Hughes. For the first time in a long time, I felt like myself in that house. I was light, my breathing easier here than in New York.

———————◆———————

My mother is now almost entirely nonverbal. I have to gaze into her eyes to get a sense of what she's thinking or feeling. Her skin gleams in the sun, and her eyes meet mine. She smiles at me. I see a hint of recognition, a glimmer of that hope. I squeeze her hand. Then I prop open the screen door. I wheel her out onto the front stoop. I want her body drenched in sunlight, covered in joy. She nods, sits back, closes her eyes, and begins to hum.

# Kicking Back
# in Key West

### EDMUND WHITE

***

**T**he poet Elizabeth Bishop lived in Key West because she said it made time seem to go by more slowly. If you're afraid of aging and dying (as she was, as I am), then torpid small-town life in the heat is the best solution—events start to creep by in a place that is almost tropical (it's the southernmost point in the continental U.S., just ninety miles north of Havana).

I was first invited to Key West in 1978 by the poet Tim Dlugos, a friend from New York who'd just published a zany collection called *Je Suis Ein Americano*. Tim, who'd been a Christian Brother, had left holy orders to lead a gay life in the big city, but there was still a part of him that liked nothing better than sitting on a front porch and soaking up the heat or chatting with a neighbor. I've never again been able to find his house, but it was one of five or six surrounded by a fence and hidden from the street in an unpretentious compound. His place had just three or four rooms, as I recall. He let me have it free for a couple of weeks in January. Soon I was going over to the neighbor's porch and smoking Kents and drinking weak instant coffee out of a blue Fiestaware cup and chatting about the first thing that entered my head and letting long silences accumulate. During that stay I went on one of my few acid trips. I remember looking at the hibiscus flowers with enthralled rapture and wondering if they were real. On the beach I studied the awkward plunges of a pelican and asked myself if it were descended from a pterodactyl.

A year later, in September 1979, I rented a big house on White Street with the writer and editor Christopher Cox, just down the road from Bishop's inconspicuous little place (she hadn't lived on the island since the mid-1950s). September is one of the hottest months there. The days were long and suffocating; cats would fall asleep in the middle of the street. The garden was a typical Conch garden (pronounced "Konk," the name for people born on the island). Now most of the houses in the Old Town start at a million dollars and the gardens are small but lush and intensely land-scaped and artfully illuminated, tropical gardens with big palm trees, but back then a Conch garden was a sort of frowsy affair with mainly useful plants, such as a grapefruit tree or a sour or-ange tree or a banana tree, swept earth rather than ground cover, and lizards suddenly coming out of a swoon and scrambling up a wall. There were trees of avocados (or "alligator pears," as the Conchs call them) and of delicious sapodilla fruit, which you slice open and eat right out of its little shell cup.

The lady next door to us on White Street would play her Ham-mond organ every day exactly at three in the afternoon behind her lowered shutters. We didn't have air-conditioning, but we did have big, lazy ceiling fans spinning day and night. We would eat very greasy overstuffed Cuban sandwiches from a bodega three blocks down and then take naps to recover. A lot of napping occurred. Across the street a Spanish-language Protestant church would lie dormant during the week and spring into noisy action only on Sundays. Often I'd sit up all night writing by hand in school notebooks. Towards dawn the roosters would start in. They're wild and beautiful and roam the streets at will, much to the annoyance of Yankees and the delight of Conchs; there's a running battle about whether they should be preserved or eliminated.

I lived in Key West for four months, until the end of January. I was very prolific and wrote the long first chapter of my novel *A Boy's Own Story*. Chris was going through a frustrating period and wrote and rewrote the first page of a story eighty times and became so angry that he was always shouting at his cats, who'd hide under the old house and refuse to come out. We'd rent bicycles and ride down to the waterfront at Mallory Square and watch and applaud the sunset along with a variegated crowd of clowns and the Iguana Man and freelance musicians, and of peddlers hawking food, souvenirs, or crafts. Most of the revelers were tourists who'd come tumbling drunkenly out of Sloppy Joe's (Hemingway's favorite bar) or Captain Tony's (where Jimmy Buffett sang earlier in the '70s for drinks).

There weren't that many tourists back then and certainly very few before December and January, the last two months of our stay. The big cruise ships that now flood Duval Street with thousands of fun-seekers didn't dock in Key West in those days. Duval Street itself, which now is mainly bars and T-shirt stores and fancy tourist restaurants serving key lime pie, then was a real Main Street, with shoe-repair shops and two five-and-dime stores and Cuban restaurants and a cinema with the nation's longest-running screening of *Deep Throat*.

Of the tourists and residents who were attracted to the island, many were gay men; the town even had a gay mayor in the '80s, one of the first openly gay elected officials in the country. Now there are still four gay bars and more than a dozen gay guesthouses (down from thirty-five in 1980), but it seems that most of the gay residents have moved away to Miami or Fort Lauderdale. The usual pattern is that gays move in as the worker ants, restoring and repairing, and then they are pushed out by older, richer straights.

I can remember in the late 1980s and early 1990s how many men with AIDS I saw everywhere in Key West. There were hospices and medical supply stores geared to people with AIDS. It seemed that every sick man who could afford it had headed for the warmth and the tranquility and the gay-friendliness of the island. Even the gay mayor, Richard A. Heyman, no longer in office by that time, died of AIDS in 1994. There are more than a thousand names inscribed on the AIDS memorial at the foot of White Street on the beach—a large number out of a total population of twenty-five thousand.

I've been coming to Key West nearly every January since the early 1980s. To be sure, the gay life is fun—the go-go boys dancing on the bars, the karaoke bar, the leather bar, the gay guesthouses with their swimming pools and hot tubs. But what has always attracted me is the place itself, with its beautiful houses from the nineteenth century covered with carved wood lace, its old cemetery where the earth is so damp that people are buried in vaults above ground, its intelligent use of every square inch of land, its rowdy seafood restaurants like the Raw Bar, where you sit right next to the harbor at night and see shadowy fishing boats slipping into the dock and you eat dozens of Key West "pinks" (small shrimps cooked in their papery shells) while the locals at the bar are all shouting as they watch a football game on TV. If you're a beach person or a golfer, Key West is not for you. Most of the sand has been imported, and the water is shallow until you've waded far out, and all the way the seafloor is covered with yucky algae and seagrass.

Being a typical New Yorker, I don't really know how to drive, and now my eyes have gotten so bad I flunked my eye exam even in Florida, where they have very low standards. Luckily you can get everywhere in Key West on a bike (it's just two miles by four miles, and it's flat). I suppose my big bottom and I look absurd teetering along on a rented bike, but when I'm alone at night drifting down the empty island streets with the leaves up above sizzling in the breeze and the clouds drifting across the moon, I do feel as free as a boy.

The big hurricanes, though they swirl past Key West, rarely make landfall, though in 2005 Wilma inundated the island with three feet of water and caused the population to be entirely evacuated (with just a few eccentric holdouts). Sixty percent of the houses were flooded. Though the salt water destroyed many of the flowers and bushes, the climate is so perfect for growing that five years later you'd never suspect the damage. Key West is the place where your sickly houseplant back in New York grows to ten feet. It's also the place where an eight-foot cactus, the century plant, produces a huge yellow flower every great once in a while, like a robot proffering a bouquet. After the plant flowers, it dies.

Key West has always attracted artists and writers. In 1928 Hemingway came with his wife, Pauline Pfeiffer. Key West, Bimini, and Cuba suited the great writer during the last three decades of his life, mainly because his favorite sport was deep-sea fishing—and because they were quiet places to write and to drink. When he arrived in the sleepy, depopulated town (by 1928 the population had shrunk from twenty-six thousand to ten thousand, and almost all of those people were on welfare), he was so struck by its run-down look that he called it "the St. Tropez of the poor." He had already published *The Sun Also Rises* and *Men Without Women*, which had made him famous, but in Key West he would write most of his remaining important books, starting with *A Farewell to Arms*.

When there, he liked to go fishing and drinking with "The Mob," which included Joe Russell, the Conch who owned Sloppy Joe's; the brilliant novelist John Dos Passos; and friends such as the poet and playwright Archibald MacLeish, who came down for a few days.

I remember taking a tour of the Hemingway house in the early '80s when the guide was a big Black woman who'd worked for "Mahatma," as Hemingway was called because he sometimes wore a towel around his easily burned head. She seemed to be in a permanent rage, but I guess that was just a manner. Anyway, she pointed out what she called "a Spanish birthing chair" that women had apparently used for giving birth and that "Mister Hemingway" would take down to Sloppy Joe's (he was usually barefoot and in shorts held up by a rope) and sit on while he got deeply drunk. The guide looked very contemptuously around her. The signifiers in that story were a bit too complicated for me to decode—I let it go and bent down to stroke one of the six-toed cats, a special breed that was already highly visible in "Papa's" day.

I never knew Hemingway, though his grandson Ed is a good friend, as is Ed's mother; many of the Hemingways still go down to Key West late every July for a festival that includes a short-story contest and a Hemingway look-alike contest. The town is suddenly deluged with tall, white-bearded, rugged men in their fifties and sixties. Ed likes to go, he says with a smile, because everything is free for members of the family.

Nor did I ever see Truman Capote in Key West (though I interviewed him later in New York). Nevertheless, he is well remembered in the "Conch Republic," as it's called, for one immortal exchange. As he later recalled, he was having drinks with friends in a Key West bar when "a mildly drunk woman ... approached me and asked me to sign a paper napkin. All this seemed to anger her husband; he staggered over to the table and after unzipping his trousers and hauling out his equipment, said, 'Since you're autographing things, why don't you autograph this?' The tables around us had grown silent, so a great many people heard my reply, which was: 'I don't know if I can autograph it, but perhaps I can initial it.'"

Why do so many writers come to Key West? The poet James Merrill (one of the heirs to Merrill Lynch) came in part to be near Richard Wilbur (former U.S. poet laureate and at age ninety the island's unofficial laureate); Alison Lurie came to be near Merrill; I keep coming back to see Alison and her husband, the novelist Edward Hower (I stay in her guest cottage), and to see Ann Beattie and her husband, the artist Lincoln Perry. We're scattered all over, but during the "season" (from Christmas on) we congregate and enjoy the intimacy of a small town and the cosmopolitanism of a wonderfully cultured and like-minded crowd.

Key West has always had a seamy side. In 1860 it was the wealthiest town per capita in America, since it was full of sailors who salvaged ships wrecked off the Florida coast (some people said the scavengers rigged up lights to lure the ships onto dangerous reefs). Drug traffickers have always been at work in the Keys, as well as overcrowded boats bringing Haitian and Cuban refugees. The corrupt "bubba system" of illegal arrests, rigged elections, real estate fraud, and flagrant disregard of ecological safeguards has held sway over Key West for nearly two hundred years.

The world of the writers and artists is fairly immune within its enclave of old houses and shaded streets and impromptu parties. The only problem it faces is that almost no younger people are coming along to fill out the ranks; it's become too expensive. Sometimes the average age at a party is seventy-five; when celebrating my seventieth birthday, I felt like one of the juniors at the assembly.

But Key West has had nothing but ups and downs over the years, and right now it seems that every other house is for sale and that real estate prices are plummeting. Given the great natural and cultural advantages of the island, it will probably become more and more attractive to the next generation. The only problem is that it is now such a social and artistic beehive that its original appeal as a sleepy town to annihilate the passage of time has been lost. Now it feels as busy as Manhattan, and the cats, rather than falling asleep in the middle of the street, race across it nervously.

# Towards a Fight

## ALEX MARZANO-LESNEVICH

The morning in February 2008 my front door freezes shut, I decide I will move from Massachusetts to New Orleans. Three years have passed since Hurricane Katrina, two since I uneasily came out as gay, when I wake to find that the drainpipe on the roof has twisted during the night, releasing its water not harmlessly down the side of the house but across my apartment door, locking the door beneath a thick, white sheet of ice. Through the window I can see it's hopeless, but I try anyway. A blow-dryer, a knife, my body thrown against it. Nothing. While my dog whines at my feet to go out, and while I wait for the maintenance man to come with a chisel, I decide: I will move.

I will move even though there is finally a girl in my bed, a tall girl with close-cropped hair and large breasts she chooses not to flatten, though the men's clothing she favors catches taut on them. From the back, Kris looks like a boy; from the front, her breasts give her away. Even now that I know what the slopes of her body feel like naked, I still sometimes pass her by on the street if her back is to me. Then my brain registers only a tall, trim boy in a Red Sox jacket, perhaps a student at one of the local colleges. A boy perhaps waiting for a girl.

The girl she is waiting for dresses every morning by reaching around to zip a dress up from the back, sliding a foot into a heeled boot, slicking a mascara wand across lashes. No one would ever mistake me for a boy; I make sure of that. I make sure of that though I have started to think—suspicion in my stomach like a mouse—that I would be happier if I stopped, that the devotion with which I daily apply lipstick has something to do with staying safe, with how desperately even in my white middle-classness I do not want to be gay and how even more desperately do not want to be the kind of different I cannot then bring myself to name.

I am accustomed to such trapped feelings. I am a writer who doesn't write. I have a law degree, though I never wanted to be a lawyer. Gay and living in the gayest neighborhood in a gay city in the first state to legalize gay marriage, I still can't bring myself to walk into a gay bar—not because I don't want to, but because then the people inside would know I was gay. Naked, between white sheets, in bed with the girl who looks like the boy I still think in my quiet heart I should be dating: That is my only refuge, body over exhausting, doubting brain.

So when the frozen door traps me inside, the metaphor is too literal for me to miss. I am stuck. When the man brings down the chisel, I take the shattering of the ice as the necessary shattering of something else. I find a subletter for my apartment and secure a leave of absence from my graduate writing program. I tell the girl who looks like a boy goodbye, that though I will miss her I need to go. I load my eighty-five-pound dog and my seven-pound kitten into my convertible, and the guitar I've never learned to play but have always wanted to, and together we hit the road. Somewhere in rural North Carolina I get a flat tire. Somewhere else in rural North Carolina the electrical system on my car quits in a rainstorm in the night. Somewhere in Alabama the cat gets sick, and then the dog gets sick, and then I get sick, too. By the end of the drive we three are all hungry, we are tired, we smell and need baths and sleep. But we make it to New Orleans.

———————◆———————

"Who moves to New Orleans after Hurricane Katrina?" A man I know back in Boston has called to say hello and instead learns I've moved halfway across the country. "Who moves to the South from the North when they're gay?" Though I've only been in New Orleans three weeks, I have answers. Kate, for one, who left her girlfriend of eight years and the tenure-track academic job she'd spent her life training for to come down here for an explicitly temporary fellowship. No car, no health insurance, no next step, and no partner. The move makes no sense, but Kate's found a pool house to rent in one of the famed Garden District mansions, can tell you where the best jazz bands are each night and where to get the best sno-ball, and has learned to ride her bike over the streetcar tracks without flipping. She's the happiest she's ever been, she says.

And Meg, a short and short-haired philosophy postdoc who still hasn't finished her dissertation, though it's been eight years. Two more and her school will stop counting her credits and she'll lose her job. Her father long dead, her mother sits in a tiny town in Texas, slowly sinking further into an Alzheimer's haze, while Meg downs bottles of Abita beer and tries to imagine herself both jobless and parentless. And Michelle. Tall and wiry, with triceps cut like electrical cord, Michelle left an Air Force post to work with FEMA redesigning the New Orleans school system. FEMA, which everybody hates. FEMA, a word you can't say in a bar without having somebody glare at you like you didn't just steal their beer, you stole all the beer in town. You especially can't say it in our crowd.

Don't Ask, Don't Tell made Michelle hide in the Air Force. Now when she puts on a tank top to show off her biceps her sexuality shows, too, in a homemade tattoo of the circle-and-cross female symbol striped in splotchy rainbow colors. Here she can wear her identity on her skin—but she can't tell anyone where she works.

And me. In this band of people fleeing one story to make up another, I find a home. I stop wearing the earrings, the mascara, the lipstick. I buy one necktie, and then I buy another. When I meet a closeted Jehovah's Witness, I'm the one to drag him to his first-ever gay bar. There are no lesbian bars here, nowhere I should expect myself to feel comfortable, and somehow this makes me braver. Not brave enough for my deeper secret, but brave enough, at least, for this one. I decide to start a social club for lesbians and advertise it on an online site. At our first meeting, there's just me, Kate, Meg, and Michelle, and we lift our bourbons to each other and make lewd jokes and I end up going home with Kate. But the next month strangers appear. Word has spread. Another month and there are so many of us we move to a bar with a patio. The patio is ringed with candles that have been pasted with pictures of dead saints, and as we laugh—new friends, strangers, refugees all to this place together—the light from the saints' faces catches our smiles, casting our faces half into shadow.

---

Each night, I walk my dog during that window of light photographers call the golden hour, just around dusk when the sun seeks refuge behind the earth and its soft glow spreads across the land like a kind of grace. I love the peace of the hour; I love the chance to walk quietly and slowly in this slow city that is rarely quiet. A sweet perfume fills the air then, and while at first I thought it was my imagination—my love for the city gilding my senses—the perfume is real, the night-blooming jasmine all across town opening its petals just as the sun sets.

Down the road from my apartment, there's a peach-colored mansion set back behind a high wrought iron fence. I live on the border between neighborhoods, in a railroad apartment that used to belong to squatters and before that was servants' quarters, but I walk my dog among the grand houses of the Garden District. The color of the peach house, garish in the daylight, softens at this hour until it's perfect against the pink-streaked sky; it looks like a set designer chose it. Even the dark gray spikes of its fence go velvety in the light. I spent the summer in New Orleans five years ago, in 2003, and I lived then in the Garden District that I live on the edge of now, but I don't remember there being as many fences then, pointed and strong. Each house now looks like its own fortress—not in the wake of Katrina, with the winds and water no fences would have held back, but in the wake of what happened to the people of this city afterwards. There were lootings, the news reported. There were murders. The crime that had always characterized parts of "murder city" spread beyond the clotted shotgun houses into the land of mansions. The effect was fractious—New Orleanian against New Orleanian, everywhere a threat—but it was also unifying. No more was the crime just something for half the city to deal with. It became everyone's problem, everyone's grief.

But even that kind of equality turned out to be fiction, a racist hallucination. While it was true some people in white neighborhoods died, far more Black people did. Now New Orleans is back in a murder spike.

Farther down the street, shaded by the leafy tops of slumped trees, is Lafayette Cemetery No. 1, visible from blocks away because of its aboveground crypts. The city lies below sea level, which means the water always wants to rise. Dead bodies buried don't stay that way. They must be interred above ground, amidst the living. When you drive out of New Orleans on Interstate 10, the pavement swoops above four of the biggest cemeteries. For a moment, the white roofs of crypts blanket the earth below you to the north, the south, the east, and the west. As a child I rode an amusement park ride in a car designed to look like a small ship. Its sail swept me over the dollhouse city of London, tiny, pitched roofs below, pinprick stars twinkling through black cloth above. I was a giant, I was forever, I was nowhere, and I flew to Neverland. The effect of the cemeteries is like that. For a moment in the sky New Orleans belongs to the dead you sail above, those who lie under pitched white roofs, whose lifelessness lasts longer than your life ever will. They will lie there until you join them, they will lie there when you do, and together you will all lie buried longer still.

Then the road dips back to green earth and the illusion shatters.

---

The cemetery in this neighborhood is smaller and has boulevards between the cement houses, each with a front door as though for visiting, a place to leave flowers. Sometimes I see couples strolling the paths hand in hand, cameras slung from their necks. Still, I don't walk my dog through it. I think she's allowed, but the idea—her sense of smell, human remains, how long is too long for anything to last?—makes me squeamish. Instead, I walk her along the tree-lined street that abuts it so we can visit the artist who lives in a small cottage catty-corner to the houses of the dead.

The artist is dying. He's on oxygen full-time now, little translucent tubes protruding from his nostrils, the silver canister trailing him like a devoted pet. But he keeps the doors to his studio open as he works at its long tables, bent over under lamplight, late into the night. This man makes metal sculptures of flowers that are, to the eye, indistinguishable from the real thing. He has lived here for decades, alone, working on his flowers. He is a neighborhood institution, and when an architect friend of mine comes to visit me from Boston, I take him to see the artist.

———————————◆———————————

We walk to the cottage on a Sunday morning, hot cups of coffee in our hands. The cemetery is alive with tourists, their voices echoing off the crypts. I've never visited the artist in the morning before, and I have never seen him look so sick. His skin reminds me of an origami elephant I once saw, the thick gray paper folded again and again until it lost its stiffness and learned to sag. He is the color of that paper. He sags. He smiles when he sees us, though, and tells us to come in, come in. For the first time, I cross into his studio. And what he says next, he says looking into my eyes, so I wonder just how many times he's watched me when I thought I was only watching him. How many times I walked past with Kate. He wants to tell us about the way New Orleans is, he says, and the way it used to be. About growing up here, living and dying here, "gay."

At the sound of the word, I flinch and then am surprised to discover that reaction still in me. I have been living openly, but it turns out I am still happier when this word for what I am is not said. My architect friend is a man I used to sleep with, right after I first came out. That was how badly I wanted not to be gay: When I finally said the word out loud, I had to flee from it. He loved me, my friend. He became my shelter. Standing in the artist's studio, I realize I've changed. I now know that this man will remain my last cis male lover. I know that it is not possible to run from who you are forever. And I know—or I believe—that I am finally finished doing so.

———————

Every evening, a man wearing a silver Mylar suit with a red felt heart pinned to his chest bicycles by my front porch and doffs his oil can hat to me. I raise the glass of wine I like to sit with at night to him, and I nod my head. Even repeated evening after evening, this moment never stops feeling like a small improbable gift. I am breathing better here in this strange town. I am breathing. I am falling in love with the city's cadences. And like a lover who seeks to delight and cajole, the city seems to arrange for needed coincidence. When I agree to go with a friend to a show downtown, the other girl in the cab, the girl I don't know, is pretty: straight brown hair cut shaggy, thin-framed and loose-limbed and easy about the world. She's the kind of girl I'd like to date, but she's the kind of girl who doesn't date trying-too-hard girls like me. She came here a year ago in February for Mardi Gras, driving with a friend from the sleepy town where she'd been living. They parked their car on the outskirts of the French Quarter and walked right to Bourbon Street, not wanting to miss a minute. For the first time they saw its neon, its rows of bright churning daiquiri machines, so many revelers. They had arrived. Then they spotted a crowd of people farther down the street. There was something in its energy—roiling, frantic. A fight, they thought. They walked towards it. Whatever the crowd was watching, they wanted to see, too. Hadn't that been why they'd come?

But it wasn't a fight; it was a man with a gun. The friend got shot in the leg. The friend went right home, says she doesn't need to ever come back.

The girl stayed. She stretched one Mardi Gras trip into a new life, the way so many do here, and she tells this story to me now as though she tells it to anyone who'll listen. "Of course," she concludes wisely, "you go towards a fight. You run away from a gun."

It's then that I understand how I can be so much happier here than I am in the home that's more explicitly welcoming to me, and why my friends are, too, through the stares we get when we walk down the street together and the stares we get when we walk down the street alone and the trash that after Katrina doesn't always get picked up and the mail that doesn't always come and all the ways that living here is harder than living at home. Why so many of us have come anyway, so many that our social club gatherings take up the whole bar and the patio, too, and the light from the candles falls mostly on faces I don't know. Somewhere in this crowd is the one I don't yet know to notice. Don't yet know I'll be asked to remember.

While being here is hard, it is also clarifying. There's an unkind formulation that says we're tourists to a tragedy that isn't ours, but that's not quite right. It's more that no matter where we are, we feel like we're fighting, trying to make lives that are true to who we are in a culture that won't wholly accept it. To be here—to have to fight openly in a place where the whole city must also fight—feels more honest. What you fight for, you love. You go towards a fight.

———◀▶———

But really the fight finds us. Late one night, Kate and I are standing on a dark street corner saying good night, the only sounds the music from the bar we've just left and the rhythmic heaving of a young white guy who drank too much and is now throwing up into a gutter. There is a cop with him, holding him up. The cop seems to be helping, not a threat, so we turn our attention back to each other. Things between us are sweet. In the bar I had her perched on my lap and my arms around her. She's in a flounced skirt with her short dyke hair spiked out, and I've got on a white ribbed tank top and men's cargo shorts I bought from a confused clerk at a suburban Louisiana mall. We feel like ourselves, like the selves we have wanted to be.

My car's parked two blocks away, her bike's in the other direction, and I am leaning into the sweet sweat of her neck, making the goodbye last as long as I can. I kiss her. I kiss her, and then I pull away just slightly.

Right into the cop's face.

He's got his head pressed six inches from our kiss—I can see the grit in his pores and saliva glisten on his lip—and he's smiling. "Now, don't get me wrong," he says, one eyebrow shooting up, "I could watch two ladies kissing all day. All," he repeats, drawing the word out, "day. But you can't do it here."

"Excuse me?" Kate asks, confused.

"You can't do it here. It isn't allowed."

The drunk guy is now actually lying in the gutter, and he is moaning. Somewhere out there in the broader city, New Orleans is still in its murder streak.

"Yes, it is," I say. "We can kiss anywhere we want."

"Not here," he says.

I will reason with this man. "Yes," I say, "of course here."

"Anywhere you want to," he says, "but not here. It's against the law."

"I am a lawyer," I say, stupidly. Because that will matter. Because he wants to argue the real law. But I have just remembered this fact, and I will brandish it as the only weapon I have. "I know the law," I say. "Tell me where in the law it says we can't kiss here. Tell me where it says you can stop us."

"It's there. It's in the law. You're not allowed to. That's my job, all right? To tell you what you're not allowed to do."

"No," I say. "Tell me where in the law it says we can't."

"Children could see," he says.

Kate sputters.

"Look, we can do this the easy way or the hard way," he says, and that's when I realize that sometime in the last few minutes I've stepped in front of Kate, shielding her from the cop. I've got my arms cocked at my sides, my chin jutted out, trying to make myself bigger.

"The easy way or the hard way," he repeats.

"Oh, yeah," I say, "what's the hard way?"

Kate's tugging on my arm now. It must be midnight, past it. The street's dark and empty. Even the drunk guy's dragged himself off somewhere. It is, I realize, not the moment to be challenging an armed officer on a power trip. Yet I can't help myself. He's wrong. We're right. We're just kissing.

But then I give up. I step back from Kate and from the cop and I let my arms go slack at my sides. I let him win. Because we do both have places to be in the morning and because, when it comes down to it, I do not want to know what his hard way will be.

For days we are angry. We telephone everyone we know and tell them the story. We spend hours in Kate's apartment and in coffee shops, poring over the right words for letters we send to the newspapers, the ACLU. We file a complaint with the NOPD and when we don't get a response, we call them, then call them again. I take Dr. Seuss's *Oh, the Places You'll Go!* and rewrite it to be a list of places gay people can kiss in public in the U.S.—everywhere—and I register a domain name to create an educational website before I suddenly, finally, realize the obvious: I am fighting a battle that doesn't exist. No one's actually unclear on the idea that we can kiss anywhere we want to. And of course the NOPD hasn't responded. The city's in a murder spike.

The future is coming; it is coming for everyone in this story. Someday that cop will turn on his TV and see the first Black president, the first president who looks like he does, say that he thinks couples like me and Kate ought to be able to marry if we want to. Which probably means we ought to be able to kiss. Before I write this essay, three states will go to the ballot and by unprecedented popular vote say that Kate and I could marry there, and when they do so, it will have been unthinkable just six months prior and obvious three months afterwards. The week I finish a first draft of this essay, I will travel to the Supreme Court to stand in front and wait while it considers our rights. With me will be thousands. By the time I first publish it, we will all be living in a changed country.

And then—while the essay exists online like a monument to a hopeful time, and I live my way into a changed body, a changed name, and a changed life, and I let myself think that maybe the fight is over—the country will swerve back again.

The future *is* coming. I believe that. But it's not coming fast enough for the artist, who will die alone before any of this happens. It's not coming fast enough for Michelle to keep the job she loves or not to feel so alone just by virtue of who she is. It's not coming fast enough for me to not have to learn to stop apologizing for—stop struggling with—who I am.

And it's not coming fast enough for the dead girl.

My months in the city add up slowly, and eventually my grad program wants to know if I'm ever coming back. I think about dropping out, but I still don't want to be a lawyer, and if I leave the program without finishing there's debt to pay but nothing in return. Hurricane Gustav materializes off the Gulf Coast, and because so many didn't evacuate last time, this time the state of Louisiana wants everyone out of the bottom half. It seems silly to evacuate only to come back and then move. So this is it, I decide. I pack up my dog and my cat into the convertible again, along with the guitar I still haven't learned how to play. I say goodbye to Kate and the others and find someone else to lead the gay group and join the line of cars on Interstate 10, which has been turned one-way—out. I pass the cities of the dead. I pass lakes and truck stops, billboards for country music radio stations and billboards with scripture and photos of newborns. Across the hours, the billboards change. The scripture and babies disappear, replaced by schools and Dunkin' Donuts. When I get back to Boston, my front door opens, but the city isn't the same for me. I'm homesick for New Orleans with a force that has me wearing fleeces in late August because I'm convinced I'm cold in the wimpy Massachusetts heat.

One day I get an email from a man who says he's a detective. He is with the NOPD homicide division, he writes. Could I please call him?

He is polite on the phone. Courteous. He even sounds tentative, but not young. Just worn out, maybe. "You founded a women's group in New Orleans, is that correct?" he says.

"Yes," I say.

"And you're all—well, you're all gay, isn't that right?" he says.

"That's why I started it," I say. "So we would have a place to come together."

"I'm calling about one of your members," he says. "A woman named—" and he reads me her name.

I don't recognize the name. I tell him that.

He sighs. "That's what I'm calling about," he says. "We can't find anyone who knew her. She was found dead in her kitchen, stabbed a couple of times. She had joined your group a couple of weeks ago online. Before the last meeting. She'd just come out as gay. The violence of the crime makes us think someone wasn't too happy about it. Whoever killed her didn't steal anything." He sighs again. "I'm not too optimistic, but would you email your members? Ask them if anyone knows anything?"

After we hang up, I do. In the email I tell them, most of them on the large online list strangers to me, that there's been a tragedy. That I've just spoken with a homicide detective. That he tells me one of us is dead. I give them the dead girl's name, and I ask them to think back to the last dark night at the bar with the saint candles, the patio. Did they see her there? Did she talk to anyone? Does anyone remember her? If you know anything, I say, write me. I plead and hardly know what I am pleading for. I tell them it's important we stick together in the face of this tragedy because that seems like the kind of thing you say in the face of a tragedy. It seems true. Please, I say, even if you don't know why you want to talk but just do, here is my number; please call.

No one does.

———————◆———————

I'd like to say that later I think of the dead girl often, that I hold on to an idea of who she might have been. But I don't. She becomes part of the tangled memory of New Orleans for me, a tangle of love and grief I don't know how to unweave. Years later, I am sitting in a gay bar with wireless internet, out alone one evening on a visit to my architect friend and the woman he marries in the small Midwestern city they move to. It is a nice city, but on the walk to the bar everyone still stares at my necktie on the street. This is what I look like now, and everyone stares, I think then. What will happen if I look like what I want to, who I want to? The press of my own secret makes me think of the girl. For the first time in years, I search for her online.

Her name's in the email from the detective, but I don't remember that clue at first; instead I look up the murders from the right month. There were so many. Male, male, male—and then there she is, a name I know immediately is hers with the words "Cold Case." Four years after she died, no one's found her killer. Online there are accounts from friends who lived in the town she left. One keeps an emotional blog on which she still writes to the dead girl regularly. I read every word, feeling all the while like I'm peering over someone's shoulder, and again I can't decide whether I'm a voyeur to a tragedy that isn't my own or whether some share of this belongs to all of us who hide.

In nothing I read, not in any news article or blog entry, not in any quotes from family members and not in any vigil photograph, do I find the information the detective told me: that there's reason to believe she was killed because she'd just come out as gay. In the stories, I am surprised to find a grieving ex-boyfriend leading the search for the killer.

My surprise surprises me. I had the architect, after all. But for the dead girl I want something else. For her I want there to have been a moment, at least, when it was simple. I want her to have gotten free.

It is both too much and too much of nothing to weave into a proper story—the dead girl, the jerk cop, the staring and the many tiny insults and the nurse in the emergency room when I fall suddenly, desperately ill and we're worried that it will be fatal and in the middle of that long, scary night the ER nurse yells at Kate to get off the hospital bed where she sits holding me, lest people get, the nurse says, the wrong idea. I know couples that send their kids to Catholic school because they want their kids to be able to read and the kids come home and tell their mothers that being gay is wrong. The only time the Massachusetts girl, Kris, did visit me, before we let distance end us, when she looked not quite like a boy and I still looked like a girl, we walked down Bourbon Street holding hands. A teenage girl with too-skinny arms and big, haunted eyes followed us through the streets for four blocks and then came close. When we turned, she said only, "Can I have a hug?" We were startled, but she looked so young and so sad that we obliged. Her arms held tight as rope. Then she whooped with joy, and started, quietly, to cry. She was from Kentucky, she said. She was gay. She'd run away from home to New Orleans a month before, but we were the first lesbian couple she'd ever seen walking down any street holding hands. She longed to someday do the same. "Oh, honey," I said, and I understood that what I was living was to her freedom and for me still contained a lie.

I couldn't offer her or myself more yet, not then. I couldn't tell her to join a group I hadn't yet started, didn't yet know to tell her that there were so many people like her, even if she couldn't see us at first. Instead, my instinct was to scoop the girl up and take her back to the Massachusetts I'd just left. As though that way I could save her from the need to fight, as though if I just brought her to a place where being gay was okay it would be okay to her, too. As though I didn't already know it didn't work that way. You didn't lose what you'd lived just because you left it.

Catching Kris's eye, I offered the girl some food, some money, but no, she was embarrassed now; really all she wanted was the hug. Really all she wanted was to know there would be a place for her.

---

It's not that I thought that I myself would die if I lived in a place that wouldn't let me marry who I loved, that wouldn't let us possibly raise children together, not without being the town freaks, the targeted or the tolerated, the lonely.

Only this: I wouldn't be able to live.

A couple of years after I wrote this essay, I finally came out as transgender. A year ago, I moved to Canada. I left the U.S. I don't think I'll ever move back.

Now as I watch the headlines from home, the country I know still is my home, subsumed in hateful destructions of queer and especially trans rights, I'm thinking of the dead girl again. I keep wondering what life she left behind and what life she found, what life she would have come to. But I know I'm not really thinking of her, not the person she was, a person I never knew, but of this problem, this knot of loneliness and grief and rage and how change can come and still not be fast enough.

The problem, in this mortal life, of what is a gun and what is a fight.

# The Museum of Us

## St. Petersburg, Russia, 2017

———————

### RALUCA ALBU

"You have your brain, your consciousness, your soul.
They cannot take that away from you."
—Nadya Tolokonnikova, Pussy Riot

The first prick of excitement hit as I passed Rembrandt's *The Return of the Prodigal Son*. The last thing I, a queer woman, expected to feel standing in the glitzy, excessively polished Hermitage, was an aching desire to peg Bishop Alder. The painting depicted an adult son, kneeling before his father, begging for forgiveness after leaving home and squandering his fortune. But Bishop Alder—the name I'd given the guy huddling over a fruit bowl in the upper right-hand corner—had all my attention. His demure Renaissance smile, the soft velvet cloak, the red glow of those cathedral candles.

Our dalliance would be consensual, of course, and absolutely elating. I imagined the easy bend of his back, the way his hamstrings would quiver with anticipation. I would remind him to stretch them out and give them room to feel alive.

"Madam?" said a woman's voice. The cruise ship's designated tour guide, Marta, had noticed I'd wandered away from the group.

She redirected me and we made our way down the stairs. My body knew the drill, we'd been at it for hours.

My partner Kate and I had flown from New York to Stockholm a week ago to board a ship for a cruise of the Baltic Sea coast. Kate's mother, a tour guide, found a great deal for us to see the countries on our dream itinerary. I know now this way of travel is not for me, but there we were. Our ship set sail from Stockholm, crossed the strait of archipelagos to Helsinki, and we were now docked in St. Petersburg for two days before we'd move on to Latvia and Estonia. Unlike the EU countries we'd easily entered, Russia had strict visa requirements. We'd mistakenly assumed the visa was included in our tour or obtainable upon arrival. But visiting Russia by cruise meant we could only enter if accompanied by an official tour guide on chaperoned tours organized between the cruise company and the Russian government.

Once on the bus in St. Petersburg, it became clear we had signed up for a rigorously monitored and heavily propagandized tour of "the most beautiful city," a phrase Marta reiterated over a dozen times in nineteen minutes. When we drove through the "real" parts of St. Petersburg—the residential areas, the large concrete blocks, the playgrounds, grocery stores, and packed commuter buses—I felt strangely blanketed by the sensation of a home I almost knew, my home city of Constanta, in Communist Romania, where I was born and lived before my parents decided to defect. This was the landscape in which I first found language, built my bones, developed an attachment style, and heard my first songs. But Marta had no information to offer about real-life daily business in the city; just distracting lore about Peter the Great, the empresses of Russia, and her engagements with the nobility in Austria. How did that muscly concrete T-shaped building come to look that way, where was Revolution Square, where did the artists spend time to feel safe, the writers? But the fog of the script took over. Marta watched us like someone was watching her.

She repeatedly compared the beauty of the Hermitage to that of the Met and the Louvre. But the Hermitage, even just architecturally speaking, was a much more ambitious beauty than either of those museum giants. It was constructed in such a way that sunlight seemed to touch everything within its walls. The marbled slate columns and whipped-cream-white staircase were warmed by thick edges of gilded filigree. Arched mosaicked ceilings promised eternal heights. Display rooms were saturated with hues of deep red, indigo, and malachite green. Ornate scenes were etched out in stained glass, prismatic crystal light fixtures dangled over our skulls, and a rainbow of collaged gemstones adorned various floors in perfect geometric alignment.

"Imagine the parties drag queens would have in here," I whispered to Kate.

"It's pageantry paradise," she said. I knew we were both thinking of the same queens when we imagined it, as we crossed through another cherub bonanza.

Kate and I hadn't touched for over an hour, ever since we disembarked. I lingered close to her now, breathing in the heat of her. She smiled here at what she probably would have laughed at at home, without her usual willing escalation into more playful terrain. In Russia, we had to be vigilant. Neither of us had visited a country yet where our bodies and desires were codified into crimes, where love could land us in jail. What would that look like here? Would security rush at us? Would Marta yell, "I knew it!"?

Our tour companions naturally dispersed each time we entered a new gallery, drawn to different works of art. Kate and I, glommed together, drifted towards the quieter corners of the room. We rounded the corner and came upon Vincenzo Carducci's *The Vision of St. Anthony of Padua.*

"Anthony!" Kate said like she had run into an old friend. "You gay, gay man!"

She was now feeling her first prickle, too.

Kate grew up in an Irish Italian family in suburban Pennsylvania; she wasn't a practicing Catholic, but she knew her saints. She would later explain that St. Anthony was the patron saint of loss, credited with accomplishing miracles that recovered lost people and things. In Portugal, Spain, and Brazil, St. Anthony is also known for his couples counseling skills and for rekindling lost love. The story goes that when his body was exhumed, all was dust except for his perfectly preserved tongue.

In the painting, Anthony is floating off the ground, heading up to the heavens with an elated grin, carnal thirst in his eyes, and spirit fingers waving at his sides. A giddy, scantily clad angel wrapped in pink velvet leads the way.

A few British tourists passed right by this documented church rave where everyone appeared to have eaten from the body of MDMA. They didn't even bat an eye—unfortunate for them, really. We muffled our laughter, our bodies instinctively drawing closer in our secluded corner. I managed a squeeze of Kate's shoulder that left me buzzing for a bit, my fingertips more aware of themselves, and my body in general, from the contact. She squeezed my shoulder back, her touch lingering just a moment too long, and we both felt ridiculous, trading meaningful glances. Under other circumstances, we would be doing something cheesy, like kissing each other in front of Anthony, thanking him for helping us find each other.

Kate hadn't been thrilled with the idea of coming to St. Petersburg because of Russia's ban on gay expression, violent antigay purges in Chechnya, and recent attacks on the biggest gay nightclub in Moscow—all prototypes to America's don't-say-gay bill in Florida and the three hundred other anti-LGBTQ+ bills introduced in state legislatures around the U.S. in 2024 alone.

"That's exactly why we should go," I said at the time. We should plant our gay bodies there, breathe out the air they breathe in, eat with their forks, pee in their toilets, be the human beings they refuse to see us as—and get away with it. I figured we would find a safe path for travel. Underground gay bars, artist circles, and activists who knew how to find each other. I didn't stop to think about logistics, like that the street signs would be written in an alphabet we couldn't read, or that we didn't apply for the right visa, that we'd be stuck with a tour guide chaperone.

I needed to be in this part of the world that fascinated me for complicated reasons. While it was not technically part of the Soviet Union, Romania was occupied by Russia after the Second World War and governed by a Soviet-style government that grew more unbearably totalitarian. In 1987, when I was three years old, my parents and I escaped Romania by illegally crossing into Austria to seek asylum. Eventually we left for the United States and became political refugees.

As a child inheritor of these experiences, who shared the status of a refugee but did not consciously process the choices of a refugee on my own terms, I craved a place in that history. I carried a desire to understand the full emotional spectrum of what it meant to be in the world we left behind—one that history itself wanted to move on from. After a decade away, when my family returned for our first visit to Romania, I showed up with my fiercest

Diane Sawyer energy, asking anyone who would talk, *Where were you when . . . What was it like to live through . . . Tell me about the summer labor camps . . .*

I was mesmerized. The idea that one kind of government could exist on Tuesday and then by Wednesday textbooks espousing that form of government could be thrown out and reset—that leaders could be ousted, public land parceled off to private ownership— fascinated me. My mother's patrilineal line was from Russia, and her maternal line was from Ukraine. I was of this place; some part of my genetic coding came from here. I needed to understand something about it, so I chased every question until I found the right one.

"There are sixteen kinds of wood in the floor of the Hermitage," Marta told us. "Wood imported from all over the world," she didn't miss the opportunity to say.

The world beyond Russia got the last word as we stepped out-side into the suddenly cloudy midsummer day. Merchants in tour-isty faux-fur hats walked up and down the street selling "McLenin" T-shirts with the infamous golden arches around Lenin's stump, three packs of Matryoshka dolls, and Ikea bags stuffed with repli-cas of Soviet-era military pins.

Back on the bus, Marta pointed to various landmarks. History always seemed to end before 1917, when the imperial government was overthrown and the Bolsheviks took over, paving the way for Soviet Communism. Marta focused the narrative on foreigners who came before, took over, brought their architectural influ-ences, and traded art from Western Europe. She shared a single anecdote about how the bread of the revolution in 1917 was only twenty percent real bread. The implication was that the Com-munist revolution that came next was all predicated on lies and

empty promises, so let's move on, let's not linger on that historical digression, a misstep, a blip—never mind that the vestiges of
the Cold War are still informing leadership styles, brutal war, totalitarian policies, that the generation still in power merely re-
packaged its KGB and secret police ranks right into so-called
democracy, free-market economy. Never mind that good things
came out of that era, too: the expansion of rural infrastructure,
free education, extended parental leave, jobs, and housing for everyone. Never mind that by papering away the history of gulags,
pogroms, class struggle, and the collective trauma of violently
imposed censorship, we don't get to bear witness to where these
things go when we pretend that they never happened.

This evasion felt familiar to me, as an American.

We passed the Pushkin House, the Dostoevsky Museum,
Nabokov's butterfly museum, the museums of bread and vodka
(replete with an anecdote about how vodka was not part of the
city's history until Peter the Great brought it from elsewhere in
Russia, dare any of us forget that this city both is and isn't Russia).
This sanitized history-telling is not unique to Russia, of course.
Imagine if New York City's Big Apple Bus Tours pointed out all the
burial grounds of people who were enslaved or the famous sites of
ACT UP protests. Nor is this the only kind of tour that is possible
in Russia—there are art crawls, Soviet-era sites, and rooftop ex-
cursions. I just did it the wrong way, for what I wanted to see. But
there was still something informative about what this one was
willing to show (or not).

———————————◆———————————

"It's so dirty," one of the Canadian tourists said of St. Petersburg.

"Yeah, not exactly beautiful," said another.

*How dare you*, I wanted to turn around and say. *Do you know what these people have been through and are still going through? This place doesn't exist for your hungry all-consuming hungover tourist asses.* I felt a sudden allegiance to the inherent beauty of this place. I didn't feel it for any government entity or loyalty but a shared trauma of the scraped-up, misunderstood, underestimated, exploited, and subjugated history. I immediately slipped into Marta's mindset—I could see why she was insisting that hey, we are just as sophisticated as the rest of you, we belong. Pander to the Western gaze, embody the logic of great achievement, no matter the cost.

Soon my conflicted rage was soothed by the views of the Neva River. The buildings lining its banks were a delicate collection of pastel hues—soft blues, pale greens, and gentle yellows. Uniform rows of perfectly proportioned windows were each framed by intricately carved pillars or ornate borders. The lullaby colors softened the strict geometry of the buildings, imbuing them with a gentle, almost dreamlike quality. They bore the hallmarks of the French aesthetic, with their graceful lines and decorative flourishes, but characterized by a distinct sense of order and discipline that speaks to the city's Nordic heritage. They stood as if in quiet conversation with one another, their facades forming a continuous, harmonious whole.

We stopped in front of St. Isaac's Cathedral. The building, designed by (you guessed it) a French-born architect, stands out with its gold dome against the rain-promising sky. It called to mind the United States Capitol, but in technicolor, with thick red-granite columns and a collection of bronze-winged angels waiting on the building's edges for their next assignment. St. Isaac's Cathedral is the largest Orthodox structure in the world. Maybe I was supposed to be feeling something—my mother is Orthodox, my aunts, too. I felt no pull to God in this moment though, just the sheer awe for what human creativity is able to render out of stone.

During the Soviet era, St. Isaac's Cathedral was converted to the Museum of the History of Religion and Atheism. The dove on top of the dome was removed and replaced by the Foucault pendulum, a device meant to visually demonstrate the earth's orbit around the sun, Marta explained. Now, I felt something. To transform a church into a monument for atheism and science was both absolutely enthralling and the kind of comeuppance I so badly crave as a queer person in America, eager for the day we arrive to a true separation of church and state. And yet—there's something overtly aggressive and imposing about housing the story of atheism in a building like this. Putin knew this. He repurposed the sanctity of the church to give people the illusion of choice, as a place to go to hope for more—the more that will never come from a place like this one.

Marta stood alone by the tour bus as we trickled out of the cathedral. I saw my chance to connect with her over a vaguely shared lineage, to go off script, to bond over Western nonsense and "Eastern" beauty.

"I'm Romanian," I said, signaling our shared past under a similar regime.

"Oh." She paused and looked thoughtful as if trying to recall some vague concept from another lifetime. "Romania," she said. "We had some tourists from Romania during the Ceaușescu era."

Finally, I thought, we could dive into the unspoken with some modicum of recognition for it, some emotional connection.

"They wore very plain clothing," Marta said. "Yes, they wore a lot of gray, some black."

I wasn't sure how to respond. Here I was eagerly consuming everything she was sharing about her city, burning with desire for more, and all she had to say about Romania is that we displayed our devastated existential souls through drab clothing choices.

"I'm part Russian," I said, awkwardly trying the identity on out loud for the first time.

She looked confused. Studied my black and gray outfit. "Do you speak Russian?"

"I don't," I said, from somewhere in the ballpark of shame and acceptance.

She smiled and motioned our group back on the bus.

Our final stop was a souvenir shop.

The store was wrapped in walls of magnets that featured images of Putin riding bears through the wilderness or holding a puppy. These images were accompanied with declarations of Putin as "The Strongest, the Most Powerful," "All Goes Well," and "The Kindest President," scribed in cursive across the scene. Other trinkets pictured Putin cuddling baby tigers, shaking hands with Donald Trump, and so on. I wasn't sure how to read this perversion of masculinity, sensuality, and power: Were these tchotchkes making fun of Putin?

I went up to one of the sales associates and asked, "Are these even legal?"

He laughed. "Yes!"

"But what do they really mean?" I asked him, hoping my eye contact was enough to communicate what I was really trying to ask: Is it legal to mock this guy, to poke fun at his maniacal narcissism? Or were these serious affirmations that people were supposed to believe?

Technically, the country's constitution allows for free speech. In practice, though, journalists critical of the regime have been threatened, attacked, or killed, which breeds a culture of self-censorship, a constant awareness of how thin the veil of ensured legalities really are. For instance, Timur Kuashev, a freelance journalist focusing on human rights, was found dead near Nalchik in 2014. Akhmednabi Akhmednabiyev, deputy editor of an independent daily in Dagestan, was shot outside his home in 2013. That same year, Mikhail Beketov, known for reporting on corruption, died from injuries sustained in a 2008 attack.

"They can mean many things," the sales associate said, clearly registering my implied question.

I knew what he meant. If you asked Putin, this store was a trove of compliments. If you asked his silent critics, they'd say it was a compliment, too, but they'd be picking at a scab when they said it.

Back on the ship, I connected to Norwegian Cruises' Wi-Fi and began researching more about St. Petersburg's Soviet history. I found my attention waning, though, and found myself searching instead about Gay Russia. Another detail Marta kept from us (poor Marta, all this pressure I projected on her!) about our homo Commie Soviet history was that many of the Bolsheviks were homos. It's part of why Stalin banned it; he hated the Bolsheviks, the rival Communist group who wanted Trotsky to lead instead. Queers literally helped overturn the tsar and supported Lenin bringing gay peasant men to the capital cities to support the new regime. It turns out we gays have long favored a socialist rural utopia.

Our community was rewarded for its ideological taste when the new Soviet code of 1922 decriminalized sex between men. But that didn't last long. When Stalin took over, he "diagnosed" homosexuality as a disease of bourgeois individualism. The Wiki entry said that a doctor "proposed the surgical replacement of a gay man's testicles with those of someone straight." (What an imagination that doctor had—I wondered if a painting inspired this proposition.) The gay nobility of the nineteenth century enjoyed their time in the bathhouses and at parties. The grandson of Emperor Nicholas I was gay. When a leader in the community felt the tides shift, he gave one final talk at the university and was showered with flowers and love "before total silence fell on Soviet homosexuality."

Multiple historical resources list the names of many famous Russian men who were part of the gay community. The lives and histories of lesbians or queer women were far less documented, far more private—I found myself weirdly proud of this fact, of their ability to maintain their boundaries and to be so clever in their ways that they could preserve them in secret. I realize it means queer women were even more suppressed than men, but it also suggested they were protected from surveillance by their invisibility.

There were no paintings to commemorate the queer women of Russia's history, no monuments to honor their struggles, and no plaques to mark their existence. As a queer woman walking these streets in the twenty-first century, I was a piece of tangible evidence. I climbed on our tiny cruise ship bed, all six feet of me, bent over to avoid hitting the ceiling, jumping around recounting all these incredible details to Kate. At some point, I am sure I screamed, "WE ARE THE MUSEUM!" Kate gamely agreed.

I pulled up a website that said "LGBTQ-friendly Things to do in St. Pete's" and sent the link to the ship's business center so they would print the list for me.

I was so genealogically feral at this point that Kate suggested we take a mental break. "Let's go hang out in the hot tub," she suggested.

To get to the pool area we would have to walk through the monstrosity of the indoor-mall-on-the-sea that was the cruise ship. It had taken two hours on board to realize we were fervently not cruise people. First of all, we were the only queer couple on board. We felt sure of this because we spent most of our waking hours on deck searching for others to no avail, muttering to each other, "Oh, maybe her, she has short hair. Wait, no, that's her husband. And she's holding him like she loves him." Kate's biggest complaint was that the ship was a monument to banal heterosexuality. Evening onboard entertainment included a male comedian cracking jokes about nagging wives and a female singer lamenting her fruitless search for Prince Charming. The ship's shopping areas were designated by gender interests: jewelry for women and golf clubs for men. I experienced my first cruise with an added layer of complexity: my cousin, who lived in Romania and recently finished law school, worked as a crew member on a cruise ship in the Caribbean where it was his job to greet the passengers, clean our American vomit, fold our towels, and wash our dishes, always with a smile. His cruise ship job kept him away from his family for six months out of the year, which he traded for a few thousand dollars. I felt shame, complicity, and the glaring divide of our family's branching paths. Not that life in the States was the dream it purported itself to be either.

"Hey," Kate said, interrupting my train of thought, "it's OK," she said.

"How did you know?"

But she always just knew.

From the top deck, the cruise ship stood out like a garish, sequined disco ball against the bleak, Soviet-era landscape around the port. Shania Twain blared over the speakers and into the pool area with its brightly colored waterslides, pool towels twisted into swan shapes and perched upon chairs, hot tubs cooking pale white bodies. After a few hours inhabiting the post-Soviet world, the cruise became an even more glaring symbol of Western excess and frivolity—a floating palace of cheap thrills and superficial pleasures, wholly at odds with the grim reality that surrounded it. It was as if a piece of Las Vegas had been transplanted into the heart of a Siberian mining town, only the town aspired to its glitz, wanting the approval and recognition of hungover Westerners clad in garish Hawaiian shirts, floppy sun hats, sunglasses, and picky superficial commentary. I imagined queers—some of them, anyway—would at least do better than this.

We waited by the tiki bar for twenty minutes until a hot tub full of retirees cleared out. Kate and I descended into the hot tub, jets to our backs, enjoying a brief respite from literally all the reality when a young woman of about nineteen ran over to us.

"Hey, I don't mean to intrude," she said, working her way into the tiny hot tub, and slipping into the nook across from us.

"I just wanted to say thank you for existing," she said. "I am just so relieved to see you two here and that you were on that tour today. It's been so uncomfortably straight on this ship, you know?"

We, flabbergasted, momentarily forgot how to speak in gay.

"You're... welcome!" Kate managed. "Are you queer?"

"I'm bi-curious. But I'm drowning here. It's awful."

"Well, don't really drown," I said, laughing at my own "joke" like a retired dad.

"It's just such a relief to not be the only one," she said, leaning back in the tub.

I understood her thirst for community, connection, the consistency of lineage.

She didn't stay long and left almost as suddenly as she appeared.

Thank you for existing, she had said, to a person who spends so much time trying to disappear.

———————◆———————

That night, we packed our bags for our second and last day in St. Petersburg. I tried to convince Kate to use our two-hour walking tour to hit up as many of these cool underground where-we-belong places as possible, but she wasn't listening.

"Shit," she said, "I can't find my passport."

Being without a passport on a ship sailing in international waters is a particular problem. Kate's passport had to be on the ship—she couldn't have boarded without it—but she would not be able to disembark until it was back in her possession.

After hours of searching and loudspeaker announcements and panicked phone calls to various embassy offices, we accepted that Kate would be bound to the ship for our last day docked in St. Petersburg, and I would spend our last day there on my own.

"I really pissed off St. Anthony," she said as she was falling asleep.

———————◆———————

Maybe Kate was a little extra saint-sensitive coming off our recent road trip through Ireland. Kate is fifth-generation Irish, and although her grandparents were actively proud of their Irish heritage, it was often entangled with Catholicism and traditional gender norms—weaponized against Kate, who was queer and not interested in feminine expression.

Kate's curiosity, when traveling, is lower stakes than my own. Kate does not travel searching for a missing part of herself, the source of family trauma, and explanations for why her parents are the way they are. She wanted to try the stews, whiskeys, and stouts. In Ireland, we chased sheep under bridges in the national park, swam in the icy Atlantic, and strolled around university campuses with no affiliations. She lingered in souvenir shops; we bought matching wool sweaters. She's an artist who paints movie sets, studied illustration, and is drawn to the Celtic knotwork for its intricate beauty.

In Ireland, I imagined what my own grandchildren and great-grandchildren would feel about a past that feels long gone and ancient, not part of their lived reality in the way mine was. My progeny will likely be more like Kate than like me. If anything, they'll likely be more curious about the history of the sperm donor we used and their paternal genetic line. I confirmed then that my immigrant eye will never see the world as a nonimmigrant, even after more than thirty years with deep roots in one country, even with no accent, even completely assimilated and with every legal privilege—the lens is the cornea.

———————————◆———————————

I set off on the tour bus again, this time without Kate. I have to bring the queer fire, I thought. I have to be a walking museum for the two of us. I will find gay community here. That would make it real.

Marta's role as tour guide was taken today by a young woman in her early twenties. Our itinerary for the day included a spicy ninety-minute walking option to shop and explore the downtown shopping district of St. Petersburg on our own. Our tour bus moved down Nevsky Prospekt, a bustling avenue strewn with restaurants, stores, vape shops, cafés (including a Starbucks, its sign written in Cyrillic), pastel buildings with Juliet balconies, black buildings with large wooden doors, fountains, the national library, a Russian art museum (praise be!), and tangles of tram lines scratching the clear sky. Every street corner was bustling, and people walked with purpose. I wanted nothing more than to get off this bus, to get lost in a courtyard, to stumble into an artist's studio, a live documentary screening, an AA meeting, a CPR class, a queer writing group working on their memoirs—anything to connect me to something true and heartfelt.

I leveled up the calculation: What makes a place? It isn't just something we walk into; it's something we bring that a place pushes back against us.

The tour guide dropped statistics on Russia's GDP, the number of imported cars in the city, new bus lines. Someone else this time—not me—asked the young tour guide about the Soviet era, something about how an avenue like this has changed over time.

Her response made me bristle: "Our history," she said, "is like history anywhere else—it's behind us."

Annoyed, I looked out the window. Emboldened by the previous night's excavations and encounters, the sizzle of the city's gay energy met me everywhere. I couldn't help but notice the erect reach of the cranes by the seaport on my way out that morning. The drawbridges slapped the sky with the two paddles of itself. As we entered the center of the city, the water fountains were alive with virility, jizzing all over themselves.

The brutalist architecture begged to be admired for its raw, rough texture, its bold, imposing form—the broad, empty open spaces, inviting echoes of moans, the hard protection of cover where two men can find themselves free to dominate each other, to release themselves to the pillars that will firmly hold them up.

A tug of guilt directed me to focus on more "serious" history, more "real" experiences. But I therapized the pressure away. My family left Romania, my father said, because it was a prison of the mind. But under my current circumstances my mind felt free to be gay in Russia. My body, no, but through sheer inheritance of trauma my mind knew how to be a place of unbounded imagination— not a cage of restricted thoughts and wills. This is what it meant for me to be a tourist here.

As the bus neared the shopping district, I pulled out the travel articles I had printed of queer spaces to explore. We had been instructed to restrict ourselves to the area for the ninety minutes of our "free time to explore," but I had other plans. During my travel research one headline had stunned me: "New LGBTQ center set to open this year." I had printed it out to read later, but as I read the article now, my proverbial nipples sank. The article mentions the famous St. Petersburg Pier and the city's environmentally friendly initiatives. That did not sound like Russia. "Fuck," I said out loud, as I realized I was holding a list of gay nightlife in St. Petersburg, Florida.

I was so American that I expected this to be easy.

Devastated, I tried to convince myself it didn't matter. I decided I was going to leave the designated area anyway, even if the tour guide forbade it. I'll stay out as late as possible, I'll find my people,

I'll take a cab back to the seaport. I'll be fine. I stepped off the bus and pulled out my phone. But my GPS map wouldn't load, the Wi-Fi wouldn't connect, the street signs remained written in the alphabet I couldn't read.

I thought, *I'll find someone who looks like they can tell me where to go.* I circled the block. I saw the museum of Soviet arcade games. *Someone in there has to be cool. They have to tell me where the gays are.* I went, I asked, they shrugged their shoulders. If they did know where the gays go, they were not going to risk their safety on sharing that information with me.

I walked the streets wondering the same things I wonder when I visit Romania—who would I have been if I was raised here? Would I have stayed in the closet, without the community of out-and-proud queers, musician neighbors, high school club leaders of Amnesty International and Women's Forum and the Gay-Straight Alliance? I would still have been the daughter of my father, who believed that Hitler was "right about the gays." This part of my identity had always been a massive spiritual and emotional barrier to fully embracing where I was from—making it difficult to accept my upbringing without feeling like I was betraying myself.

I turned a corner and found myself face-to-face with the absolute queen of the architectural drag ball: The Church of the Savior on Spilled Blood. Nine beautiful, seemingly jeweled onion domes with ornate spires flirted with the sky. They were ornamented with bright blue, green, white, and yellow candy-like studs, incredibly punk, suggestively genderqueer—likely to my eyes only, but still...this was not your typical church. This drama for the eyes was at the level of a flirtatious Renaissance painting—playful, fearless, spiky, busy, and totally chaotic. It was Madonna in her cone bra era, amphibian-color couture.

That the shiny shell of these domes is just glass coated onto metal at high heat—vitreous enameling—is truly the godly thing to me. A collision of elements, a human feat of impossible mastery: what it must have taken to place these large structures on svelte cylindrical supports all the way up there, only a few feet short of where heaven was then. I will never tire of the realization of how before we invented conveniences such as elevators, electricity, and deodorant, we found ways to build, transport, place, and shine such giant domes. It took twenty-four years of human hands, feet, and pumping hearts to build The Church of the Savior on Spilled Blood to completion.

All around the upper brick façade of the church, between the cap and the bell tower, a series of tiles, 134 of them, illustrated the coat of arms of different areas—full of medieval imagination, ambition, and fantasy. The Church of the Savior on Spilled Blood was, too—like the Russia I was now attempting to find—constructed and made possible by desire.

Inside the church a bath of mosaics against every wall, one of the largest collections of mosaics on the continent, illustrated (somewhat homoerotic) scenes that linked the death of the tsar, somehow, to the crucifixion of Jesus. Yes, OK! I'll go with it. History is a narrative, its links ours to connect. These images, rendered by the once-only-sketches of more than thirty artists (imagine the parties, the conversations, the undocumented intimacy of it all), blasted their vision to me across space and time.

I stood in the middle of the chamber and let my head loll back. Each onion dome formed a convex circle towards the sky. In each deepened orb lay scenes of resurrection, of Jesus's (socialist) lectures, his friendship with sex workers, with the poor, with his fellow refugees. All of it played out right there, in Caribbean blue, phoenix bird orange, tarot card gold, acid green filigree, with metal chandeliers tethered to the ceiling by what I could only compare to a long metal string of anal beads.

It was here; it was everywhere. Take me home to St. Patrick's Cathedral, to DeSantis's Florida, to Romania's ban on same-sex couple adoption, to my mother saying she doesn't believe that's a real family. Take me to all of it, and I will put a studded bra on it and St. Anthony will say, you found it. It's here. It was, and is, always here. Вы уже найдены.

# Future Past

## CALVIN GIMPELEVICH

There is a queer urge—in the communities I know, which is to say, a queer American urge—for utopia. For an escape from the violent or subtle pressures of societies ill-designed for homosexual or transgender comfort by creating or moving to places that serve our particular needs. One sees this urge in art and theory, in the queer flight to cities with active subculture; in events creating temporary alternate space—nightlife, parades, festivals; and in the carving of self-fitting niches in rural privacy. When I was twenty-two, in 2011, this longing for utopia brought me to Berlin.

I came to Berlin imagining a blank space, a queer space, in which to feel free—despite tangible familial connections to the city's exceptionally unblank history—and despite, ironically also, having been raised in San Francisco, a city so tied to queerness in the cultural imagination that queer people flock to it, with their own utopian dreams, from all over the globe.

But San Francisco was too solid for me: a place of corporeal relatives instead of mysterious dead ones; of commutes and underfunded schools and subway shutdowns; of chamomile growing weedy through the sidewalks; of disappointments, groceries, politics, laundromats, friends. Queerness did not leap from every corner, eliminating the mundanity of daily things. A place instead of no place. So I flew across the world to meet Germans in queer clubs, who spoke rapturously of my home city, who dreamt of road-tripping or living in California.

I scammed my university into paying for the trip with an essay explaining the importance of time in Berlin to my future white-collar career. I say "scammed" because there was no scholastic need for travel. I had all the credits, courses, and department signatures necessary for graduation—everything but the petition informing the school I was done. I did not mention that I had dual citizenship with Germany and hardly needed the school's help to get there—that my interest revolved less around scholastic pursuits than the all-night or even three-day or weeklong techno parties. Specifically, I'd heard of a thriving queer nightlife and was eager—newly identifying as transgender—to go.

So I first went to Berlin as a student in a formal study abroad program designed for Americans. The notebook I kept during that time is thick with flyers for art events, parties, and clubs. It is a journal of seemingly never sleeping, dozing on benches and trains and couches, coming home in the early mornings as commuters started their day; a document using *fucking* as a verbal accelerant too often, that tells me I went on a field trip to Sachsenhausen concentration camp hungover on three hours of sleep after negotiating a tryst for a non-German-speaking friend. The school organized weekend trips of social-historic importance, listed on a syllabus whose details I did not always read, and I arrived to meet my cohort bleary, early, for what might be an excursion to a death camp or an Enlightenment-style garden.

My friend, Sibylla, lives in a three-story German vernacular building with white walls and dark beams crisscrossing the outside, enclosing a courtyard at its center. A shop for hearing aids takes up the ground floor. Sibylla is on the second floor with her girlfriend, Sina, who was born in another country, one which no longer exists: East Germany, or the German Democratic Republic (GDR) or Deutsche Demokratische Republik (DDR).

More than a decade has passed since my last trip to Berlin. I am thirty-three and here with my wife, Markel, on a pandemic-delayed honeymoon. It is supposed to be a vacation but, in reality, we both are working. She has an art commission with attendant meetings, deadlines; I am researching a novel. There is a strange pressure on the trip because we are testing Berlin as a place we might live—an ironic pressure because the reason Berlin is tempting is the same reason we are both working on the first vacation either of us has taken in ten years: Germany's social services and funding, its friendliness to artists, makes art a more financially viable career. This is the utopian aspect of my second trip: the desire to have health insurance and stable housing in a place we can be easily visibly queer.

Sibylla and Sina kindly, insistently, vacate their apartment for a week, going to Sibylla's parents', to give us a free place to stay. Thick, dark beams divide the living room into segments of clay brick, white brick, and smooth wall. More beams support the ceiling. The building is three hundred years old.

Markel and I arrive at night, exhausted by travel. The first thing Sibylla and Sina show us, after hugging and helloing and hugging again, before explaining the keys or locks or necessary parsimony with electricity in their retrofit flammable building, is a small brass plaque, ten centimeters square, laid into gray cobble-

stone. HERE LIVED AND WORKED GUSTAV SIMONSOHN, BORN
1894, ARRESTED APRIL 1, 1941, DETAINED AT POLICE PRISON
ALEXANDERPLATZ, MURDERED SEPTEMBER 12, 1941 IN BUCH-
ENWALD. The text is in German, the dates numeric, commemorating a Jewish veteran and paint seller who died in the Holocaust.
*Stolpersteine*, or stumbling stones, are set at a person's last volun-
tary address before their transportation, extermination, or flight
from Nazi terror. Simonsohn's last address had been Sibylla and
Sina's apartment; the hearing aid shop on the ground floor had
housed his paint store. More of these plaques—nearly one hundred thousand more—dot Berlin and the rest of Europe, forming
the largest decentralized monument in the world. Each plaque is
handmade, individually installed, in an attempt to rehumanize
those exterminated en masse, stripped of names and given numbers. Each sits on the ground. Once you notice the memorials,
they are inevitable, everywhere, like the bullet holes still pocking
buildings from the final days of that war.

Sibylla hands me a printout detailing the history of this particular victim, from the city's *Stolpersteine* database, along with
neighborhood maps, the wireless password, and Wikipedia articles about Frederick the Great and his palace, things we're planning to see. Sibylla knows our itinerary better than anyone, better
than I do: She called a month in advance and we made it together.
After herding Americans professionally as a student assistant in
my old study abroad program, she knew we would not book tours
or tickets in advance on our own.

---

I have no memory of *Stolpersteine* from my last trip—incredible,
as they are actually everywhere, shining among Berlin's cobble-

stones, ubiquitous to the point that I am not sure how it is possible to visit Germany and miss them. It makes me wonder, in
spite of documented physical traversals, if I actually visited the
country or spent that semester within the projections of my own
mental fog.

In truth, I was fairly dissociated before gender transition, and
spent much of my life in an abstracted haze wherein physical reality had only the vaguest pertinence to my being. For the entire
decade between my first puberty and the second, I had a tendency
to get lost trying to find my own house on my own street, to realize I had left the house with my shirt inside out, and to knock into
the sides of doorframes as I passed through. Dissociation exacer-
bated my sense of living outside the present, as if I were a discor-
porate ghostly being hovering above the current moment, looking
for a future—the queer future—where my body could land.

Berlin is the most densely historically symbolized space that
I've encountered, but it's hard to tell how much this compression
of centuries impacted my first stay. The only hint comes from
notes for a story, never written, in which many histories happen at
once. In this story, a character resembling a stripped-down, purely
observant version of myself wanders Berlin as simultaneous eras
play out: Imperial, Nazi, Communist; the period restricted to
buildings or districts or rooms, so by walking the protagonist time
traveled, or by watching saw multiple contemporaneous times,
somehow coalescing to a story as the barriers thinned between
different eras; the protagonist-narrator buffeted by an eternal
present in which a citizen of the GDR, shot while attempting to
scale the wall, gasping her last breath in the death strip between
nations, impacts the arc of a sixteenth-century Berliner debating
the monk Martin Luther's enflaming treatise; where the gay Nazi

and Brownshirt leader, Ernst Röhm, flies through gritty '90s sado-masochistic nightclubs before his assassination during the Night of the Long Knives, Hitler's intraparty consolidation of power and purge.

I wrote these notes towards the end of my first trip. I remember going out at night in the first weeks, trying to find the right party, right people, right place for the queer paradise that must be hidden somewhere, where my life could begin. I defined myself wholly in terms of queerness, transness, and was surprised to meet Germans who treated me, because I am Jewish, the way I would treat a grenade: like something delicate, explosive, and rare.

◆

The Memorial to the Murdered Jews of Europe sits in the middle of the city, a two-hundred-thousand-square-foot installation filled with concrete slabs, or stelae, arranged in a grid. The stelae are rectangular, roughly coffin sized on top, and of varying heights, reflecting their position on the sloping field. From a distance they seem an identical grid, but from the ground it's clear that some slabs are knee height and some tower over your head.

Markel and I are here as part of our strange honeymoon. It is the most depressing place I am willing to visit on my second trip to Berlin, having rejected Sibylla's suggestion that we go to Sachsenhausen concentration camp, whose exhibits continue to populate my nightmares. Security and metal detectors slow entry to the interior space, for the same reason Hitler's office and bunker have been repurposed, unmarked: (Almost) nobody wants them to become flash points for contemporary fascist organizing. Most of the visitors seem like tourists or pilgrims—though a few are clearly just here to use the center's bathrooms, afterwards debating if they should view the exhibition as well.

Markel and I want toilets before moving on to the photos and testimonies. I read my first Holocaust memoir in middle school, have seen it depicted in some unknown number of films, read about it in history books; I've visited Israel's overwhelming memorial, Yad Vashem, and found my surname in its list of victims. Even so, I have trouble keeping this particular horror separate from the general file in my head labeled "atrocity and state-sanctioned terror," mixing the Germanic terror with Slavic pogroms with colonialism and the gulag system and American slavery and the Armenian genocide. The period of my life I spent reading the most harrowing Holocaust testimonies was also the period I encountered exhaustive accounts of the My Lai massacre perpetuated by U.S. soldiers in Vietnam, perpetually linking the two in my consciousness; so I am in Berlin, looking at a photograph of piled Ukrainian Jewish corpses and recalling the details of Vietnam War crimes, wondering why I feel compelled to study these things when there is only, at some point, the shame of being human and the fear (and certainty) of monstrosity recurring. The fear is always personal, always rooted in the imagining of myself and loved ones in the situations detailed. I still cannot figure out if my sense of vulnerability is normal or not, if many people feel they could as easily be bludgeoned, maimed, terrorized as the people in those photos, or if it has something to do with being Jewish, or being the child of a Soviet refugee, or simply having an active imagination.

What strikes me during this second Holocaust memorial visit is not what happened in the camps or Eastern Front, so much as the tightening of existence just before they occurred. It seemed to me, as a younger person, that at some point the historic moment must have overshadowed the minutiae of living, and people transformed from jobholders or parents or students into victims or resisters or collaborators—into the kinds of people written about or whose photos were shown in exhibits. I'd lived with the belief that one should maintain vigilance for the tipping into historic scale. Now, conversely, I sense no reduction, for the people concerned, of individual selves into grand narrative arcs; no point minutiae disappears.

The two things disturbing me most are how personally relatable I find the Jews and homosexuals of Weimar Berlin, how full their lives—so full that, even knowing the history, it seems impossible they could die in camps—and the gap between the Nazis' rosy utopic visions for their own Germania—blushing mothers and children in verdant forests—and the reality of their means. That the Nazis, professed animal lovers, outlawed vivisection on nature's creatures, while proving all too willing to mutilate their prisoners of war for medical experimentation.

Perhaps this is where I should mention that, before the Nazis, Berlin was a place of Jewish optimism: where German Jews had the option to assimilate and (sometimes) grow rich, where Eastern European Jews fled from violence and repression. The Jewish quarter boasted an opulent domed synagogue capable of holding three thousand worshippers and a college serving as the intellectual center of Reform Judaism. Yiddish, Hebrew, and German mixed, as the secular and religious mixed, in a place that seemed finally—maybe—ready to let that specific demographic thrive.

More than 2,500 concrete blocks form the looming installation. The blocks are flat, gray, uniform; reminiscent of tombstones, of dehumanizing bureaucratic order, of buildings in a gridded city. As one walks downslope, towards the memorial entrance, the stelae become larger, soon towering overhead. The result is eerie, fearsome: Gray blocks consume your vision, providing narrow paths to walk through, with slivers of light in between. The cold, dark, shadowed walkways contrast with the sky overhead. Sound is muffled; one becomes isolated from the sights of Berlin, provided brief glimpses—hope or respite—before continuing.

The memorial was described to me by Sibylla as a physical metaphor mimicking the darkening prospects of European Jews as Nazi power escalated, driving them ever downward, ostracizing them from regular life, creating an atmosphere of separation and terror—a metaphor that squares with my own sense of the space, though I find, later, the design is intentionally open to interpretation. The memorial has been controversial from inception to present, with criticisms ranging from its not being *enough* (could anything ever represent the millions dead?), to the vagueness of brutalist symbols, to the absence of names or other markings on the upper stelae identifying the monument to passersby, to the very fact of its backwards-looking existence, pointing forever towards guilt. The cobbled floor is not a flat slope, but undulating, wavelike, so the visitor is never quite sure where they stand. This ground is reflected in the information center's concrete ceiling, so it is as if, by being in the center's blunt nonabstracted exhibit, one has entered the graves.

Stelae are in one sense metaphoric, literal in another: concrete blocks situated at the heart of the capital. Sunbathers lie on the lower, knee-height towers; children climb and toddle on them. Some jump between the higher pillars or play hide-and-seek among them. Several friends mention the website *Grindr Remembers*, cataloging hookup pictures taken in the field of columns: shirtless, sometimes pantsless images of chiseled abs and rounded buttocks. Men stand between columns, lean on them, hang from them, sit atop, and pose athletically in between. Like many brutalist structures, it photographs well. One of the founders of *Grindr Remembers* describes the memorial as having a cruise-y feel—likely from the sense of anonymity and privacy in the public sphere. Both homo- and heterosexual couples have been found copulating, which, in conjunction with painted swastikas, urination, and fireworks resulted in security patrols.

Tiergarten, a historic cruising park to the immediate west, has its own memorial to queer persecution: a concrete cuboid containing a video showing originally intimacy between men that was eventually, with controversy, amended to add lesbians. Degrees of victimhood and, by extension, memorialization are still debated: the imprisonment, torture, and murder of gay men in the Nazi era being more aggressive than they were for women or the gender nonconforming. There is something innocent if offensive about sexual play so near to a monument commemorating the victims of fascist murder. The cuboid's cavalier placement speaks to a recovered sense of safety—the freedom *not* to think or worry about outing oneself as queer or where you geographically are. Berlin is permissive. It was, for a sliver of the twentieth century, the most inviting place to be queer in the Western world.

Markel and I happen to arrive in Berlin the week after Christopher Street Day, German Pride, its name a sort of verbal anti-memorial. Germany was home to the world's first homosexual rights movement—in the sense of homosexuality as a medicalized subtype, an identity as opposed to action. I am working on a book concerning Weimar and Nazi Berlin, which is the reason I know about figures like Dr. Magnus Hirschfeld, Jewish and gay, whose Institute for Sexual Science researched and provided services for orientations of all types, including trans people, while lobbying to remove Germany's antisodomy law. They were close to successfully repealing the statute when the Nazis came to power; Hirschfeld fled, and the Institute was shut down and its records destroyed. Libertine Weimar gave way to abductions, castrations, and worse. Much of the local queer history was erased. Today, Berlin commemorates the 1969 Stonewall Riots on Christopher Street in New York instead of their own milestones.

"Berlin," the city's most famous sex tourist, Christopher Isherwood, said, "meant boys." Working-class boys, "nearly all out of work," who "stripped off their sweaters or leather jackets and sat around with their shirts unbuttoned to the navel and their sleeves rolled up to the armpits" because it excited their clients. After the economic and social devastation of World War I, German society fractured. The monarchy abdicated, the unstable Weimar Republic began, veterans flooded the streets, Communists and conservatives warred. The sudden loss of Imperial censorship led to a flourishing artistic awakening, Berlin the center of Europe's avant-garde. Isherwood sought refuge from stifling upper-class Britain in the city, temporarily living at Hirschfeld's institute and patronizing male sex workers. The musical *Cabaret*, based on his *Berlin Stories*, features a thinly veiled version of him staying with a German woman made destitute by inflation and war, who used to keep a maid and take summer holidays, but who was now reduced to sleeping "in the living-room, behind a screen, on a small sofa with broken springs," forced to let out her rooms. Isherwood left with his lover after Hitler's ascension. I am reminded of him when I think about all the people who come to explore for a week or a weekend, to party and cruise in a city that's regained its tolerant image; of myself coming to what seemed, in my early twenties, like an open place to escape what stifled at home.

———————◆———————

Do Berliners feel overwhelmed by the constant reminders of history? I am thinking of the flamboyant first manifesto of futurism (written in 1909) when a group of young Italian men declared their unwillingness to live within their country's multitudinous cultural artifacts, to be buried by the actions of predecessors, when they desired excitement, motor cars, aeroplanes, speed.

> It is in Italy that we are issuing this manifesto of ruinous and incendiary violence, by which we today are founding Futurism, because we want to deliver Italy from its gangrene of professors, archaeologists, tourist guides and antiquaries.
>
> Italy has been too long the great second-hand market. We want to get rid of the innumerable museums which cover it with innumerable cemeteries.

How tempting it must have been for them, feeling their own vitality, to throw off the stifling weight of the past; how relatably American, in fact, to emphasize a blank slate on which to build dreams. Unfortunately, the futurists wound into Italian fascism, quixotic sayings justifying the physical actuality of Il Duce's dictatorship, which perhaps should not be surprising given the manifesto's ninth point: "We want to glorify war—the only cure for the world— militarism, patriotism, and the destructive gesture of the anarchists, the beautiful ideas which kill, and contempt for women."

Neither of the two most enduring memories of my first trip made it into the journal.

First: election season, particularly the posters of the far-right party, Alternativ für Deutschland (AFD). These posters had to be placed very high in the dead of night, to keep their members from being attacked and the adverts ripped down. It seemed a strange mutual game: Where would the AFD images appear next, and how quickly could leftist and centrist Berliners get them down? One had an illustration of a multicultural-seeming group of people, including head-scarfed women, on a flying carpet that said, in German, "Enjoy the trip home." Another showed a middle-aged German-looking man on a motorcycle with the text *Gas Geben*, or "Give it Gas," ostensibly referring to politics, speed, and the motorcycle, with its inescapable echo of the chambers of Holocaust death, Jews herded into "showers" pumping murderous Zyklon B. This, in a country where swastikas are illegal and Holocaust denial a jail-able offense.

Second: with Sibylla in a huge industrial club, sunk into concrete couches; the music—techno—more physical than aural, vibrating the bones and the skull, watching the smoky black silhouettes of men penetrating each other before returning to the dance floor. The shock of exiting into light, at 9 a.m. as if from a dream, having never stayed up that late nor witnessed anonymous bobbing tumescence in shadow form.

Hohenschönhausen is, on the second trip, as I remember. The Stasi prison, where Germans—mostly Germans—were interrogated

and held by secret police. It is a bleak concrete structure amidst concrete apartments in a neighborhood that still leans Communist—
meaning conservative—in East Berlin. Conservatism, in this context, is a comfort with state power, an unwillingness to criticize or
part with their former regime. About a third of the tours are given
by former inmates, though as time progresses and survivors become fewer, their numbers shrink. I toured Hohenschönhausen
with the school program and now again with Markel. The memories immediately turn to a shapeless montage of bleak repressive
concrete: featureless cells in the basement, airless confinement,
torture, depersonalization, despair. What lingers is the pointless-
ness of it, Communist surveillance turned against its own people,
an estimated ratio of one informant per 6.5 citizens: round-the-
clock secret spying on families eating and watching TV, paranoid
men measuring the angle of satellite dishes to discern if they were
gathering signals of political programs (or rock music) from the
West. The perversion and death of utopian meritocratic ideals.
The attempt to take the leveled—if not blank—slate of postwar
demolished Berlin and make Communism, in the form of Soviet
client-state, appear.

Mass deaths occurred while the Soviets controlled this place:
malnutrition, exposure, murder, all of it becoming subtler when
the Stasi took over with their preferences for isolation, sleep
deprivation, and threats. Hohenschönhausen is unlike any of the
other memorials we visit—there is no relationship between it and
its surroundings, no porousness between the prison's reality and
any other. No children play, no cruising happens. The space is too
effective at being itself, just as East Germany effectively gave citizens its own unique version of history and culture by imprison-
ing, deporting, or killing dissidents and forbidding contact with

foreigners. The Stasi could not believe it when East Germans rebelled, their state collapsed, and Germany sutured its cleft. Erich Mielke, the Stasi's head, personally responsible for the destruction of thousands of lives, gave a baffling final speech as the revolution ousted him, proclaiming, "I love all—all humanity! I really do!" while the audience jeered.

But who can blame the experiment in Communist sameness immediately after the war? It was pressed upon them by the Red Army, but this pressing came after the disaster of fascism and losing a second world war; after the Holocaust and collective guilt—who wouldn't want to start fresh? Germany had the biggest Communist party, outside Russia, in the Weimar era; Communists and fascists fought in the streets, power teetering between them, before the Nazis finally won. Some of these Communists helped build the German Democratic Republic after the war, bringing with them the skills of Weimar street fighting, of the concentration camps they were stuck in, of Soviet training, and used them to make a prison of their burgeoning state. The official line, in East German history, was that the East and West were always culturally separate, the East full of Communist heroes, the West stuffed with Nazis and capitalist exploiters; under Nazism, East Germans were victims, but now stood Nazi-free—a fiction allowing Nazis to reinvent themselves as good Communists, responsibilities shunted, for people to forget and move on.

I am standing with Markel in a padded room in this Stasi prison with a small group of international visitors. Our tour guide is Belgian: a tall man with a tonsure and flyaway hair. He was never imprisoned, but is intimate with victims and seems as indignant and angry as if he had been. He describes a situation in which it seems reasonable to lose one's mind or become suicidal, explain-

ing the ways people would try to kill themselves—but be unable
to—while wearing straitjackets, locked in this rubbery window-
less cell. The protests included ramming one's head repeatedly on
the wall and smearing defecation. I am thinking of a helplessness
so profound the only way to exert control is by shitting yourself,
and about the people going about their ordinary lives before being abducted by an unmarked van; I am relating, I am horrified,
but also a little bit bored. The bludgeoning sameness of this place
throws everything together, stories becoming as repetitively indistinguishable as its cells.

———————◆———————

*Vergangenheitsbewältigung*, literally "coming to terms with the
past," refers to Germany's attempt to understand, digest, learn
from, and analyze historical culpability, primarily regarding Nazism and the Holocaust, but also Communism. The truth is, yes,
Germans often find history overwhelming. The question is periodically raised whether the emotional centricity of Germany's
past impedes their present; whether (from the Right) atrocities
are overblown and harm the confidence of innocent moderns,
or (from the Left) it obfuscates contemporary issues of race, religion, and class pertaining to Muslim migrants, or has ossified
into an ideology wherein the only atonement for German guilt
is unconditional support for the State of Israel, which has led
to the bizarre situation of non-Jewish anti-antisemitism com-
missioners, charged with protecting the Jews, calling Jewish—
including German and Israeli Jewish—critics of Israel antisemitic, and taking undemocratic measures with regard to Palestinian conversations and symbols; treating Palestinian flags, for
example, as anti-Israel and thus antisemitic—too dangerous to

claim public space. On top of all this lies the question of whether Germans can finally proudly and responsibly (antinationalistically) wave their own flags when their country makes it to the Women's World Cup.

Online, I subscribe to a militant gay Communist account posting homoerotic Soviet posters, beautiful pictures of Russian and East German boys. It reminds me that the GDR had laxer homosexual regulations than the capitalist West—which retained reimprisoned gay men "liberated" from camps, retaining the Nazi-strengthened antisodomy laws; that the GDR funded gay films. The profile neglects to mention the Communist disappearances, prisons, or belief in the moral weakness of same-sex attraction, linked to bourgeois excess.

But the beautiful revisionist history and dream! Homo-utopic. No violence or hostility or trans panic. None of the overt or subtle humiliations experienced when one's gender cannot be visibly parsed. Financial supports and health care; interclass access to all life's pleasures and needs. I think about the overwhelmed former Communists seeing shelves upon shelves of varyingly branded mayonnaise at capitalist groceries, wondering if this was what the West offered in place of socialist fraternal ambition. If they could have equality without surveillance or puppet state or suffocating lack of freedom. I relate to the plaintive texts by those late East Germans saying they want something in the middle. Something better than nihilistic profit or centralized power; better than all of our pasts.

It's difficult to imagine what my own queer idyll would look like, beyond the list of freedom-froms. The shoes-off gallery and ambient listening bar in Kreuzberg might be a good representation, with its amorphous cloudlike installations and trans bartenders and listening space and pillow-laden social room, where Markel and I sit on the floor with an old and intimate friend. The more I try to visualize it, the more I get staccato images of sexuality, art events, picnics, nightlife—the things romanticized in the books and photos and movies that built my idea of queer space in the first place, which I cherished and felt outside of and hoped Berlin could provide. This is why it seemed, when I was twenty-two watching men copulate in techno basements, that I might have arrived.

The unflattering sense of myself as an Isherwood swirls up from the first trip. That wealthy British man seeking freedom in an economically shattered country. Less dramatic, but I am American— despite dual passports—and the United States occupied Germany, with varying degrees of sensitivity, for decades—the legacy of which includes my ability to navigate Berlin, on the first trip and second, with the linguistic prowess of a German toddler. As a barista tells me (in English), "Did you know, after the war, we were inundated with American corn? A grain which is not part of the German diet? It is because, when the Americans asked an official what the people needed, this man did not know the term for 'wheat,' so he used the German word: *korn*. And now we have to learn English in school."

The only grammar for these failed utopias is the future past tense: Life *would have* been better; we *were going* to attain. In the grammar are the lost dreams. They have destroyed my faith that history arcs inevitably towards justice, or that our optimism brings good—the faith, but not the hope. In the background of all these thoughts is a quote that I have known to imbue so many queer people with a sense of potential, but which fills me with despair. It is from José Esteban Muñoz's *Cruising Utopia*:

Queerness is not yet here. Queerness is an ideality. Put another way, we are not yet queer. We may never touch queerness, but we can feel it as the warm illumination of a horizon imbued with potentiality. We have never been queer, yet queerness exists for us as an ideality that can be distilled from the past and used to imagine a future. The future is queerness's domain.

I don't have enough faith in the future to wait. For me, queerness has to be here.

---

The doorman looks at Markel and asks if she knows the name of the event we are trying to enter.

"Hello Daddy," she says. This is a bearish event; he's asking because the two of us together look straight. He provides stickers to cover our cell phone cameras. The location is semi-industrial, East Berlin, off the main strip. Inside are sweaty, hairy Arabic- and German- and Hebrew- and English-speaking men with their shirts off. It's noon. The party has been going since the previous night and will last another two days. We make our way through the smoky warren, a maze that leads to bathrooms and a dance floor, to a bright patio with a second DJ.

We are here instead of at the exhibit in another club on Tresor, Germany's first postreunification electronic venue. After Communism, formerly forbidden Western musicians ventured east to make clubs. East Berlin was full of abandoned industrial spaces; of buildings expropriated by Communists or Nazis whose ownership became uncertain, unclaimed. Tresor started in a bank vault. The exhibit is described as a mixture of sound installation, history, and active nightclub, with an apparent one-to-one scale beige sand recreation of the club as it stood before shuttering. It turns out the club scene is not timeless or modern, but bound in history in its own way. Berlin's techno clubs are officially recognized cultural institutions, like theaters and museums, reflecting their centrality to the city's economy and culture.

The centrality is hard to argue. On one evening Markel and I—trying to find DJ friends—climb three sets of identical piss-scented, glass-and-graffiti-covered stairwells to find three bored-looking bouncers guarding the entrances to three different clubs whose only difference is the subgenre of techno playing, too subtle for me to distinguish. In truth, I would rather be at the exhibit, contemplating dance music's role in reunification culture, than partying. Queer community, in my life, wound up being more about support and friends and meal trains, about organizing art shows and signing petitions; in other words, about continually responding to the reality of circumstances and carving a niche within them. These alternative spaces are just one aspect in a larger practice of site repair.

I am thinking of the moment I flew across the United States for a family crisis, with no luggage and no sleep, to a city whose queer community I had invested heavily in and who came out for me in a moment of need: lending clothing and cars and cell phone chargers, listening, cooking, shipping my hormones, making up guest beds. Nothing about that week was utopian, but in the flawed present, built on flawed past, queerness offered respite, a way of being inside the storm. That care, as much as the temporary and explicitly queer spaces made in nightlife and other niches, allows survival and expansion within the happenings of the world.

At the Hello Daddy party, a few men are naked, drugs—powders—proliferate in the restrooms. Apart from this, nothing is guarded by the stickers on our cell phone cameras, but it isn't bad to escape the realm of selfies and digital record, to be wholly in this queer pocket in an alternative space.

Daylight drenches the patio, but inside the main space holds darkness, smoke machines, artificial changing lighting, the loss of perception of time. Repetitive music, sets bleeding into each other, heightening timelessness—this present bleeding into my last trip, to any point, day or night, at any rave. I am in a dark room pressed with bodies, and we are dancing, dancing.

# Lessons in Digging and Replanting

## SARA OROZCO

I was alone in a jail cell in Charleston, South Carolina. A metal bunk bed with thin, lumpy mattresses, no pillows, was pushed against a wall of vanilla-colored cinder blocks. The yellow hue from the hallway lights illuminated dirty floors. I couldn't figure out who to call. My friends, if they'd made it home, were at a rented beach house twelve miles away with no working phone. I knew no one else in Charleston. I couldn't call Mami. Not only was she far away in Miami; she wouldn't be able to speak English to the staff, nor did she have the money to bail me out. I also didn't want to face her disappointment. Now I was not only a lesbian: I was also a criminal. Though, in Mami's mind, these things were one and the same.

It was Saturday night. A police officer explained that someone would walk me to the courthouse on Monday morning, where I would face the judge. I had never felt so alone and disgusted with myself. I sat on the edge of the bottom bunk, my head flat against the cool wall, my knees against my chest, my arms wrapped around my legs. A few hours earlier I'd danced wildly on a dance floor, laughing with my friends, feeling invincible. It never occurred to me that the Charleston police knew exactly where the one gay bar in town was, and that they might raid it from time to time. I didn't know how much worse these raids on gay bars had gotten with the AIDS panic. They were looking for reasons to arrest gays that night in 1985. I had made it easy for them.

I pressed my head against my knee and closed my eyes, but the cramping in my stomach was too much to hold, and I had no choice but to lower my pants and squat over the hole in the middle of the floor. The police paced back and forth outside my cell unfazed. In cells on either side of me, women screamed profanities and rattled bars. For hours, the sounds of a guard's jingling keys, followed by the entrance of a new woman into the holding area, accelerated my heart. Would they put her in my cell? Would she beat me up for being gay? But they kept me in my cell alone until morning, when a cart with wobbly wheels stopped at my cell door.

"Breakfast," a man said, sliding a plastic tray underneath my door: dry toast, apple juice, and pale scrambled eggs on a paper plate. My stomach cramped again. Sweat built on my upper lip and forehead. There was nothing in my stomach to throw up. When I was little, Mami spread VapoRub on my chest when I felt sick. I imagined Mami with her warm hand caressing my back and telling me I would be okay. I needed her now. I knelt on the hard floor, placed my own warm hand on my chest, took deep breaths, and cried for what I'd lost.

━━━━━━━◆━━━━━━━

For a while, during the time I transitioned away from Miami and into my college life, things between us had been happy. Mami decided to make the drive with me to the mountains of North Carolina, where I'd won a volleyball scholarship to attend the University of North Carolina Asheville, and help me settle in. It was the first time in years we were able to experience a real mother-daughter road trip with joy.

I'd originally chosen the school because Asheville was as far away a place as I could imagine from Miami, from Mami. Now, the reality of leaving her felt painful. I couldn't advance into adulthood, it seemed, unless she loved all of me, including the part that was gay. She would never be okay with it. Jesus would never be okay with it, as she made clear. But it was out in the open now, which felt like finally breathing mountain air after a lifetime in a muggy sea-level city.

Our car tipped upwards as we began our ascent into the mountains, and Mami began moaning in fear. She had always been terrified of heights. She'd only lived on the coasts of Cuba and Miami—flat places. While I drove along the Blue Ridge Parkway marveling at the mountain views, Mami spent most of our drive with her hands on the dashboard, head down, crying out, "*Basta*, Sarita!"

I laughed at Mami's overkill. "It's not my fault you have to drive up mountains to get to Asheville," I said, though I did have to lean against the steering wheel when we drove up with our windshield full of the sky. It felt like our car was a marble rolling up a ramp, that at some point, it would have to stop and roll back down. The Blue Ridge Parkway was itself a journey through unpredictable, awe-striking beauty. More than once the road carried us into a stony tunnel and momentary darkness, then shot out into an expansive view of light-struck treetops and mountain crags. It was about as different from Miami as a place could be. Maybe it would be my place.

"We only have another hour to go," I said, glancing at my mother. Her curly brown hair had smoothed in the dry, chilly weather. But she still clutched the dash.

Mami worried. She had always worried about my crushes on girls. She knew, more recently, there was something suspicious about my friendship with Tammy. She did not know about the clubs, the drinking, the cocaine—that part of my life would stay secret from Mami, hopefully forever. But I was desperate to connect with her before I left home. When I came out to her over pancakes at Denny's, she responded with flat denial, despite the years she fought me for my tomboy style, the obsessive crushes on girls.

"You are not like *that*," she said, her tone thoughtful. Both of us were unable to say the word *lesbian*. It felt like profanity.

"I am like *that*," I said, looking at her. Mami glanced away, uncomfortable. I'm sure she was concerned for me and my happiness and safety, but more than anything, I knew it was her deep faith in Jesus that would never allow her to see me *that* way.

"I want you to try to be different," she said. "This is not who you are." I saw the sadness and disappointment in my mother's face. I knew I was a sinner. "Please, tell me you'll try to like boys?"

I didn't have a fighting chance. I couldn't hurt her, and I couldn't undermine her faith. "I'll try," I told Mami, and I meant it.

———◆———

The Blue Ridge Parkway was dotted with scenic overlooks. Mami begged me not to stop, but it was too breathtaking not to. I closed my car door and gaped at the blue line of mountains in the distance. Mami shuffled slowly towards the metal barrier protecting us from the edge. "Hold me so I don't fall off," she said.

"You aren't even close to the drop-off," I said, but took her arms as she asked. This was how we connected: by going through the motions that confirmed our filial devotion, even if it meant her pretending she was in danger and me pretending I was saving her. Sometimes laughing about it, sometimes not. To Mami, everything felt close to the edge. A hurricane warning meant the imminent destruction of our house; my learning to drive meant an inevitable, tragic car accident; my moving away to college meant she would never see me again. I held her tight and reassured her she wouldn't die that day by falling off the mountain's end.

We looked at the vast open skies and the scattered small towns below. I felt hopeful. I knew what I had to do. I needed to put behind my attraction to women. It wasn't worth hurting Mami by being *that* way. I needed to put my drug use behind me, too. Self-sacrifice, pain, and disconnection had been core to my family's narrative ever since fleeing Cuba. Why should my life be defined by anything else?

My mother saw that my tiny ears were pierced before I could crawl, maybe even before I left the hospital. It was important to my mother that I act like a girl and look like a girl. Unfortunately for me, Mami, and her two child-free sisters who projected their feminine aspirations onto me, I wasn't good at being a girl. I preferred shorts over flowery dresses. I ran with the neighborhood boys, often beating them at different athletic contests and wearing my resulting cuts and bruises like badges of honor. My mother's disappointment rose each time I rejected her attempts to peel me away from the pack of boys so I could spend time instead with their boring sisters, flipping through movie magazines and playing dress-up. Even as my mother and tías reassured themselves that we weren't in Cuba, that my unfeminine behaviors might be expected in America, I knew I was an embarrassment to them.

In fifth grade I zeroed in on a girl wearing sneakers and shredded, faded denim overalls over a white T-shirt that read *Keep on
Truckin'*. Her name was Robin, but everyone called her Robbie.
I felt shy around Robbie. When she talked to me at school, the
words in my head ran away. At home, I talked about her nonstop
to my mother, who was delighted to hear that I was finally making friends with a girl. Then she met Robbie, and her ballooning
enthusiasm collapsed.

"She's a *tomboy*," I overheard her say on the phone to one of my
tías. A streak of fear ran through me. I knew being a tomboy was
terrible. I dropped the friendship immediately. Somehow I understood it was time for me to show interest in boys in more typical
ways. The parade of best intentions began—chaperoned dates,
love notes from boys, and invitations to awful school dances that
lifted my mother's mood and standing in the neighborhood.

In eleventh grade I again fell hard for a girl. Tammy was my team-
mate on the volleyball, basketball, and softball teams. She wore her
hair so short you could see her pink scalp. Her brown eyes disap-
peared when she smiled, and her blue polyester Adidas tracksuit
pants dragged on the ground. We told no one we were girlfriends.
I continued to hang out with the popular straight kids and even
dated a boy during that time, taking him home occasionally so
Mami could feed him pastelitos de guayaba. Tammy and I could
only be alone together in the early mornings when we skipped
homeroom to snuggle and kiss at her house before rushing to
school for first period. The secrecy was painful for both of us, the
lies necessary to sustaining secrecy eroding my sense of self.

I excelled at sports, and the many practices and away games
gave me reasons to be out of the house. I lied to Mami and stayed
out late for other reasons. It was the early 1980s, and cocaine was

everywhere in The Magic City. I made friends Mami would not have approved of and snuck with them into gay bars in Ft. Lauderdale. One new friend worked in a mail distribution center, and when she came upon an envelope with no return address, she assumed the package contained drugs and snuck it into her purse. She was usually right, and she loved to share the wealth. I hid this all from my mother by avoiding her, and then I felt guilty for the distance between us.

I was relieved we'd salvaged our relationship before I left. She helped me unpack in Asheville, and when she left to catch her plane to Miami, we hugged goodbye for a very long time. She called me every week or two on the dorm's pay phone. Just before Thanksgiving, I ran down the stairs to take her call. "Como estás?" I greeted her happily.

"You are not my daughter," she said, all of her old anger and hurt bleeding through the phone.

I was speechless. "I found a picture in your room," she continued. "A picture of you and Tammy holding hands!"

I froze in fear, caught. I searched for the lie that would get me out of this situation. Any lie would do. "Mami—"

"I did not raise you to be that way. Do not come home!"

I begged to come home for Thanksgiving. I promised to see a psychiatrist with her, as she wanted. Back in Miami for Christmas, I sat on the psychiatrist's couch next to Mami and denied any queer feelings to them both. The doctor faced us from behind his desk, upon which sat a picture of his three sons, each holding a tiny Cuban flag.

"It's possible that having grown up without a good male role model might be a factor in you not liking boys," the psychiatrist said. "You are afraid of intimacy with males because you don't trust men." Mami nodded. I nodded, too. It was something we could agree on, at least in theory. We could add this to all the ways Papi had failed us. I promised them both I would work on my trust issues. With effort, I steered clear of girls my freshman year. But Mami and I remained estranged.

By my junior year I stopped going to Miami for school breaks. I stayed in Asheville and took summer classes while working at a macrobiotic café where the food was so organic that I once saw a moist worm wiggling out of a cauliflower, to a customer's delight. I fell in love with an older woman named Sue. We spent all our time together, dining out, exploring nearby towns, running, hiking, making love. I settled into my gay identity and knew *this* was me. I was part of a community, dancing at Womyn's Festivals, camping out for three- or four-day outdoor music events where great singers like Holly Near, Ferron, Meg Williams, and Chris Williamson played to multiracial crowds of feminists and lesbians. We frequented gay-owned O. Henry's Restaurant. The laid-back, sometimes ghostly feeling of downtown greatly contrasted with the lit-up feeling I had walking downtown Miami with its electrified skyscrapers. I sometimes missed the energy of the gay bars I frequented in Ft. Lauderdale with loud beating disco and doing cocaine with my friends. But here, especially hiking in the mountains, I felt connected to the earth.

My favorite hike was Looking Glass Rock, a six-mile round loop trail with a 1,700-foot climb. The trail started smooth, but towards the top climbers navigated boulders and steep switchbacks. I was careful climbing those rocks, as the drop-off was sudden—four hundred feet to the valley below—but I craved the adrenaline of the climb. At the summit an exposed massive white-granite rock jutted into the sky. I carried a notebook with me and sat on the granite, surrounded by panoramic views above the forest trees. Being at this elevation inspired me to write, especially on those foggy mornings I walked through mist and arrived at the exposed rock, clear blue sky above me, clouds below. I wrote the truth in my notebook and composed a different story about my life for Mami. I found the best way to manage my relationship with Mami was to tell her what she wanted to hear while I lived a separate life that was my own. I felt she loved me in so many other ways that I no longer ached for her unconditional acceptance.

Sue and I eventually transitioned into friends, and college reached its end. Six of us rented a beach house on Isle of Palms to celebrate our graduation. I attended my last college class and stopped one last time at the student center for my mail before racing south to join my friends at the beach house.

"An envelope came for you," the mail room work-study student announced. He handed me a bulging FedEx envelope. The handwriting was Jenny's—the Miami friend who worked in the mail distribution center. She periodically sent me some of what she'd confiscated of the mail with no return addresses, along with a note that said something like "Look what I found. Thinking of you." I immediately knew what was inside.

"We are gonna party this weekend," I said with glee, as the student who'd handed me the envelope raised his eyebrows conspiratorially. Jenny usually sent me a gram of cocaine, maybe two. I opened this envelope and peered down at nine grams of cocaine, individually wrapped in mini reclosable plastic bags. I pulled out her note: "Look what I found. Congratulations on finishing school. Move back to Miami. We miss you." What was I going to do with so much cocaine? I ran to my car and carefully placed the envelope far underneath the driver's seat.

I cranked up my Donna Summer cassette and plotted my trip on the paper map. The party was in full swing four hours later when I arrived at the house, by which time I had completely forgotten about the envelope under my seat.

The house was creaky but cute, perched in a field of tall grass next to a dune, with bunk beds, a refrigerator, and not much else, not even a working phone. Someone handed me a margarita. We flung our bodies into the hot and steamy coastal air. We dubbed ourselves the WOWS: the Wild Women of the Waves. In the evening we smoked pot and then had the brilliant idea of driving thirty minutes to find Charleston's only gay bar. Someone had a piece of paper with directions written by a friend in Asheville. The six of us piled into two cars. I drove my car and Ellen took shotgun. "This is for later," Ellen said, producing a perfectly rolled joint, opening the glove box, and hiding the joint under a stack of paper and a couple of parking tickets. We blasted the AC and Donna Summer, turning down the music only when someone needed to alert me of an upcoming turn.

We circled several abandoned warehouses before we found the one emanating pulsating dance music and approached the unmarked door. Inside, disco lights spun bright colors. The heat and energy absorbed us. I downed a Sex on the Beach, followed by a Long Island Iced Tea, and then pulled my friends to the dance floor. Poppers circulated the room. I inhaled, and within seconds my head felt like it would explode, my heart raced, and then a warm sensation flowed down my body. I danced wildly with my friends. I never wanted the night to end.

Overheated, I made my way through bodies to the entrance, but the outside air still felt suffocating. My car was parked close by. I slipped inside and cranked up the AC and music. I leaned into the vent, the cool air on my sweaty neck. I remembered the joint Ellen stashed and reached to open the glove compartment. I had just located the joint and was feeling around for a book of matches when there was a loud banging on my window.

"Put your hands where we can see them!" a police officer yelled through the glass. I panicked, closed the glove compartment, and dropped the unlit joint.

"Both hands up!" the police officer said angrily, slamming my window with the palm of his hand. My mouth went desert dry. I couldn't swallow. The cop aimed his gun at the window to the side of my head.

"Please don't shoot," I begged.

The officer opened my door, and I stepped out of the car. I put my hands on the hood as I was told. I was sure he hadn't seen the joint before I dropped it. I had been in a parked car, not even driving. What did he think I'd done? That's when I noticed the other police officers pouring out of the empty parking garage across the street from the bar. They banged their batons on car hoods as they descended upon the warehouse. It was a raid.

Police officers charged into the bar. "Step away from the vehicle," the officer told me, and I waited for a female cop to frisk me. I had nothing on me. I allowed myself a small, shaky sigh of relief.

An officer spotted the joint under the dashboard. It didn't take long for the search team to discover the Federal Express envelope under my seat. I stood motionless and watched my life blow up. The officer read me my rights as he pushed me into the back of the squad car to take me to jail.

As the squad car slowly pulled towards the exit, I watched through the window as people from the bar ran for safety. Several sprawled face down on the ground as police searched their pockets. It felt like a horror film, the only soundtrack the wail of a siren. A drag performer fell to the ground, the heel of her right pump broken. Her friends clung to her and encouraged her to keep moving, but she just lay there sobbing, police officers all around her, pushing patrons out of their way. I spotted my friends gathered in the corner of the parking lot. I prayed they would be okay. As far as I could tell, I was the only one in handcuffs. A tow truck driver attached a hook to my car and prepared to haul it away.

---

My friends appeared on Monday morning in the courthouse. "We got you a lawyer," they said. I was speechless with gratitude. The five of them held hands in solidarity. "He's waiting for you in the courtroom. We have to go home, but call us if you need anything." I felt shame, vulnerability, and overwhelming love for them. *They stayed* was all I registered. I was not alone.

"Thank you," I squeezed out before being pulled into the courthouse and led down a hallway thick with cigarette smoke. A handsome man in a dark-blue suit with graying hair approached me.

"You're so little," he said with surprise, looking me up and down. "That's good."

My lawyer, whose name was Tom, explained what would happen in the courtroom. "Let me do all the talking," he said. I sat silently next to him and faced the judge. I wanted to run out the door and return to my life in Asheville. I couldn't stop thinking about Mami, who would probably be packing to attend my graduation in just a few days. I imagined her face upon finding out why I wouldn't be at my own graduation. I had ruined both our lives, and so carelessly.

The prosecutor's brown suit was baggy and wrinkled in contrast to my lawyer's impeccable suit. He stated his case against me. "Judge and the people of the court, the plaintiff was seen inside her car acting suspiciously. A police officer approached the vehicle and saw the defendant hiding something in her glove compartment. She was asked to step outside while officers searched the car. Underneath the front seat, the officers found nine grams of cocaine in an opened Federal Express envelope. She was arrested and charged with drug possession with intent to distribute. We ask for no less than five years and a penalty of $25,000." The prosecutor sat down, stretched his legs, and tossed my file folder behind him.

My lawyer stood up. "Your Honor, may I approach the bench?" The prosecutor joined him. There was a lot of nodding and headshaking. My lawyer returned to our table, gathered some paperwork, and approached the bench again. There was more mumbling and back-and-forth, this time between the judge and prosecutor. Then they all looked at me. I stared back, unsure if I should smile or cry. My lawyer and the prosecutor returned to their seats, and the judge turned towards me and then read from his paper.

"The court finds Sara Orozco guilty of drug possession with intent to distribute, a felony that carries up to fifteen years in prison and a fine of $25,000." I heard myself gasp and then cry. My knees shook. My life was over. Tom put his hand on my shoulder.

"The judge is not done," he said. "Look up."

"As a first-time offender, I sentence you to two hundred hours of community service, random drug testing, and a $2,000 fine. Your record will be expunged one year from today if no more violations exist. Case dismissed. Next." Tom packed up his papers, and we walked out into the hallway. I wanted to hug him. He helped me set up a payment plan at the clerk's desk. He handed me a plastic bag containing my shoelaces, wallet, belt, and a business card from the tow company who would release my car for a hundred dollars. I looked inside my wallet and found one ten and one five.

"I can pay for the tow and add it to my bill," he said. "I'll drop you off at your car." I was scared to ask how much I already owed, but I felt so indebted to him that I would've paid him any amount he asked. I felt filthy—like a dirty dog—sitting on the white leather seat of his car. I asked about my community service, wondering how long I'd have to stay in Charleston, and Tom delivered his final blessing.

"The judge agreed to you doing your community service in Asheville," he said. "At the Billy Graham Center. Call them in two to three days and they will set you up."

I gawked. *Billy Graham?* The Christian evangelist megapreacher? The one who referred to his antigay preaching as a *crusade*? At his compound where Christian zealots could gather to learn about the Scripture?

*Mami*, I thought. Of course she had nothing to do with it. But it felt like a joke she was playing on me. I prepared for the pain of my repentance.

———————◆———————

At the Billy Graham Center I was assigned to a Christian counselor named David. He was pale, skinny, knobby-kneed, and only a few years older than I was. He often pointed at a small black Bible in his front pocket as he spoke. Every morning David dropped me off at the side of an unpaved dirt road on the mountainside. My job was to dig up ferns from the forest and leave them by the side of the road. David collected the ferns and delivered them to the Center grounds for replanting. The Center had a mission to blend their landscaping with the natural landscape of the surrounding area, and the plan was to replant these ferns along the Center's walkways.

On those damp mornings I walked the dirt trails that curved through shady fern-filled forests, thick bushes, and tall trees. Bare branches scratched my arms and neck and my abraded skin burned with sweat. This was part of my repentance. As he drove me up or down the mountain, David talked about how Jesus can help the lost find their way back home.

"I'm not lost," I said. "And I don't know where home is anymore."

"Home is here," he said, gently tapping his chest. There was an innocence to David. He was corny, earnest. I didn't want to like David. When I looked at him, I saw my own mistakes. I thought about how stupid I was to have cocaine in my car. But he was gentle, and he softened me.

I became familiar with the root systems of ferns. To transport a fern, David taught me, I had to carefully dig up the fern with its entire root system.

"Carefully work your tool around the perimeter of the plant," David instructed. "A fern with its roots can be transplanted immediately." Some ferns yielded easily from the earth. Others were stubborn, not wanting to be lifted; for these I used the garden trowel to loosen the soil encircling the plant. Lifting a plant without proper care might tear its roots, compromising the replanting. When I pulled at a small fern and heard the pops of snapping roots

I was flooded with guilt. I had to stop doing damage. I carried ferns to the nearby trail and lined them up for David to collect.

I thought about the pessimism of broken roots, and the satisfaction I felt when I extracted a plant intact, its roots clean and whole. Maybe that was my problem: My origins weren't healthy. My family had been torn from their country and half-heartedly planted themselves somewhere else. I started life with my roots already distressed, in a place my parents did not intend to stay. I'd sought out better soil, replanted myself, and for a while I'd thrived. But those tumultuous beginnings left something important unresolved.

Every day at noon, David found me for lunch and drove us in his open-top black Jeep to a picnic table on a ridge at four thousand feet. He packed peanut butter and jelly sandwiches on white bread and cartons of cold whole milk. I was still in awe of the Blue Ridge Mountains, the deep green of the closest mountains fading to a baby-blue haze in the distance. I felt absorbed into the peace and quiet. I remembered driving up the Blue Ridge Mountains that first time with Mami and gaping at the unspeakable beauty while Mami clutched the dash, her eyes squeezed shut. I remembered driving her to Looking Glass Falls a few days later, just before she left to go home, and how she refused to get out of the car. A road ran adjacent to the sixty-foot waterfall, ending at an observation deck at the top of the waterfall, and she agreed to go to the top of the falls on the promise that she wouldn't have to hike. Tiny water droplets floated through our open car windows and landed on our skin, light as ladybugs. I parked at the observation deck. Water plummeted over a stone cliff into a stream of rocks below.

Mami said she'd wait in the car while I got out to look. "It's just a few feet from the car, Mami," I pleaded. She joined me on the observation deck for three minutes, then returned to the car and shut herself inside to wait. I turned towards the falls. It was late summer. The breeze off the waterfall felt cool against my skin. I had already fallen in love with Asheville.

David was a budding preacher, and I was his assigned pupil. He said things to me like "God will guard your heart and mind," or "If you sit still and close your eyes, you can feel Jesus in the breeze." I wasn't interested in Jesus. I was interested in completing my community service and forgetting all about my criminal past. I worked twenty hours digging ferns under the summer sun; at night I waited tables in Asheville. At this rate I could complete my community service in ten weeks and start paying off my debts.

I liked David, despite how eager he was to save my soul. His path to salvation involved thoughtful discussion, at least. His calmness helped me think.

One afternoon he announced, as if he'd finally solved a problem, "You have been walking an unplanned path." He was excited. "There's a better plan for you."

Oh yes, God's plan. I'd once been a perfect Catholic school student; I'd worshipped the nuns and believed everything they said. I memorized every fable and revealed my soul to the priest twice a week, confessing to riding my bike to the 7-Eleven without telling Mami, or about how I secretly kept a pet lizard in a jar by my bed because I was afraid of the dark. When I was ten and confronted my first crush on a girl, I somehow knew not to share this information with the priest at confessions. This was something monumentally sinful. Something God might not forgive. I could end up in hell. I prayed for years, made dozens of desperate promises to myself, to God, and to my mother, but my attraction to girls wouldn't go away. Eventually I believed none of it. I stopped going to church and waited in vain for my mother to find room in her heart for both God and me. I worshipped at the altar of Donna Summer, guided by the holy spirit of cocaine and disco lights.

Mami found me selfish—choosing my own needs over the laws of God. I thought she chose God over me. I thought God turned Mami against me.

But maybe David was right about the unplanned life part. Once I rejected Mami's plan for me, I'd been traveling the streets of my life at random, not bothering to read the signs before I turned. Maybe I needed an actual map for living. I'd been acting as if I had no control over my life. I believed myself somehow immune to accountability.

During my time at the Center, I obediently reflected on my choices and my future. I didn't want to continue lying to others and myself, and I didn't want to continue hurting my mother. But I hadn't found anything to replace God, and without anything to believe in, I felt unsettled and hollow. I no longer had God to talk to in my head when I was in trouble or happy or lonely. I no longer had my mother.

At the moment I had David, who, unlike God or Mami, might actually provide a satisfying or at least direct answer to a difficult question. "Where does Jesus stand in relationship to gays?" I asked David. I knew what to expect from his answer, but I wanted to hear what he thought.

David skirted the issue with one of his platitudes. "God loves everyone."

I balked. "How can someone love you and demand that you be different than you are?" I said. "What kind of love is that?" Some days, like today, I was mad at David. Billy Graham. Cubans. Miami. Mami, my lawyer Tom in South Carolina, and even the judge who sentenced me to work at the Center. I felt pushed away from the central artery of life on earth. I was an outcast.

"Just because someone believes they are gay, that doesn't negate God's love for his children," David said.

"David, you sound like a robot," I said. "Is this where they send the gay people to work off their homosexuality? Do you really think it's going to work?" David looked hurt. Exposing this unspoken truth between us seemed to still the wind moving through the treetops, flattening the view and any hope he had been offering.

I looked out over the mountains that rose indifferently around us. I felt anxious about finishing my community service and not having a place to go. Miami meant returning to the closet; this was no longer an option. I had loved my years in Asheville, but recently all I could see were its boarded-up buildings and reminders of my friends who had moved on. The Blue Ridge Mountains once felt like shelter. Now looking at them made me feel shame.

David took the Bible from his shirt pocket, flipped through the pages, and paused. "Do not judge, or you too will be judged. For in the same way you judge others, you will be judged. Matthew 7:1–2."

I waved off the book and stared at him, whispering with intensity, "I don't care what that book says. What do you think, David? YOU?" He seemed startled by my angry desperation after months of agreeable service, as if I'd ripped the script from his hands. I started to shake in the face of his uncertainty, barely holding back my tears. He stepped closer and touched my shoulder. "I believe we are both children of God, Sara. That is enough. It has to be." His voice wavered. I closed my eyes and imagined it was Mami saying these words. In my mind I heard her say them. It had to be enough.

I finished out my service by replanting ferns along the Center's pathways. Rows of billowy ferns guided visitors decisively through the grounds, then blended wildly into the forest where they'd first emerged. Now it was time to find new ground for myself. When I left the Center, David and I hugged goodbye for a very long time. Slowly, carefully, I withdrew my roots.

# The Proudest Texan
# in Mérida

## KB BROOKINS

On the worst of days, when I don't win the award or get the review I wanted, when I find myself envy-scrolling Twitter (I refuse to call it X) and learn that another talented writer friend has gotten the spread in some flashy magazine, when I witness others being called a "force," a "big deal" beyond their local community, I think of this Kevin Hart skit: the one in which a fan calls Kevin a "local ass bitch."

Kevin and friends are at some dingy, dimly lit bar. The fan, who is really a hater—as so often happens to fans when their fave gets too big—states, "I'm a fan, but only in America. You ain't shit until you perform in Paris." Kevin and the bar's patrons look confused. The man looks Kevin up and down while hurling an insult that stings: "Ol' local ass bitch!" As this escapes the man's lips, everyone in the bar hoots and hollers. Kevin's posse hurls epithets at the man as Kevin calls security. Security drags the man out of the viewer's frame. Kevin leaves the ego-murdering scene to pace the bar's patio alone.

"Why can't I enjoy myself?" he asks no one particular. His hands are in his pockets as he looks at the ground; he then brings them to his temples. It's a comedy sketch, but the frustration in his eyes is palpable, genuine. Despite his expensive clothes, his homies' quick defense, and his ability to buy out an entire venue to celebrate a year spent getting richer, Kevin is disappointed by the idea that he can only make an impact, be important, have a community of people who love and embrace his point of view in one small patch of the world. That the only people who get him will be people to his left and right.

I, too, would go on a spiral after being called a local ass bitch. While it's true that many writers (including myself) consider love from one's own community the real indication that you've "made it," let's be honest. Deep down, we'd all like the nationally recognized awards. Large advances, translation deals—for someone in some faraway country to take a selfie with our book and say "loved it." Deep down, we all secretly wanna be the Pitbull (Mr. Worldwide!) of our respective genres.

I, too, want people to love me wherever I go.

The conflicting thing about this admission is, well, I *am* a local ass bitch. Every biography I've composed includes a mention that I'm from Texas. Most of my work—in poetry, nonfiction, visual art, and otherwise—makes clear that I've chosen, for better or worse, to spend my life in the Lone Star state, a geography routinely in the news for being where the worst things happen and the worst political decisions are made. But I embrace Texas, even when its elected representatives attempt to snuff out my Black, trans, queer self, even when the state turns its back on all the things that I see through my loving, weary eyes. Texas is home to my family—both chosen and blood. We have queens in cowboy boots and food trucks brewing BBQ and slang that slurs words together like the best mole of your life consumed at Tex-Mex cantinas decorated with Christmas lights; this state is my heart. It contains everything that makes me comfortable in this uncomfortable world.

I write down things that have made me stay in Texas this long so that *my* Texas can be shared with others. It's the place I belong, even when I don't. In my youth, leaving the state rarely crossed my mind. I grew up in a household that didn't have funds for lavish family vacations, and my parents are also scared of planes, so when we did venture out of town it was to a place accessible by car and usually where family lived. Waco. Malakoff. New Orleans. Because it's easy to get exhausted from sitting in a car for hours on end and according to my mother "gas costs an arm and a leg," our vacays lasted three days max.

I'd never even left Texas until I turned twenty, thanks to a fellowship that paid for a scholarly excursion to New York. Though I found New York aesthetically beautiful, it was way too different from what I knew. Trains as a primary mode of transportation? Walking no matter the weather? Noises and unfamiliar smells galore? No thanks. When I asked for a sweet tea from a Harlem-based soul food spot, they looked at me like I'd cursed them out. I could've run to LaGuardia right then. It wasn't until I got a partner more adventurous than I that I first made plans to venture abroad. I was twenty-six, and Gaby wanted to take me to Mexico.

I know what you may be thinking. Mexico is *so* close to Texas. Texas is land literally stolen from Mexico, so how could it have taken me twenty-six years to cross such a nearby threshold? Listen. When money is an issue and you have seemingly everything you need, it's easy to lack a sense of wonder about the world beyond what you can see. I understood early that travel required money and curiosity, neither of which I possessed, so I kept myself landlocked and satisfied with a rotation of dissecting, celebrating, and denouncing the intricacies of Texas. But Gaby has family in Mexico she tries to see once a year. I considered the trip an opportunity to deepen our relationship—you learn so much about a person when you (a) meet the people who knew them young, and (b) travel with them; truly, I've wanted to break up with exes because of the way they pack luggage.

We read up on Mérida, a landlocked city in Mexico and the capital of the Yucatán. Photographs showed brightly colored arches and busy markets. Its culture around food and live music made it sound like a sister city to Austin, where I'd moved three years earlier, drawn to those very things. But it was different enough in nature and culture that we could do and see multiple things that don't exist in Texas. This would give me the chance to understand whether I was a lifelong local ass bitch. I was excited.

Gaby came across a listing for Mérida Pride. The timing was perfect: Pride coincided exactly with our travel dates. My happy jitters turned nervous. From eighteen to twenty-four, I'd probably attended Prides in major Texas cities more times than I could count on two hands; my conclusion was that Pride sucked. By a certain point, I could not look past the centering of whiteness and cisness, the straight gaze dictating what manifestations of queerness were "appropriate" and not, the presence of cops, the presence of Christ-wielding counterprotesters holding up signs saying "God hates gays," the lack of accessibility for disabled folks—the list goes on.

The faces at Pride were not the same faces I'd see when my friends and I confronted drag bans, anti-trans legislation, and the general fuckery that comes with being queer in the States these days. Corporations emblazoned their brands on Pride floats and the lanyards they tossed from them, only to pull the LGBTQIA+

merch from their shelves when pressured by conservatives (*coughs* Target). Since the tragic mass shooting at Pulse in Orlando, Pride also became the setting in which I'd been my most hypervigilant—heightening my fear that being amongst a group of queer people in a queer space meant a target on my back. Plus, I'm sober, so I can't rely on drugs to help me artificially elevate a lackluster experience.

So I stopped going to Pride celebrations. These spaces weren't made for me, and I doubted queer people who weren't rich had a comfortable place in any Pride anywhere; the admission fees climb with the years.

Gaby was thrilled at the idea of celebrating Pride in Mérida. "I don't know about that," I hedged.

"I mean, it's happening while we're in town, so we might as well," she coaxed. Her dark brown hair swooped over her freckled face. One look into her almond-shaped eyes is usually enough to talk me into something, but I struggled to be swayed on this one. Would I blister my feet walking miles in the sun just to be let down again?

"What if it's a wash?"

"Then we leave," she said, not skipping a beat. Her soft hands were on my back, as they are when she sees that I'm anxious about something. After some haggling, like the lover boy I am, I caved. I figured, at least, that I could go and expect nothing.

———◆———

Four weeks later we drove into Mérida from Playa del Carmen. I gasped at its architecture; the mostly clay structures were drenched in an assortment of pinks, blues, yellows, and greens. It was like a scene out of a movie, only somehow more regal. The

Texas city I called home was once vibrant like this, strewn in color, eccentric, but its uniqueness has fallen to the gray blocks of gentrification. Vines grew down from balconies, and Mérida's buildings were beautifully stained with age. Absent were construction zones and six-lane highways. Mérida was, for lack of more honoring words, breathtaking.

From the rental car's passenger seat, I extended my arm out of the window and breathed in the fumes of our temporary place of residence with open palms. The streets smelled of dulce and cigarettes; people moved through downtown areas as if they'd walked those streets all their lives. The efforts taken to preserve Mérida's buildings and traditions visibly honored its history, and despite its beauty and allure the city seemed to have avoided becoming choked out by tourism. Some 1,500 miles from home I'd discovered a completely new world.

We dropped off our bags at our Airbnb and walked to a local OXXO store for enough five-liter water bottles to last us through our trip. Because we were tired of being in a car, and tired of the amusing but generally reckless nature of driving in Mexico on streets with little to no signage, we elected to spend the rest of the night on foot. We strolled past bustling clusters of houses, cathedrals, mercados, a bronze monument of Mérida leaders, and arrived at a row of restaurants, where we perused menus before landing on one that fit our needs—arrachera tacos for me and a cheese-stuffed chile relleno for Gaby. We followed our glorious entrées with a stop at a dulcería y sorbetería, where I was graced with some of the best ice cream of my life. With newly sticky hands and locking arms we waddled aimlessly around the modestly sized downtown area, full of happiness and wonder. Our gaze was drawn to a raucous huddle of people across the tan-tiled street, and curiosity pulled us toward the crowd.

Once we were close enough to peep the fashion (tall tees and too-tight jeans), faces (unwrinkled and overly manicured), and smells (must and OXXO perfume), I knew exactly what we'd stepped into. Some fifty Mexican teens huddled in a circle; in the center, a boy held up a Bluetooth speaker. It was half his size, half blown out, and maybe functional enough to be heard by those in the first three rows of the crowd. An electrical cord connected the speaker to a microphone held by a boy in sagging pants and a black tee. The crowd cheered every time the boy announced the names of people to his left and right. After the boy's speech, hip-hop beats played as opponents took their places. We had happened upon a rap battle.

It's not that I believed rap was confined to the U.S. Because of Gaby's affinity for Bad Bunny, I'd learned a great deal about reggaeton and its rap-influenced, Panamanian origins. It surprised me, however, that this braggadocious subsection of rap, with its underground, improvisational nature, its old-fashioned trash talk, had found its way into the hearts of Mérida teens, as it had mine in the 2010s. The difference between this night and any old night I spent at an eighteen-and-up bar in my hometown of Fort Worth, Texas, was the makeup of the crowd and the language they spoke. I was accustomed to all-Black crowds; this one, save for me, was all brown. Passersby were unfazed by the gathering, which to me communicated that these battles were a regular occurrence. I was curious and excited about this cultural exchange that I could recognize, even with my struggle-Spanish. When I missed things, Gaby, being the multilingual queen that she is, could be counted on to translate for me. Gaby and I blended into the crowd, trying to make out about every other word emitting from the muffled speaker.

Each teen had three rounds of freestyles to woo the crowd and create a spectacle for anyone walking this little street in Mérida. I caught snatches of daring lyricism—"your mother's my bitch" and "no MC can stop me"—bitten from young lips. We struggled to hear but stayed anyway, relishing in magic lyrics made off the dome, breathing in the brandishing of rhymes improvised to prove that the one brave enough to speak is better than you.

To my unsurprise, all of the battle rappers were male. Hip-hop—no matter where, it seemed—was a sport that thrived in the brandishing of masculinity. Who's the wittier man? The richer? More good-looking? Better with the ladies (who are called, in the world of battle rap, anything but ladies)? Who's the *least* feminine out of us two? Though it surely wasn't always this way, hip-hop has become a rumination on the possible ways to one-up and out-man. This battle was no different. I'm a Black, queer, assigned-female-at-birth hip-hop listener, so I've learned to contend with the genre's conventions. When I get tired of suspending my morals I find rappers who are interested in better things. What kept me listening to these Mérida teens, and to hip-hop in general, was the unmitigated talent with words that the art of rap opens space for. When I could translate quickly enough in my head, I was amazed by the rappers' ability to improvise. When one rapper flamed another for wearing "rags," his opponent quickly composed double entendres about his opponent's mother.

Three rounds in, a young man entered the circle, eager to gain a victory and advance to the next round of the competition. He looked rugged and perhaps seventeen years old. His short hair swooped over his downturned eyes, which daggered his opponent —a pip-squeak of a boy who looked no older than fourteen—with vengeance. The older boy put his mouth on the mic when the beat dropped and declared with all the gumption in the world, "ningún maricón me ganará." You could see spit coat the mic as he continued.

"Ugh," my partner said.

"What happened?" I whispered.

"He said the *f* slur," she told me in a disappointed tone. Of course, the inevitable. Approval from the crowd filled the air around us: *ooooh*s and *ahh*s from guys; giggles and, at best, indifference from girls. "Do you want to go?" Gaby asked. At that moment, I was stuck to the spot; all I could do was think.

If I were to distance myself from every rapper who's ever been queerphobic and not apologized for it, I'd have to turn away from many greats (Tupac, Biggie, Eazy E). I'd have to eliminate a good chunk of current-day rappers (Yung Thug, Rick Ross, J. Cole, Drake), too. I'd need to cross off women (Sexy Redd) and even some queer rappers (Tyler, The Creator); from "no homo" to "pause," from old-school slurs to "sassy," queerphobia colors so much of hip-hop that it's impossible to avoid. Queer rappers (Saucy Santana, Lil Nas X) say that some men in the industry won't work with them. Even in subsections of hip-hop like reggaeton, a genre that took root in Panama, queer hate sprouts and blooms. Despite being a socially conscious genre, its consciousness only extends so far, and rarely into areas of gender and sexuality. Often, I'm left to decide what I can ignore or what I must denounce. So I had to think.

—◆—

Did I want to let one rapper stop me from basking in this otherwise fun experience? Was what he said indicative of the whole space, given that no one responded with disapproval but us? Did others share our disgust but not feel safe enough to voice it? Here I was, in a new space, the day before Pride would kick off two blocks from where we stood, contemplating what level of queerphobia I could tolerate.

Ordinarily, this would be the time I'd be ready to pack it up. I'd chalk up the experience to another indication that the world is fucked up and that it's not a good idea to attend any more Prides. But these were kids—surely they could grow out of this BS in time. And where else at home, or in the States in general, would I get to see an all-Spanish rap battle? By the time I finished thinking, two more rounds had rolled by; the homophobe advanced to the finals. We left and told ourselves it was because it got late, but we knew. We always must know.

---

The next morning we found a perfect parking spot in front of a municipal building. There were even more unoccupied parking spots around us. "Do we have to pay?" I asked Gaby, accustomed to shelling out an arm and a leg to borrow space in the center of a city. To both of our surprise, we didn't. The street was as clear as the sky; the sky beamed in a way that felt like a kiss, rather than the suffocating hug of the Texas sun. I had rested well, growing okay with being in another flawed place. We held hands as we crossed the street and walked toward signs in the distance. "Marcha de la Diversidad Sexual Mérida," they said. The signs donned inclusive Pride flags in their corners. Street vendors hailed us as we neared the streets blocked off for the parade.

"Aguas, amigas!" one said. She'd made a sign from a big Pride flag: COLD WATER, LOVE IS LOVE.

"*Mom*," the child of the street vendor said, in that tone only a child who's embarrassed of their parents could give.

"Lo siento," the vendor said. "*Amigues!*" This correction, how easily she'd shifted into gender neutrality, dispelled the constant contention that gender-neutral Spanish isn't spoken outside the States, that words like "Latinx" or "Latine" made no sense in the Spanish-speaking world. After the correction from her child, the woman spoke this allegedly unspoken Spanish with ease. I smiled, then bought an overpriced water. After this interaction I tuned my ear to the ends of words as they were spoken around us; often, folks spoke with an "-e" in place of the "-a" or "-o" that gender words in Spanish. It was music to me, the speak of *novies* and *esposes*. I walked with my lover to the sounds of a queer worldview.

We walked until we found a big group of people all looking toward the street, where drunk partygoers danced and threw beads from their rooftops. For every four or five floats there was a pickup truck blasting music from a stereo on its bed, vibrating Selena and Bad Bunny while straps wrapped around them. We claimed a piece of sidewalk and watched the floats roll by.

Kids—goths, cheerleader types, and some jocks—huddled in their respective cliques. They held signs, some handmade, some printed—a touching number of them reading "Support trans youth." Among them, uncles, drag queens, abuelas, and—my personal favorite—Latine Dykes on Bikes. Young people marched next to their elders; babies danced next to old trans guys who happily showcased their bare chests—without being met with puzzled stares like the ones I get anytime I dare to be shirtless. I'd never experienced a Pride so intergenerational. No one kissed in front of signs that said "God hates gays" because those signs weren't there. I saw no cops, or guns, or counterprotesters. No "LGBT-friendly" police union.

I breathed in, and out. In, and out; there was no constriction overpowering my lungs. No instinct to scan the premises for a lone gunman. Upon experiencing this—a few hours of true, queer happiness—a tear involuntarily fell from my face.

I'd been staring at a banner, unaware the tear was forming. I guess I was mourning all the Prides I missed, all the Prides I wasn't privy to. I was crying for what no longer seemed possible in the States: Pride for All, a celebration that makes good on Pride's initial promise. I thought back to the last time I'd felt so uncomplicated— not an identity nor a target, not a hard lesson nor a nuisance. At this moment I was just a person who happened upon a good thing.

Later, after smashing some surprisingly amazing Korean food —unbeknownst to me at the time, there's a solid Korean presence in Mérida—we went to a sapphic party hosted by Igualdad Sustantiva Yucatán. The club was a clay house, its floor-length windows free of panes. From outside, the open windows framed montages of beautiful people dancing while sipping from their glasses or whispering in the ear of a soon-to-be intimate. Old lesbians sat outside with their cards holding cigarettes they let burn to the filter; young lesbians laughed and hugged their friends as they yelled outside. The party was nearly spilling into the streets.

The city of Mérida contained stretches of land that could hold buildings but decidedly didn't. In the urban landscapes of Texas, developers see a patch of land that isn't a park or landmark and absolutely *must* build on top of it—so it was unbeknownst to me that you could pick a part of town and exist in its open space. The club was on a street lined only by trees to its left and right, so the sapphics could be as loud, as raunchy, and as real as they wanted to be. No neighbors motivated to alert the police, no one likely to frame a party as "loitering" or "disturbing the peace" or to demand the dimming of their pink and orange lights. Nothing to stop them from blaring, loving on old and new loved ones all night.

"Should we go in?" I asked Gaby. It's typical of me to get cold feet about parties, especially when the partygoers are people I don't know.

"We're already here," she said. "But we can do whatever you want if you don't want to stay." She's patient with me when my crowd shyness activates. I stopped to think. Though we had a beautiful day, were we setting ourselves up for sadness? Was this day, like the day before, too good to be true? *We're already here*, I told myself, trying to coach away the excuses I always come up with to leave.

Inside, too, was spacious. Though I'd expected, from the outside, that we'd be packed in like sardines, torn-up seats were available at the bar, and the tiny-but-mighty kitchen-turned-dance-floor held vacancies. We ordered sparkling waters and sipped them in front of the window, the air from outside brushing our faces.

I moved my limbs side to side as my partner lightly twisted her hips to the music. I like to dance, but I rarely do. I'd blame my stiff-ness on the music (*how do you dance to this?*), or the mood (*well, other people aren't dancing*), but the truth is I was used to the om-nipresence of phones ready to record and embarrass you anon-ymously on social media. I was also regrettably accustomed to the threat of someone snickering, simply because someone they don't deem beautiful dares to dance in public; such was the state of mainstream American dance clubs. So a simple left-to-right, a sign that I can at least keep pace with everyone around me, is often the most that I'd do.

But then I looked around me. A pair performed dances I'd never seen, which required them monopolizing half of the small dance floor. Two lovers shimmied their shoulders at each other while they kissed. Three homeboys did what looked like multiple rounds of tango. Though clearly improvised, everyone was perfectly in sync. In the zone. Unconcerned with what was happening around them; interested only in each other. The DJ blared Spanish house music, then transitioned into Britney Spears's "Toxic."

"Oh my god," I yelled to Gaby. Despite my initial shock of encountering Britney's magnum opus in a club in Mexico, I realized this was inevitable. We were at a gay party, for Christ's sake. The girls and the gays everywhere love this song. "I'M ADDICTED TO YOU, BUT YOU KNOW THAT YOU'RE TOXIC" erupted from the lungs of everyone. Then, and only then, did I realize that I was in a safe space.

And I don't mean safe space in the "we've taken trainings and know all the right lingo" way. I mean that I was free—of people's judgment, of want to be anywhere else; I felt safe in my want to kiss, to dance sloppily under the sweltering Mérida humidity, to be the queer that I am, that I haven't unleashed since . . . well . . . ever.

My solemn right-to-left turned into fist pumps, robots, running mans. I looked ridiculous, but I was happy! Gaby joined me in this fun charade, doing her signature.

"Ay, mierda!" the DJ said, nodding in our direction. The DJ stood on a podium over multiple mixing boards, wearing wired Beats headphones, red lipstick, a short cut, and tripp pants—her body draped in chains and adorned with stick-and-poke tattoos. "Viva la fiesta!" she furthered, shuffling into Beyoncé's "Alien Superstar." She pivoted backwards into an ecstatic frolic and spin.

Admittedly, it had been a while since a person younger than twenty-five was impressed with something I'd done, so I wanted to bathe in this moment. To bottle it up, rub it in, feed it to my future children. How cool was it to be singled out and not freeze up. How cool it is to be where people agree to move their bodies around in their free time with strangers while another stranger curates the vibe. I looked up at her glistening face and beamed.

I wondered what we looked like to the few passersby on the street. Two lovers, making happy in a new queer home? Or a song—perhaps "Toxic" by Britney Spears—that turns off the moment we drop eye contact, or some tourists, visiting Mérida, who stumbled across a lesbian bar? To me, we were proud in a foundational sense: experiencing the pleasure, the self-respect, of our effortless state of being.

Mérida is now a city I search for at every Pride. Its imperfect vision of what it means to be queer. To be young, old, alive, unburdened by surveillance, the eyes around us filled only with love. The city that offered me moments I wish away and others I wish for in my dreams. Love erases the boundaries of the local, and welcoming acceptance can make any place feel like home. We all deserve to be loved wherever we go. Me, and my Gaby, and all the queerdos in Texas and beyond deserved a place in which to feel truly proud. I'd left Texas, and now I knew what to ask from it when I returned.

# Acknowledgments

The editor would like to gratefully acknowledge Savannah Rush, research assistant on *Edge of the World*, and the Department of Writing, Literature, and Publishing at Emerson College for supporting her work on this project. Additional editorial assistance was provided by Katherine Standefer.

Edmund White's "Kicking Back in Key West" was originally published in *The Guardian*.

Alexander Chee's "Mirador" was originally published in *The New York Times* under the title "In Spain, Secrets and a Possible Betrayal."

Alex Marzano-Lesnevich's "Towards a Fight" appeared in a previous form in *The Rumpus*.

# About the Editor

**ALDEN JONES** is the author, most recently, of the Lambda Literary Award nominee *The Wanting Was a Wilderness*. Her travelogue *The Blind Masseuse: A Traveler's Memoir from Costa Rica to Cambodia* was longlisted for the PEN/Diamonstein-Spielvogel Award for the Art of the Essay and is a volume in the Big Ten Open Books gender and sexuality studies collection. Her story collection *Unaccompanied Minors* won the New American Fiction Prize and was a finalist for a Lambda Literary Award and the Publishing Triangle's Edmund White Award for Debut Fiction. A longtime travel educator who has lived, worked, and traveled in more than forty countries, Alden is assistant professor of Writing, Literature, and Publishing at Emerson College, and also teaches in the low-residency Newport MFA. She lives in Boston with her family.

# Contributors

**RALUCA ALBU** is a writer, teacher, editor, and advocate. She has been a Center for Fiction Fellow and a New York Foundation for the Arts Fellowship finalist, and has written for *The Guardian*, *BOMB*, *Guernica*, *The Village Voice*, Doctors Without Borders, Authors Guild, and others. A once-refugee, she lives in New York with her woodworking wife and their two floofy, goofy Samoyeds.

**KB BROOKINS** is a writer, cultural worker, and artist from Texas. They are the author of *How to Identify Yourself with a Wound* (Kallisto Gaia Press, 2022), *Freedom House* (Deep Vellum, 2023), and *Pretty* (Alfred A. Knopf, 2024). Follow them online at @earthtokb.

**ALEXANDER CHEE** is most recently the author of the essay collection *How to Write an Autobiographical Novel*. He lives in Vermont and teaches creative writing in New Hampshire and is at work on a new novel.

**GARRARD CONLEY** is the *New York Times* bestselling author of the memoir *Boy Erased* and the novel *All the World Aside*, as well as the creator and coproducer of the podcast *UnErased: The History of Conversion Therapy in America*. His work has been published by *The New York Times*, *Oxford American*, *Time*, and *Virginia Quarterly Review*, among others. He is an assistant professor of creative writing at Kennesaw State University.

**ANDREW ELLIS EVANS** is an author, travel writer, and lecturer. As *National Geographic*'s Digital Nomad, Andrew reported live from all seven continents. His award-winning memoir *The Black Penguin* was named one of "summer's best travel books" by *The New York Times*. He lives in Virginia's Blue Ridge Mountains.

**CALVIN GIMPELEVICH** is the author of *Invasions,* an NEA Fellow, and the recipient of a Lambda Literary Award. His work has been recognized by

Artist Trust, Jack Straw Cultural Center, 4Culture, CODEX/Writer's Block, Studios at MASS MoCA, and the Kimmel Harding Nelson Center for the Arts and has appeared in *Ploughshares*, *Kenyon Review*, *A Public Space*, and *The Best American Essays 2022*.

**DAISY HERNÁNDEZ** is the author of *The Kissing Bug: A True Story of a Family, an Insect, and a Nation's Neglect of a Deadly Disease*, which won the 2022 PEN/Jean Stein Book Award and was selected as an inaugural title for the National Book Foundation's Science + Literature Program. She is also the author of the award-winning memoir *A Cup of Water Under My Bed* and coeditor of *Colonize This! Young Women of Color on Today's Feminism*. She is an associate professor in the English Department at Northwestern University.

**GENEVIEVE HUDSON** is the author of the novel *Boys of Alabama*, which was a finalist for the Oregon Book Award. Their other books include the memoir-hybrid *A Little in Love with Everyone* and *Pretend We Live Here: Stories*, which was a Lambda Literary Award finalist. They've received fellowships from the Fulbright Program, MacDowell, Caldera Arts, Sitka Center of Art and Ecology, and the Vermont Studio Center.

**NICOLE SHAWAN JUNIOR'S** creative nonfiction appears in *Oprah Daily*, *Guernica*, *The Rumpus*, *The Massachusetts Review*, and elsewhere. They have attended residencies at Hedgebrook and Tin House and have received fellowships from Lambda Literary, the New York Foundation for the Arts, and more. Born and bred in Brooklyn, Nicole lives in Philly with their foster children and feline familiars, Octavia E. Tuxfur and LA Blacks.

**ALEX MARZANO-LESNEVICH** is the author of *The Fact of a Body: A Murder and a Memoir*, which received a Lambda Literary Award and the Chautauqua Prize, as well as several international awards, and was translated into eleven languages. A 2023 United States Artists fellow, their essays appear in *The Best American Essays 2020* and *2022*. Their second book, *Both and Neither*, is forthcoming from Doubleday and publishers internationally.

**DENNE MICHELE NORRIS** is the author of *When the Harvest Comes* and editor in chief of *Electric Literature*, winner of the 2022 Whiting Literary Magazine Prize. A 2021 Out100 Honoree, she is the first Black, openly trans woman to helm a major literary publication. Her writing has been supported by MacDowell, Tin House, and the Kimbilio Center for African American Fiction, and appears in *McSweeney's*, *American Short Fiction*, and *ZORA*. She cohosts the critically acclaimed podcast *Food 4 Thot*.

**SARA OROZCO** is a first-generation Cuban American queer writer and licensed psychologist. Her essays have been published in *The New York Times*, *Brevity*, *River Styx*, *Voices de la Luna*, *Delmarva Review*, and many others. She is currently working on a collection of essays on how her Cuban exile experience, her family's political obsessions, her childhood growing up gay in a Miami barrio, and a series of unhealthy relationships led to her being a better family and couple's therapist. Sara lives in Boston with her wife, Lori, and their dog Buddy.

**PUTSATA REANG** is an author and journalist whose writings have appeared in *The New York Times*, *The Mercury News* (San Jose), *Politico*, and *Ms.* magazine among other publications. Her memoir, *Ma and Me* (FSG/MCD, 2022), won the Pacific Northwest Booksellers Association Prize for nonfiction and was a finalist for a Lambda Literary Award and Dayton Literary Peace Prize. She teaches memoir writing in Seattle-area public schools and is a speaker at college campuses, corporations, and conferences.

**ZOË SPRANKLE** is a writer based in Brooklyn, New York. Her nonfiction has been nominated for a Pushcart Prize and featured in Roxane Gay's *The Audacity*, *The Bellevue Review*, *Quarter After Eight*, and *Go Magazine*. She holds an MFA from the Newport MFA at Salve Regina University.

**EDMUND WHITE** writes novels, essays, biographies, poetry, and plays. His many accolades include the National Book Foundation Lifetime Achievement Award and the PEN/Saul Bellow Award for Achievement in American Fiction. He lives in New York City.